PERSPECTIVES

Readings on Contemporary American Government

CloseUp®

Staff

Director of Publications:
Patricia Bandy

Managing Editor of
Academic Publications:
Joellen M. Fritsche

Senior Writer:
David R. Zack

Researcher/Writer:
John Carwile

Manager, Art Direction
and Production:
Joan Petruska

Editorial Assistant:
Ann F. O'Malley

Photographers:
Renee Bouchard
Hilary Schwab

Researcher:
William Garber

Acknowledgments
The editorial staff wishes to thank the
many people whose concern for citizenship education made this book possible. The contributing authors gave freely
of their time, energy, and creativity. Former CLOSE UP editors John Carland and
Elisabeth Good provided valuable editorial guidance. Peter, the cartoonist,
made the book sparkle. It is our hope
that this book will help citizens realize
that their involvement in government will
make a difference.

Library of Congress Cataloging in Publication Data

Close Up Foundation
  Perspectives: Readings on Contemporary American Government
  1. United States policies and government, 1945
and onward. 2. Periodicals.
ISBN: 0–932765–04–1

Additional copies of *Perspectives: Readings on Con-*
temporary American Government (at $14 each, with
special rates for large orders) and information about
other Close Up Foundation publications are available
from: Educational Publications, Close Up Foundation,
1235 Jefferson Davis Highway, Arlington, Virginia
22202.

Close Up Foundation
Stephen A. Janger, President
The Close Up Foundation was established in 1970 to encourage
high school students and their teachers to gain a better understanding of our government and their role as citizens.

Since that time, the Foundation has engaged in a variety of
activities, from bringing students and teachers to Washington
for weeklong government studies programs, to outreach efforts
involving local programs, publications, older Americans, and
cable and satellite technology.

The Close Up Foundation is nonprofit and nonpartisan. It has
no affiliation with any branch of government, political party, or
interest group. Members of the Foundation's Board of Advisors
hold a variety of political viewpoints and include representatives
of both major political parties.

Contents

★★★★★★★★★★

THE CONSTITUTION

1. The Constitution

In This Chapter

I magine that you were asked to create a new form of government for the United States. Where would you begin? What issues would you raise and how would you decide their importance? These are not easy questions, yet they are exactly the ones that faced the men at the Constitutional Convention in 1787. Our government is a result of how the authors of the Constitution answered these and other questions about the purpose and principles of the proposed government.

The Constitution creates the basic institutions of our national government and spells out the powers of these institutions, the requirements for holding office, and the rights of citizens. In addition, our Constitution is the fundamental law of the land. It is the basis for laws written by federal, state, and local legislatures.

The Constitution has its roots in the dissatisfaction many Americans felt with the government under the Articles of Confederation—a government that was very limited in its powers and ineffective in dealing with the problems facing the new nation. Under the Articles the national government could not raise its own money and the enactment of legislation required the agreement of all thirteen states. The goal of the new Constitution was to strengthen the national government in order to promote the economy and protect against foreign invasion.

A Strong But Limited Government

America's founders were very suspicious of strong government. After all, the government of Great Britain had used its powers to take away the colonists' liberties. Could not a strong American government do the same thing? The authors of the Constitution shared this suspicion to a point. But they also wanted a government to be strong enough to protect liberty and keep

George Washington presides over the signing of the Constitution in Philadelphia in 1787. Washington served as president of the Constitutional Convention after he was unanimously elected by the attending delegates.

order. The conflict between the need for a strong, effective government and the desire to prevent a repressive government was solved in several ways.

Considerable power was given to the national government, especially to regulate commerce, raise money, maintain armed forces, deal with foreign nations, and pass laws without the consent of the separate state governments. But this authority was distributed among different institutions (Congress, the president, and the courts) rather than concentrated in one body or person. This is the principle of separation of powers. Moreover, the three branches of government were each given opportunities to block the action

of the other branches. This is the principle of checks and balances. The Constitution thus created a government that was strong in many ways but could be readily prevented from abusing power. It reflects the belief that government should have power only in certain areas and only when many different interests agree that such power ought to be exercised.

Federalism

The national government was intended to be strong but limited; beyond its authority, power would reside with the states. This distribution of power between the central government and the states is called federalism, and like the separation of powers, it spreads out political authority to prevent power from being concentrated in any one group.

The division of power between the national government and the states was one of the most delicate tasks the authors of the Constitution confronted. Federalism has always involved two somewhat contradictory ideas. The first, expressed in Article VI, is that the Constitution and the laws of the national government are supreme. The second principle, contained in the Ninth and Tenth Amendments, gave to the states or the people all powers not delegated to the national government. These include control of state, county, and city governments, supervision of education, and local police powers. The conflict between national supremacy and states' rights came to a head in the Civil War when southern states claimed they had the right to secede from the Union. Even with the resolution of that crisis, the question of division of power between national and state governments remains a fundamental issue.

The Bill of Rights

The Constitution provided for the protection of certain rights, but it lacked an explicit statement protecting such basic liberties as freedom of speech and freedom of the press. The first ten amendments to the Constitution, called the Bill of Rights, guarantees the protection of civil liberties and civil rights.

The Bill of Rights grants certain positive rights such as freedom of religion, speech, the press, and assembly, the right to petition the government for redress of grievances, and the right to bear arms. It also guarantees certain procedural rights such as no unreasonable searches and seizures, no double jeopardy, no excessive bail or cruel and unusual punishment, and the right to a speedy and public trial.

The Bill of Rights gave citizens protection from the national government, not state governments. The First Amendment, for example, requires that "Congress shall make no law respecting an establishment of religion"; nothing is said about state legislatures, many of which enacted Sabbath laws and other discriminatory legislation. After the Civil War, the Fourteenth Amendment was adopted, which says in part that no state shall deprive a person of life, liberty, or property without due process of law or deny a person equal protection of the laws. This amendment

has been used over the years to extend the Bill of Rights to the states and increase the protections granted in the Bill of Rights.

The Constitution Today

That a system of government created in the eighteenth century has survived until the present is a remarkable accomplishment. An important reason for this survival is that the Constitution is flexible enough to meet with changing circumstances. The Constitution was not written as a detailed and rigid document. Although Congress is given the power to declare war, for example, the president is commander-in-chief of the military and has considerable discretion in the exercise of this authority. Because the Constitution did not precisely define the meaning of "commerce" when it gave Congress the right to regulate trade, Congress can deal with such modern areas of commerce as air travel. This adaptability is strengthened by the provision of a formal method for modifying the Constitution: the amendment process. Although it has not been used frequently, the ability to amend the Constitution means that if a provision of our government is not working the way we want it to, we can legally change it. For example, when the original method of selecting the president and vice president became unworkable, the Twelfth Amendment was passed in 1804.

The Constitution is the framework of our government, but more importantly, it is the symbol of the ideals of the American people. The substance of the principles in the Constitution ultimately rests on the American people and what they do with it. The people have the constitutional right to demonstrate against a government policy and can thereby change that policy. The press has the constitutional right to publish the truth that can bring an end to government corruption. The people have the constitutional right to criticize public officials and can elect a more responsive government. Viewed in this way, the Constitution is a document with meaning for all of us.

Why Has the Constitution Endured So Long?

Representative Don Edwards

Don Edwards (D-Calif.) has been a member of the House of Representatives since 1962. Representative Edwards is a member of the House Judiciary Committee, which reviews proposed amendments to the Constitution, and chairs the Civil and Constitutional Rights Subcommittee.

In the summer of 1787, a group of 55 remarkable men came together in Philadelphia to produce one of the greatest documents ever written—the United States Constitution. The Constitution established the four principles upon which our government rests: the separation of powers among three equal branches of government (executive, legislative, and judicial); a system of checks and balances; federalism, which divides power between federal and state governments; and the principle that ours is a nation ruled by laws, not men.

The four principles were the product of the insights and experiences the delegates brought with them to Philadelphia. The colonial experience and the war for independence taught the framers of the Constitution that concentration of power in the hands of one person often resulted in tyranny. At the same time, six years of life under the Articles of Confederation proved that a weak central government was inadequate to govern a large and diverse nation of thirteen states, each jealous of its own powers and prerogatives.

Under the Articles of Confederation, the decisions of Congress were little more than recommendations to the states. On important matters, the approval of each individual state was required before action could be taken. For example, Congress had to prevail on each state for funds for the National Treasury, but lacked the power to enforce payment. In matters of commerce, both foreign and domestic, the states often acted individually to the detriment of other states and the country as a whole.

Faced with a rapidly deteriorating financial situation and the inability to act, the country's leaders recognized the need for a stronger central government. The states agreed to gather in Philadelphia in the summer of 1787 to revise the Articles of Confederation. Instead, the framers created an entirely new document, and in the process, a new form of government. It is federal, in that it is made up of sovereign states, which retain power over their own affairs, and it is national, in that there is a central government to "provide for the common defense and promote the general welfare."

The framers of the Constitution recognized, based on their experience with the English king, that people could not be trusted with unlimited authority. Thus, power was divided among the three branches of government. As James

Madison said, in framing a government for people and not angels, "you must first enable the government to control the governed; and in the next place oblige it to control itself."

At the same time, by carefully enumerating the powers and responsibilities of each of the three branches, the Constitution also established the system of checks and balances to assure that no one branch could usurp too much power. To accomplish this goal, each branch of government had to be given the means and the motives to resist encroachment by the other. Again, in Madison's words, "ambition must be made to counter ambition."

By delegating power between the national government and the states, the framers of the Constitution granted the states the authority to govern themselves in internal matters, while the federal government would provide for general needs of the nation. The Articles of Confedera-

tion made the rights and duties of the national government easy to perceive and define—primarily, the power to wage war, levy taxes, and regulate commerce among the various states.

Another fundamental principle established by the Constitution is that ours is a government of laws, not men. In many ways, the most significant provision of the Constitution is the clause that says "this Constitution . . . shall be the supreme law of the land." It is not merely an agreement between sovereign states, but a law enacted by the people, backed by the armed power of the entire nation, and ultimately enforceable in the courts.

Thus, the common denominator of all three branches of our national government is the law. The legislature writes the laws, the executive branch enforces the law, and the courts interpret and resolve disputes under the law. All of our executive and judicial officers swear their loyalty not to any monarch or other individual but to the Constitution—to an idea made into law.

Why did the Constitution succeed where the Articles of Confederation failed? One reason is that the Articles of Confederation depended on a group of independent and often selfish states to run the affairs of the nation. The Constitution deals directly with the people themselves, deriving its power solely from the consent of the governed. The Constitution was formulated on the theory that the national government should possess only those powers set out in the Constitution. All other powers remained with the states or with the people. While this concept was not articulated in the Constitution itself, but in the Tenth Amendment, which was adopted with the rest of the Bill of Rights, it nevertheless is one of the principles underlying the creation of the Constitution.

Equally fundamental to the Constitution's endurance is the fact that the framers did not intend for the Constitution to set out every detail of government or to answer every question that might arise over the next several hundred years. Indeed, such a task would have been impossible. Instead the Constitution sets forth certain general principles designed not only to address the problems facing the framers in 1787, but also to address unforeseen problems in the future. By creating a framework for government rather than a rigid set of rules and regulations, the framers of the Constitution established a govern-

Constitutional Distribution of Powers

The Constitution grants the national government the power to:	The Constitution grants national and state governments the power to:	The Constitution grants state governments the power to:
■ regulate commerce with foreign governments and among states ■ coin money ■ declare war ■ create and provide for an army and navy ■ establish uniform laws regarding naturalization and bankruptcy ■ establish a postal service	■ levy taxes ■ borrow money ■ establish courts ■ make and execute laws	■ establish local governments with sole jurisdiction over institutions such as police departments and schools ■ hold elections ■ regulate intrastate commerce

ment that changes and adapts to the growing needs of the nation.

For example, the delegates to the Philadelphia convention were lawyers, farmers, and merchants. They were all white property owners. Women couldn't vote, and slavery not only existed, but was recognized and in some degree protected by the Constitution. And yet, partly through application of the original Constitution and partly through amendments to it, we have seen the groups of people brought within its protection expand. Indeed, that expansion is a by-product of the system established in Philadelphia in 1787.

It is a tribute to the Constitution's vitality that, despite the built-in mechanism for change, there have been few modifications over the years. Madison and his colleagues gave us a framework for experimentation and peaceful, rather than violent, change. Indeed, Madison forcefully defended the idea that one of our greatest virtues is that we have not hesitated to experiment, to take steps for which there was no real precedent: The Constitution is in keeping with that idea. It is not, as some would have us believe, a work of divine origin, forever fixed in both content and meaning, but rather, a practical, workable document planned to meet certain immediate needs, and subsequently adapted by an ingenious people to meet the changing requirements of the times. Because of the framers' willingness to experi-

ment, we have enjoyed unparalleled stability as a nation and have grown from thirteen "nation states" of a few million people to fifty states and 230 million people. We have made the transition from an agrarian society to a post-industrial, space-age society; have weathered enormous political, economic, and social upheavals; and still survive as a nation.

There are those who might argue that strict adherence to constitutional principles hinders the efficient operation of our government. Government today seems to many to be costly, burdensome, and grossly inefficient. There is always inefficiency in bureaucratic institutions, public and private. But the Constitution does not create efficiency or inefficiency. It sets up the basic framework of our government and leaves it to individuals to make the framework function smoothly. And for the most part, it does. One has only to look at other countries to see that we are a model of efficiency. In this country, things work because the system works.

Others argue that the Bill of Rights in particular hinders effective government. For example, the police can't do their job because of the Fourth Amendment right against unreasonable searches or the Fifth Amendment right against self-incrimination. And there hasn't been a president of this country who hasn't wished—at least in private—for the ability to curb the press, regardless of the First Amendment.

7

But these rights were so vital to the framers that, although they were not included in the Constitution itself, they were added soon after and are viewed by many as an integral part of the original document. Several states ratified the Constitution on the assurance that a Bill of Rights would be added. The Constitution was to be free of the tyranny of the English king—who quartered soldiers in peoples' homes, and whose officials searched people's houses without warrants, jailed them without trials, and restricted the press. For the framers, no evil was worse than a tyrannical government. They drafted the Constitution to assure that that evil never returned. They were successful beyond their dreams.

Questions to Consider

1. Why were the Articles of Confederation inadequate for governing the new nation?

2. What do you think is meant by the statement "ours is a nation of laws, not men"?

3. In your opinion, why has the Constitution changed so little over the past two hundred years?

States' Rights and the Constitution

CLOSE UP asked two distinguished Americans to comment on the principle of federalism, which divides the power to govern among national, state, and local governments.

Governor
Mario Cuomo

Mario Cuomo is the Democratic governor of the state of New York. Governor Cuomo views federalism as a balance of power that must be maintained between the national government and state and local governments.

The term "federalism" is used to describe our fundamental ideas about how responsibility and authority should be divided among the three levels of government—federal, state, and local. It grows directly out of the Constitution, which our nation's founders forged in 1787. That compact established the three branches of the federal government and gave specific powers to each branch to oversee and assist the states. The president, as commander-in-chief, is charged with the national defense. Congress is given powers to tax the people and regulate commerce among the states, and the Supreme Court is authorized to resolve controversies between states and between citizens of different states.

While the Constitution established a system of checks and balances among the three branches of government, at the same time it established a balance between the federal government and the states. The Tenth Amendment to the Constitution reserves to the states whatever powers were not specifically granted to the federal government. The Tenth Amendment became the constitutional basis of the doctrine of states' rights. From the beginning of our nation, we traditionally have treated the states and the local authorities as the building blocks of our country, the level where government has stayed closest to the people. But there has always existed a tension between the federal government's authority and that of the states. The history of our federal system is really the story of the constant interplay between Washington's legal reach and that of the states.

Let's look at this history briefly. As the nation grew—in size and strength—the federal government grew, too. Recovery from the Civil War centralized power around the federal government. Railroads and industrial growth called for broader regulation. In the 1930s and 1940s, President Franklin D. Roosevelt's New Deal brought the nation out of the Great Depression with major new federal programs in agriculture, industry, and social welfare. Subsequently, the New Frontier and Great Society programs of the Kennedy and Johnson administrations in the 1960s extended even further the federal government's involvement.

For some people, these developments have been a necessary and effective use of governmental power to protect the people. However, some critics denounce this growth as "intrusive" and call for a rollback of federal authority. They talk about a "New Federalism" that would "restore" the primacy of states' rights. No one questions the need constantly to reexamine the balance between the federal government and the states, but it is a mistake to see the two entities in some kind of standoff where one cannot succeed without the other relinquishing power.

The fact is, I think, that the states today are alive and well. The last hundred years do not necessarily represent a history of the states' diminishment. On the contrary, the states have grown alongside the federal government, and there is widespread agreement today that the federal government and the states are dividing up responsibility and authority in a reasonable and practical manner. Ironically, those who want to cut back federal power wish to accomplish this by reducing programs that in fact strengthen the abilities of states to govern.

I think it is fair to say that certain tasks are appropriate for the federal government—e.g., looking after our national security, such as protecting our sea lanes or stopping the importation of drugs into the country. Other tasks are similarly appropriate for the states—e.g., administering public education and providing basic services such as road construction and employment programs.

We also expect a constant shifting of responsibilities between the levels of a federalist system. What is it that determines whether and when the federal government or the states are more appropriate? There are many complex factors, among which are who has the resources and what is the most efficient scale. The federal government has greater, more diverse assets and therefore can undertake tasks on a large scale. The states, on the other hand, are able to focus on particular needs and therefore can tailor programs to meet those needs more closely and efficiently.

Often, the states and federal government encourage and complement each other in fulfilling their respective tasks. The states serve as laboratories for innovation and change, trying out new ideas and programs. The federal government takes the ideas that work and helps spread them throughout the country. Thus, many of the programs for employment, health, and income security that the federal government now operates began first in the states. Recently, my own state of New York introduced two ideas to limit the dangers of driving. New York laws now

---

Origin of the Term "Federalism"

Before 1787, the terms "federal" and "confederal" meant the same thing. Both referred to a loose association of states that governed without a strong central administration, like the Articles of Confederation. But at the ratification convention, supporters of the Constitution appropriated the term "federal" and gave it their own meaning: a government that is neither entirely centralized nor entirely decentralized, but a combination of the two. Thus, people who favored the Constitution became known as Federalists. Today, the term "federal government" means the national government but "federalism" refers to the division of power between the national and state governments.

---

require automobile drivers and passengers to wear seatbelts and prohibit the sale of alcoholic beverages to anyone under twenty-one years old. This approach to making our roads safer is spreading to other states—and may soon influence legislation in Congress.

In short, federalism means that each state is strongest, and the nation as a whole is strongest, when we help each other, and when no state stands alone, when no state gets back only what it puts in but what it needs. The strength of our country is in its diversity: different people, different regions, and different ideas. Federalism is a way of bringing these differences into harmony. It encourages states to develop solutions to problems independently and then helps the states share in each other's successes. Every state has its own special needs and problems, but every state also has something unique to offer to the rest of the nation. We stand separately but not apart. We provide for ourselves, but we cooperate with each other. We see federalism as a family matter.

Representative Newt Gingrich

Newt Gingrich (R-Ga.) was first elected to the House of Representatives in 1978 after teaching history for eight years at West Georgia College. Representative Gingrich believes that the growth of federalism has led to a liberal welfare state that reduces the amount of control people have over their daily lives.

Our nation's founders understood that, in a democracy, power should be kept decentralized. They wanted the states to retain as much power as possible. That is why, when in doubt, they preferred power to be maintained at the state level or in the people themselves. The framers of the Constitution were very concerned about centralized power leading to dictatorship.

Yet, the framers knew that the problems in their world could never be centralized. They could never have conceived of an age with nationwide television, instantaneous computers, telephone communications, and jet airplanes that link us together in only a few hours or a few seconds. Still, we too have learned that most problems should be solved as close to home as possible, where people understand the community they're trying to govern.

Independence and self-reliance run deep in our culture, and they are surviving despite the best efforts of the liberal welfare state to destroy them. If we obeyed every bureaucracy, implemented every Washington-invented plan, and adhered to every Washington politician's centralized vision, we would rapidly become a country incapable of sustaining our freedoms. Every step toward centralizing decisions in Washington

undermines local and state opportunities to practice self-government.

The liberal welfare state is committed to the development of a strong, central bureaucracy in Washington. In the model liberal welfare state, professional bureaucracies in Washington hire technocrats who solve the country's problems by applying the best knowledge they can find after much study and thorough analysis.

In the last fifty years, however, we've learned that technocrats are only human and that no one knows enough to run a complex, continent-wide nation with 250 million people from one national capitol. We've learned the hard way that there is more flexibility, greater opportunity for innovation, more new ideas, and more exciting experiments in government at the state and local level. We've learned that fifty state capitals collectively have far better ideas than one national capital. Legislators in the states are closer to the people than the members of Congress in the national capitol. Being outside Washington often allows people to see simple truths that are obscured by the high-powered lobbyists, news media, and complex systems of Washington, D.C.

What I call the "opportunity society" is almost the reverse of the welfare state. The opportunity society places greater value on self-government. Whenever possible, the opportunity society would allow each citizen to be involved in reshaping the processes of government so that the power to make decisions is given back to the people.

The opportunity society would also emphasize individual and local self-reliance. Every effort would be made to balance the federal budget so that citizens would pay fewer taxes and therefore have more personal resources to behave as their own masters. This is truly power to the people.

By focusing on opportunity and strength rather than victims and welfare, the opportunity society creates an expanding range of possibilities. The welfare state is limited to the central bureaucracy as a resource. The opportunity society begins with each of us as individuals. To develop solutions, the opportunity society turns first to the power and strength of the family, the neighborhood, volunteer associations (including churches), and finally the free-enterprise market. It only turns to government—first local, then state, and as a final source, the federal bureaucracy—as an absolute last resort.

A free society is strong and durable because of its ability to solve problems and create opportunities at many levels. The greatest danger of our current centralized welfare system is the dependence it creates. However, in the opportunity society, which I advocate, the entire society is considered a resource. The result would be a much more flexible, durable system of self-government.

Questions to Consider

1. Compare how Governor Cuomo and Representative Gingrich view the relationship between the federal government and state governments. How are their two views different? How are they alike?

2. Do you think Governor Cuomo would support Representative Gingrich's concept of the "opportunity society" in the United States? Why or why not?

3. Do you think the federalist system established by the nation's founders is still an effective form of government? Why or why not?

Civil Liberties and the Constitution

Arthur Spitzer

Arthur Spitzer is the legal director of the Washington, D.C., chapter of the American Civil Liberties Union, a nonprofit, nonpartisan organization dedicated to protecting civil liberties and civil rights through litigation, lobbying, and public education. He has practiced law in Washington for ten years.

Can a board of education decide that next year all black students will attend East High School and all white students will attend West High? Can a public school class begin the day with the recital of the Lord's Prayer? Can a teacher demand that a student open her handbag because the teacher suspects there is marijuana inside? If a student circulates a petition in the lunchroom calling for repeal of the school dress code, can she be ordered to stop?

The answers are no, no, no, and no. The reason is the United States Constitution—specifically the Bill of Rights. Strictly speaking, the Bill of Rights includes only the first ten amendments to the Constitution (added in 1791). In practice, other amendments also fit within the Bill of Rights, including the Fourteenth (1868), which requires the government to treat people equally regardless of their race, sex, or other characteristics; and the Fifteenth, Nineteenth, and Twenty-sixth, which extended the right to vote to black males (in 1870), to women (in 1920) and to eighteen-year-olds (in 1971).

Public schools cannot be racially segregated because the Fourteenth Amendment to the Constitution prohibits the government from discriminating against people based on race. It also prohibits discrimination based on other characteristics that are irrelevant to a person's qualifications, such as sex, religion, or national origin.

Public schools cannot begin the day with prayer because the First Amendment guarantees each of us freedom of religion—both the freedom to practice our own religion (or to practice no religion) and the right not to have to practice someone else's.

A public school teacher cannot inspect a student's handbag or backpack at whim because the Fourth Amendment protects each individual's right to privacy and requires the government to have a factual basis to suspect someone of violating the law before the person can be subjected to a search.

A public school student has a right to circulate a petition because the First Amendment prohibits the government from interfering with a person's peaceful expression of his or her views.

Of all the sections of the Constitution, the Bill of Rights has the most direct impact on the everyday lives of all Americans. Most of the Constitution is a blueprint for the structure of the federal government—how officials are elected or

appointed and what their duties are—but the Bill of Rights deals with the relationship of the government to its citizens.

In a sense, the Bill of Rights stands in conflict with the main body of the Constitution. The basic philosophy of our government is democracy—a government of the people, by the people, and for the people, in Lincoln's words. Decisions in a democracy are made by majority rule, either directly, as in the election of the president and members of Congress, or indirectly, as when laws are passed by the legislature. But the purpose of the Bill of Rights is to put some matters outside the majority's rule: to say that there are some decisions the majority cannot be allowed to make.

But why shouldn't the majority always rule? The answer comes from the Declaration of Independence—that there are "certain inalienable rights" to which each of us is entitled as an individual. The philosophy of the Constitution is that a person's religion is his or her private business, not the government's; that "a man's home is his castle"; and that the government should treat all its citizens fairly and without prejudice. The Bill of Rights protects those rights for each of us, individually, so that they cannot be taken away by a majority that may hate our particular race or religion or political activity.

People who are in the majority at any given moment often don't understand why they shouldn't be allowed to have their way. The simple answer is that by respecting the rights of others, they are protecting their own rights in the long run, because tomorrow, or next year, or ten years from now, they may be in the endangered minority.

History is replete with examples: when labor unions began organizing in the 1920s and 1930s, when civil rights workers began marching in the South, when people began demonstrating against the war in Vietnam, they were often called communists or traitors and local authorities often attempted to stop their activities. Yet ultimately, their causes prevailed. New religions—from Christianity 2,000 years ago to the Christian Scientists and Mormons of the nineteenth century to the Scientologists, Hare Krishnas, and "Moonies" of today—have almost always been despised and persecuted by the existing majority. Yet many religions that were once new and radical are well-established and accepted by society today.

Ten years ago, when a Nazi organization wanted to hold a march in Skokie, Illinois, the city council tried to prevent them. Many people couldn't understand why a group that advocated the extermination of Jews should be allowed to demonstrate in a mostly Jewish town, but the courts upheld their right to conduct a peaceful march. Just imagine what might happen today if the courts had ruled the other way: the city council of a town where most voters disapproved of abortions might ban meetings or other activities by pro-choice groups on the ground that they also advocate mass murder. The lesson of history is that the only way to protect the rights of any of us is to protect the rights of all of us.

In addition to the provisions of the Constitution, many federal and local laws also perform an essential function in extending the protection of civil rights and civil liberties to the private sector. One of the most important facts about the Bill of Rights, and perhaps the least understood, is that it applies only to action *by the government*. That is why the examples at the beginning of this article were all set in the public schools. The framers of the Constitution were worried about governmental tyranny, not private conduct. Thus, for example, it is no violation *of the Constitution* for a private company to engage in race or sex discrimination.

However, we have decided as a society that such private discrimination is unacceptable, and so Congress has passed laws prohibiting it. Other laws in some places protect people against private discrimination based on age or sexual orientation, or against having their privacy invaded by the use of telephone taps or lie detector examinations.

Because there will always be unpopular minorities, the fight to protect civil rights and civil liberties will never be completely won. But with the Bill of Rights to shield us from majority tyranny, the United States is likely to remain one of the freest societies that has ever existed on the face of the earth.

Questions to Consider

1. According to Mr. Spitzer, why does the Bill of Rights conflict with the rest of the Constitution?

2. "The only way to protect the rights of any of us is to protect the rights of all of us." Do you agree with this statement? Why or why not?

3. Do you think freedom of speech should be denied to individuals or groups who advocate beliefs—such as racism or sexism—that infringe on the constitutional rights of others? Why or why not?

Five Prominent Americans Reflect on the Constitution

The Constitution is the most important document of the United States. Besides establishing the framework of our government, it protects the basic freedoms that people the world over have come to associate with this country. CLOSE UP asked five prominent Americans to reflect on how the Constitution influenced their lives and what changes they would recommend for the Constitution.

Senator Strom Thurmond

Strom Thurmond (R-S.C.) has been a U.S. senator for more than thirty years, having been first elected in 1954 after a career in South Carolina state politics. He was president pro tempore of the Senate from 1981 to 1986. Senator Thurmond is also a member of the Commission on the Bicentennial of the U.S. Constitution.

Our Constitution has had a profound effect on my life, both personally and professionally. At an early age, I developed a love of public service and government, and as I studied our Constitution, I developed a deep and abiding respect for the document, not only because it is the basis for our form of government, but because I consider it to be one of the centerpieces of man's great struggle for self-determination. Next to the Bible, I believe our Constitution is the greatest document in history, and it certainly remains the finest, most magnificent political document ever conceived.

Professionally, the Constitution has had a great impact on my life. My respect for the authority of the Constitution, and my belief that the federal government has improperly and unconstitutionally involved itself in areas left to the states, has been the driving force of my public service career. Since my election to the U.S. Senate in 1954, I have been fighting to ensure that the federal government remains faithful to and consistent with the precepts and mandates of the Constitution; specifically, that the federal government exercise only those powers delegated to it by the Constitution and that the states retain all other powers. That system of federalism was and is the cornerstone of our government. It must be carefully adhered to if we are to prevent the accumulation of too much power in Washington.

I am the sponsor or principal co-sponsor of several proposed amendments to the Constitution. First and foremost, I support an amendment that would mandate a balanced budget for the federal government. Congress has consistently shown its inability or outright refusal to pass balanced federal budgets (our nation has had but one in the last quarter-century), and it is quite clear that statutory approaches mandating a balanced budget are ineffective because they can be overridden by other statutes. However, the Constitution is the "supreme law of the land," and no statute can conflict with it. Therefore, a balanced budget amendment to the Constitution continues to be the only truly effective way we have to end the disgraceful practice of deficit spending and to stop shouldering future generations with a huge national debt.

Secondly, I favor an amendment that would restore the right of students to *voluntarily* pray in public schools. The amendment would in no way mandate or require prayer. In fact, it specifically states that no compulsory prayer, or state-composed prayers or meditations, would be allowed. The amendment would simply restore the right of purely voluntary worship that has been denied to public school students through misguided decisions by the U.S. Supreme Court.

Third, I support an amendment that would allow the president to serve only one 6-year term of office. This would allow the chief executive to make decisions without worrying about reelection and enhance his ability to make long-range public policy in controversial areas. Having to run for a second term currently discourages some of those decisions from being made. What is unpopular at the time—but good for the country in the long run—is often the best course, but political considerations many times stymie those decisions.

Our Constitution's future is a bright and promising one, as long as our people never take it for granted. For more than 200 years, our Constitution has sustained this nation in some of its most turbulent times, and it remains for the world a shining symbol of freedom and hope for all people. That is perhaps our Constitution's greatest strength: its ageless wisdom and application. Our Constitution is firmly rooted in the principle that power is ultimately vested in the people—that they, not the government, are the real reservoir of sovereignty. Our citizens convey on their government certain rights and responsibilities, and in this day where dictators and tyrants seek to use government as a tool for control and domination, that is a great and wonderful gift. It is my hope that the American people never forget how great a system of government we have, and cherish forever the legacy of freedom and human dignity our forefathers carved out for us more than 200 years ago. Our Constitution will continue to stand strong for centuries to come if we are willing to fight for its survival.

Judy Goldsmith

Judy Goldsmith, former president of the National Organization for Women (NOW), is actively involved in the effort to mobilize support for women's rights. She is a native of Wisconsin and taught college English at several universities around the country before becoming a national NOW officer in 1978.

The Constitution was not something that I was ever consciously aware of in my youth, except as I studied it in high school civics classes, and later in college. I certainly did not perceive it as a "living document" with any relevance to me. It was not until I became an activist in the women's rights movement that I came to understand the profound impact of the Constitution on my life, as well as that of all citizens.

My first real awareness of the Constitution was of a serious deficiency in it—the lack of any fundamental statement ensuring the rights of women under the law. It was that awareness that motivated my involvement in the fight for the Equal Rights Amendment (ERA), the proposed constitutional amendment that would have corrected the deficiency and established in the Constitution the principle that discrimination on the basis of sex is unacceptable under our laws.

However, in the course of the campaign to pass the ERA, I also became much more familiar with the Constitution in general, with its history, with the amending process, and in particular, with the protections for the rights of citizens that it does offer.

As an activist for change, for example, I came to fully appreciate the protection for the rights to free speech, to assemble, and to petition the government for redress of grievances. Along with all the others provided in the Constitution, these were rights that had always seemed academic and abstract. For me, it took direct contact with them to understand how real, personal, and vitally important they are. The Constitution isn't perfect (it doesn't yet have the Equal Rights Amendment!) but it is a wisely constructed document for governance, a working tool that we can use in the ongoing effort to form "a more perfect Union."

Certainly, the first amendment I would add to the Constitution is the Equal Rights Amendment: "Equality of rights under the law shall not be denied or abridged by the United States or by any State on account of sex" (with the same second and third sections providing for it to take effect two years after ratification and enabling Congress to pass legislation to enforce it). Inequality of opportunity and economic disadvantage for women persist in the second half of the 1980s. Women continue to make only about 62 cents for every dollar made by men for comparable full-time work, and two out of three adults living in poverty are women. The ERA is needed to give constitutional grounding to the laws that were—and will be in the future—designed to protect women against sex discrimination. Without that constitutional foundation, such laws are, in effect, written in sand and may be rescinded, indifferently enforced, or gutted. The full and equal protection of the laws for women should be consistently available nationwide, and the Equal Rights Amendment would ensure such a standard.

The second amendment I would add to the Constitution would be to make the District of Columbia a state. It is unconscionable that the District, with a population exceeding that of several states, does not enjoy the same representative form of government as the rest of the country.

Yet, though the amending process has made passage of these two amendments extremely difficult, I do not think that making the amending process easier is desirable. The difficulty of the process has protected us from countless frivolous or even dangerous amendments.

Phyllis Schlafly

Phyllis Schlafly is a member of the Commission on the Bicentennial of the U.S. Constitution. She is a lawyer, author of twelve books, a syndicated columnist, and radio commentator. Mrs. Schlafly is also the president of Eagle Forum, an organization that promotes policies to support and protect the family, homemakers' benefits, better education, and a strong defense.

The United States Constitution is the most important document in my life next to the Bible. The Constitution is the fountainhead of the religious, political, and economic freedoms all of us enjoy in America. It is impossible to overemphasize the decisive role the Constitution has in shaping the way of life, the opportunities, the freedom, and the security we all take for granted. It is why we have the freedom to attend the church of our choice without penalty or discrimination. It is why we support the political policies and candidates of our choice without fear of reprisal. It is why we have the choice to pursue a particular career, change jobs, or move from one end of the country to the other without anybody's permission.

My life is testimony to the opportunity all Americans have—if they use it—to start from humble beginnings and have a successful and fulfilling life. What makes this possible is the vast amount of freedom that flows from the unique system of checks and balances designed by the founding fathers which restricts the power of government over the people.

I would amend the Constitution in the following ways:

1. An amendment to Article III to end life tenure for all federal court judges. I think they should be appointed for a term (perhaps ten years), and then stand for reelection on a "retain or do not retain" ballot. This system has worked well for many state court judges. Life tenure has given federal judges too much power in relation to the other branches of the federal government.

2. An amendment to repeal the Twenty-fifth Amendment which was added to the Constitution in 1967. The Twenty-fifth Amendment set up the procedure under which Gerald Ford became president of the United States without ever having been elected by the people. It is contrary to American principles of self-government to have as president a man who was not elected to that position by the people.

3. A Human Life Amendment to declare that unborn babies are persons entitled to the full protection of the law. The worst example of judicial activism was the 1973 Supreme Court decision in *Roe* v. *Wade*, which gave women the right to kill their unborn babies. It has resulted in the national tragedy that a million and a half unborn babies are killed every year. Just as it took a constitutional amendment to end slavery in the last century, we need a constitutional amendment to stop the killing of innocent lives.

Barbara Jordan

Barbara Jordan holds the Lyndon B. Johnson Centennial Chair in national policy at the University of Texas. She served as a U.S. Representative from Texas from 1972 to 1978. Ms. Jordan rose to national prominence as a member of the House Judiciary Committee which conducted hearings on the impeachment of President Richard M. Nixon.

To say that the Constitution has influenced my life is an understatement. I have an extraordinary reliance on and almost personal attachment to the Constitution. At one time I felt that the Constitution did not include me. It is clear that the seven articles that comprise the basic structure of the Constitution did not include blacks or women. It was only through the process of amendment that blacks and women were included in that document. The Thirteenth amendment to the Constitution freed slaves, and the Fourteenth Amendment granted blacks citizenship. The Nineteenth Amendment extended to women the right to vote. These amendments provide early testimony to the flexibility of the Constitution, and in a concrete way increase my daily pride in being an American.

The basic freedoms guaranteed by the Bill of Rights and the Fourteenth Amendment allowed me to become the best I could become without the specter of suppression and restraint. As a lawyer starting a new law practice in Houston,

Texas, I knew that I was not consigned to practice law in the ghetto forever. If I could prove to others my competence as a lawyer, there were no limits to the goals I was free to pursue. The Constitution personally and professionally gave me a solid platform for achievement.

I think the Constitution has worked very well since its adoption in 1787. It has supported the integration of schools and the right of women to control their own bodies, among other important legislation. Yet there are those who would like to add new and quarrelsome provisions to this document. It is my belief that we must resist emotional tampering with the Constitution at all costs. It is not easy to change the Constitution, and that is good. Basic rights and liberties should be kept secure from transitory events and political currents.

I would not add any amendments to the Constitution. The flexibility of this document has made it an instrument that has served us well. There are those who would amend the Constitution to balance the budget, render abortions illegal, and include persons already addressed within its articles. There are others who would write the existing structure of our bureaucracy into the Constitution to give it a firmer base. Still others would like to make substantial changes in the form of government established by the Constitution. They would opt for a parliamentary government (in which the nation's leaders are chosen by the majority party) rather than our present form of representative democracy (in which public officials are directly elected by the people).

My view is that our framework of government with its three branches and our separation of powers is sufficient for the governance of the people of this country. If the Constitution as amended is found wanting, we in America have both the creativity and the political structure that allow us to address needs as they arise without changing the fundamental law. If I can in any sense be called a conservative when it comes to altering our framework of government, I am one.

Representative Tom Lantos

Tom Lantos (D-Calif.) was elected to the House of Representatives in 1980 after working as a foreign policy advisor to Senator Joseph R. Biden, Jr. of Delaware. Prior to his political career, Representative Lantos was a professor of Economics at San Francisco State University.

In the history of our great Republic, 11,092 men and women have served as members of the United States Senate or House of Representatives. Of that number, I am the only one who has lived under both fascist and communist dictatorships. I am the only survivor of the horrors of the Holocaust to be elected to Congress. Those experiences shaped my life and shaped my love and respect for the United States Constitution.

Just two months after my sixteenth birthday—in March of 1944—the Nazi Army occupied my native Hungary. Even before formally taking control, however, Nazi Germany dominated the Hungarian government's foreign relations and directed its domestic policies of discriminating against Jews and stifling all opposition to the fascist regime.

Twice, along with thousands of others, I was sent to a forced labor camp. We were required to perform heavy labor on projects under the supervision of fascist troops. Many of those who were consigned to these camps were later sent to extermination camps at Auschwitz. Thanks to my "Aryan"-looking blue eyes and blond hair and my strong will to survive, I managed to escape from the work camps. I was able to return to Budapest, where I lived in a "safe house" established by the Swedish diplomat Raoul Wallenberg. Through his courageous and daring efforts in just seven short months, Wallenberg saved an estimated 100,000 Hungarian Jews from the "final solution." My exposure to Wallenberg was a critical turning point in my life—my concern with civil and human rights stems from these early experiences.

In January 1945, Budapest was taken by Soviet troops after six weeks of house-to-house fighting. I had the opportunity to see the local Soviet leaders at first hand. Members of the high command of the Red army were interested in learning English. Through a series of coincidences, I found myself tutoring the top Soviet officers in English. Every morning a large black Soviet car sporting the Soviet flag picked me up and I spent an hour or two giving English lessons.

During this period of time I saw the tragic consequences of the denial of free speech, the subversion of the electoral process, and the imposition of a nondemocratic government by foreign troops.

In the summer of 1947, at the age of 19, I left Hungary to study in the United States. America was the land of promise, a land of opportunity—in stark contrast to the declining possibilities that I saw in Hungary. America was a land of liberty, where freedoms and democratic rights were enshrined in the Constitution.

One of the happiest days of my life was the day I became a U.S. citizen—five years after my arrival here. I call myself "an American by choice"—I am not a U.S. citizen simply because my parents happened to live here. I really *wanted* to be an American.

The United States Constitution embodies and guarantees the principles that are so important to me in my personal and public life. I know of no document so well designed and crafted. Two principles of the Constitution are especially dear to me because of my own experiences: freedom of speech and respect for civil and human rights.

As a teenager in Hungary, I learned the value of free speech. The fascist and communist governments controlled newspapers and radio in an effort to control the minds of the Hungarian people. Criticism in the press of the regime's denial of human rights and its disastrous foreign policies was not permitted. I listened to the Voice of America and the BBC (the British Broadcasting Company) which provided then—and in fact still provide—information in areas of the world where freedom of information does not exist. During that period, I had to listen clandestinely because the government did not want Hungarians to hear other views. As I compared what I saw with what I heard from the West, I came to know the importance and value of free speech and a free press.

Both the fascist and communist governments trampled on individual rights. People were arrested without warrant; were punished on false charges without due process of law; and were denied the right to assemble, to discuss new ideas, and to practice the religion of their choice. The denial of these rights was implemented through courts controlled by the fascist and communist regimes.

In contrast, the Constitution gave the United States a government that is accountable to its people. For the first time in history, the principle was established that government is responsible

Let's see... EQUAL RIGHTS... then one for a BALANCED BUDGET... GUN CONTROL would be a good one. And MANDATORY PROM DATES is a must AMENDMENT.

NATIONAL AMENDMENT WRITING CONTEST
☆ ☆ ☆
BE THE FIRST STUDENT IN YOUR SCHOOL TO AMEND THE CONSTITUTION.

to its citizens. One key feature of the Constitution is that it upholds individual rights and respects the dignity of human life.

Protecting the human rights guaranteed by our Constitution remains one of my most basic concerns as a citizen and as a congressman.

Questions to Consider

1. Make a list of all the constitutional amendments proposed by the writers of this article. Which amendment do you think should become part of the law of the land? Why?

2. Examine what each writer has to say about the impact of the Constitution on their lives. How do they compare? How does the Constitution affect the way you live?

3. After reading Representative Lantos's article, do you think Americans take for granted the freedoms given to them in the Constitution?

22

Extending the Right to Vote

During the summer of 1787, delegates from twelve of the thirteen states met in Philadelphia to revise the Articles of Confederation. After initial discussion and debate, those who favored scrapping the Articles in favor of a stronger, more centralized government became leaders of the Philadelphia Convention.

Under the Articles, any amendment or change required the unanimous consent of the states and, consequently, no changes had been approved. The fifty-five men laboring in Philadelphia that summer realized the problems of unanimous consent, and as they drafted the new document—the Constitution of the United States—

they were determined to provide an avenue for change.

Article Five explains how the Constitution can be changed. Amendments may be proposed by a two-thirds vote of both houses of Congress, or by a national convention called by Congress at the request of two-thirds of the state legislatures. Proposed amendments must be ratified by either an affirmative vote of three-fourths of the state legislatures or by three-fourths of the state conventions called to vote on the amendment. The choice of ratification is left to Congress. Thus far, all amendments have been proposed by Congress, and all but one have been ratified by state legislatures. That Amendment, the

Twenty-first, which repealed prohibition, was ratified by state conventions.

During the past two hundred years just twenty-six amendments have been added to the Constitution. Three of these amendments were enacted to extend suffrage (the right to vote) to groups previously disenfranchised, and two of the three were adopted in this century. The Nineteenth Amendment gave women the right to vote, and the Twenty-sixth Amendment extended the right to vote to eighteen-year-olds. Although the process through which both these amendments passed was similar, the political climate in both cases was vastly different. This case study will explore

Suffragettes marching in a parade to support the passage of the Nineteenth Amendment. The right to vote was extended to women only after a seventy-two year struggle.

how and why these amendments were added to our Constitution.

The Nineteenth Amendment

———

In the new code of laws...I desire you would remember the ladies and be more generous and favorable to them than your ancestors. Do not put such unlimited power into the hands of husbands. Remember, all men would be tyrants if they could. If particular care and attention is not paid to the ladies, we are determined to foment a rebellion, and will not hold ourselves bound by any laws in which we have no voice or representation.

Abigail Adams, 1777

———

A woman's brain involves emotion rather than intellect; and whilst this feature fits her admirably as a creature burdened with the preservation and happiness of the human species, it painfully disqualifies her for the sterner duties to be performed by the intellectual faculties. The best wife and mother and sister would make the worst legislator, judge, and policy.

Speech at an anti-suffrage meeting, 1896

———

The campaign for women's suffrage had its beginnings in London at the 1840 world convention of the Anti-Slavery Society. Elizabeth Cady Stanton and her husband Henry were part of the American delegation. The British, however, were horrified to learn that the American contingent had women members, and after much discussion, the convention voted against seating the female delegates. The women were allowed seats in the balcony where they could listen to but not participate in the proceedings. Elizabeth Cady Stanton walked out rather than be seated as a spectator, and several male delegates, including abolitionist leader William Lloyd Garrison, walked out in support of the women.

It was on that eventful visit to London that Elizabeth Cady Stanton met Lucretia Mott, a Quaker schoolteacher and ardent abolitionist from Philadelphia. The two women became good friends and resolved to hold a women's rights meeting in the United States. Eight years later, in 1848, Elizabeth Cady Stanton organized a women's rights convention in Seneca Falls, New York. The three hundred attendees quickly adopted resolutions calling for women's rights to own property, obtain a divorce, practice free speech, and enjoy equal opportunity in commerce, the professions, and education. Elizabeth Cady Stanton's

August 26, 1920. With state officials and women suffrage workers looking on, the governor of Tennessee, Albert H. Roberts, signs the state's ratification bill and the Nineteenth Amendment becomes law.

last resolution, calling for granting women the right to vote, became the cause of much debate. Even Lucretia Mott feared it would create an uproar and make supporters of women's rights look foolish. However, abolitionist Frederick Douglass, a famous orator, spoke in favor of it, and the resolution was adopted by a slim majority.

At the same time that Lucretia Mott and Elizabeth Cady Stanton began to call for women's suffrage, Lucy Stone was graduating from Oberlin College at the age of twenty-nine. Born to a poor farm family in Massachusetts, Lucy worked as a teacher and as an aide to pay her way through college. Upon graduation she became a public speaker for the Anti-Slavery Society at a salary of $25 a month. However, her interest in women's rights soon led her to take a $15 pay cut to speak weekdays on abolition but weekends for women's rights.

A fourth woman, Susan B. Anthony, became involved in the struggle for women's rights twenty years

later when she met Elizabeth Cady Stanton. A schoolteacher and an ardent advocate of prohibition, Susan B. Anthony resigned from her work with the American Temperance Union to devote all of her time to the women's rights movement.

These four women, whose names are synonymous with women's suffrage, began the campaign for voting rights for American women. Though none of them would live to witness the ratification of the Nineteenth Amendment, they all labored tirelessly for the rest of their lives toward the enfranchisement of women.

In 1869, Susan B. Anthony and Elizabeth Cady Stanton founded the National Women's Suffrage Association (NWSA). The goal of the NWSA was passage of a constitutional amendment to enfranchise women, and Susan B. Anthony traveled across the country giving speeches on behalf of women's rights.

During that same year, Lucy Stone founded the American Women's Suffrage Association (AWSA) with abolitionists Julia Ward Howe and Henry Ward Beecher. The goal of this rival suffrage organization was to win voting rights for women within each state by working with individual state legislatures, rather than attempting passage of a national constitutional amendment. In 1890, these two organizations merged under the title of the National American Women's Suffrage Association (NAWSA), and Susan B. Anthony served as president from 1892 to 1900.

The first victories for women occurred in the West. In 1869, Esther Morris, mother of three sons and the wife of a Wyoming settler, asked the president of the Wyoming territorial council, William Bright, to grant women the vote. Before the opposition had time to organize, a bill was passed by both houses of the legislature and signed by a sympathetic bachelor governor. It seems appropriate that women would first win the right to vote in a western

territory, where women worked side by side with their husbands clearing land and building homes and were considered equal partners in marriage.

In 1890, when Wyoming applied for statehood, some members of Congress tried to get the territory to annul their women's suffrage law. The Wyoming legislature wired Congress, "We may stay out of the Union for 100 years, but we will come in with our women." And so Wyoming was admitted as the first women's suffrage state.

By 1896, three additional states—Utah, Colorado, and Idaho—had also granted women the right to vote. However, between 1896 and 1910 no new states passed suffrage amendments. To be sure, some states had granted women partial suffrage (e.g., women might be allowed to vote in school board elections), and many people seemed to believe in full voting rights for women. On the national level, a women's suffrage amendment was proposed in Congress many times. However, the opposition to women's suffrage was strong, and the proposed amendment was rejected each time.

By 1913 five more states had enfranchised women. Alice Paul, a young Quaker from New Jersey who had been active in the British suffragist movement, advocated working at the national level to pass a women's suffrage amendment. She formed the Congressional Union (CU) within NAWSA. There were philosophical differences between the majority of NAWSA's two million members and the CU. While NAWSA leadership advocated the use of moral pressure and persuasion to change the minds of the president and Congress, Alice Paul and the CU wanted to rely solely on political protest.

Alice Paul began her protest movement with 10,000 demonstrators marching in a women's suffrage parade in Washington, D.C., on the day before president-elect Woodrow Wilson's 1912 inauguration. Many members

Women Voters In Presidential Elections

Only about one-third of the women eligible to vote reported voting in the 1920 presidential election. Many waited until the 1928, 1932, or even the 1936 election to cast their first ballot. The chart below shows the percentage of men and women who said they voted in the last four presidential elections.

Year	Men	Women
1972	64%	62%
1976	59	58
1980	59	59
1984	59	60

Source: U.S. Bureau of the Census

of the NAWSA opposed the action on the grounds that it would alienate sympathetic congressmen.

In 1915, Carrie Chapman Catt was elected president of the NAWSA, and Alice Paul was expelled from the organization. Paul and other members of the Congressional Union formed a political party, the Women's Party. It had just one goal: women's suffrage. With headquarters in Washington, the Women's Party continued to demonstrate for suffrage in front of the Wilson White House. After a few months, many of the protesters were arrested and jailed. As newspaper stories about prison conditions circulated (the cells were filthy and overcrowded and insects were found in the food), sympathy for the women spread, and money for the movement began to pour in. The arrests and convictions were later invalidated in the courts, and the protesters were viewed as heroines.

In 1917, the United States entered World War I. Under the leadership of Carrie Catt, women mobilized to support the war effort. In addition to hospital work, they took over jobs men had held before the war.

By the end of the war, Congress began to sense a change in the mood of the country. After all, Russia had given women the vote—why not the United States? In New York, the most populous state, a suffrage victory helped influence many congressmen to support a federal amendment. President Wilson declared his support for the amendment and both the Republican and Democratic convention platforms advocated women's suffrage. As demand for a constitutional amendment increased, NAWSA president Carrie Catt revealed a plan that assigned at least two women to lobby each congressman. After an intense lobbying effort, the Rules Committee of the House of Representatives finally agreed to bring the amendment to the floor for a vote.

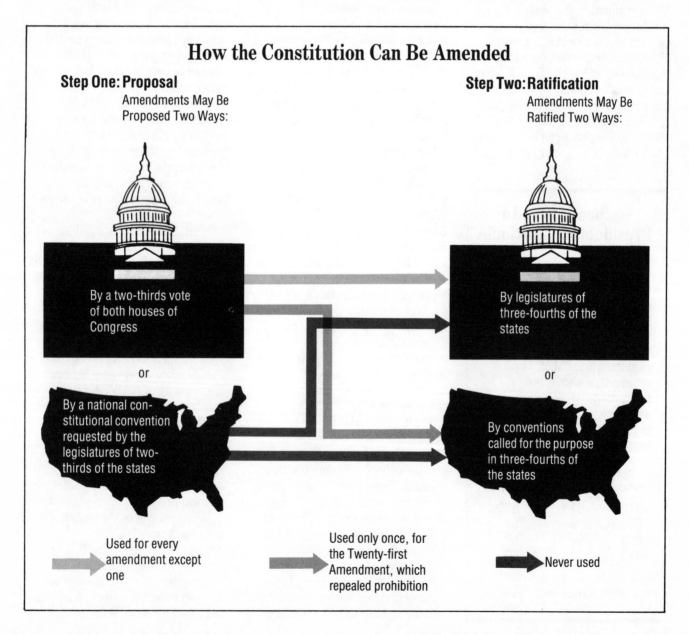

How the Constitution Can Be Amended

Step One: Proposal
Amendments May Be
Proposed Two Ways:

By a two-thirds vote of both houses of Congress

or

By a national constitutional convention requested by the legislatures of two-thirds of the states

Step Two: Ratification
Amendments May Be
Ratified Two Ways:

By legislatures of three-fourths of the states

or

By conventions called for the purpose in three-fourths of the states

Used for every amendment except one

Used only once, for the Twenty-first Amendment, which repealed prohibition

Never used

On January 10, 1918, the first woman to serve in Congress, Jeanette Rankin of Montana, opened the House debate on the proposed amendment. Congressmen who supported the amendment vigorously lobbied their opponents. Some congressmen made special efforts to be in Washington for the historic debate. A representative from Illinois left a hospital for the first time in months to vote for suffrage. A New York member came from the deathbed of his wife, a suffrage worker, to support the amendment. On the third vote, the amendment passed in the House of Representatives with only two votes to spare.

The suffrage amendment was short ten votes in the Senate. Believing a Senate vote was mandatory before the fall elections, the suffragists set about trying to secure those votes by the end of the summer.

Women came from throughout the United States to Washington for the vote. The debate lasted five days. President Wilson addressed the Senate, making an eloquent plea for suffrage.

On the day following Wilson's speech, the Senate rejected the amendment by two votes. Immediately, suffrage workers went to work on Senate campaigns to elect suffrage sympathizers and to defeat anti-suffrage senators.

In May 1919, the newly elected Congress was called into special session by President Wilson to consider once again the suffrage amendment. That same day the House passed the amendment and sent it to the Senate. This time the debate lacked the drama and passion of earlier days, and on the third ballot, the Senate passed the amendment 66 to 30.

Although many states voted for ratification in the days immediately following passage, it soon became apparent that ratification would be an additional struggle for the suffrage workers. States in which suffrage had been won years before had disbanded their organizations and now found it difficult to regroup

and petition their legislatures for ratification. However, by March of 1920, thirty-three states, just three short of the required thirty-six, had ratified the amendment. Then came the news of ratification in West Virginia and Washington. Only one more state was needed—and Tennessee offered a favorable prospect.

The governor of Tennessee called the legislature into special session. Carrie Catt went to Nashville to deliver a speech and remained six weeks fighting for women's franchise. She traveled across the state speaking in towns large and small. In Niota, a small town in eastern Tennessee, an elderly woman who read of Mrs. Catt's speeches wrote her twenty-four-year-old son, recently elected to the legislature:

And vote for suffrage and don't keep them in doubt. I notice some of the speeches against. They were very bitter. I have been watching to see how you stood, but have noticed nothing yet. Don't forget to be a good boy and help Mrs. Catt put "Rat" in ratification.

Harry Burn voted "yes" as his mother had requested, and the amendment passed the legislature, 49 to 47. After a seventy-two-year struggle, the amendment granting women the right to vote was law.

The Twenty-sixth Amendment

————

The right of citizens of the United States, who are 18 years of age or older to vote shall not be denied or abridged by the United States or by any state on account of age.
Senator Jennings
Randolph, 1942

————

Since ratifying the Constitution in 1789, Congress has extended the right to vote three times through the amending process. In 1870 the Fifteenth Amendment granted

former slaves the right to vote and in 1920 women gained the right to vote after a seventy-two year struggle. Using these two amendments as a precedent, the Twenty-sixth Amendment was adopted in 1970 to grant eighteen-year-olds the most basic of democratic rights.

The Twenty-sixth Amendment has its roots in America's involvement in the Vietnam War and the subsequent political activism of young people in the 1960s. During the mid-1960s, the United States increased its commitment to the Republic of South Vietnam to defend it against a communist invasion. Young men—many of them eighteen or nineteen years old— were drafted into the military to fight the war. Some people thought that if a young man was willing to die for his country, he should also have the right to vote. At the same time, many young Americans became increasingly involved in political issues such as race relations, women's rights, and protection of the environment. Without the power of the vote, young people could only voice their concern over these and other issues through protest marches and demonstrations. As the protests grew, some national leaders thought the time had come for eighteen-year-olds to be given the right to vote. Congress used the pending expiration of the Voting Rights Act in 1970 to grant eighteen-year-olds the right to vote.

The Voting Rights Act (VRA) provided for direct federal intervention to assist blacks and other minorities in registering and voting. Literacy tests and poll taxes (used to prevent blacks and other minorities from voting) were abolished in six southern states. The act also provided for federal examiners to observe and monitor elections in states covered by the act.

In 1970, Congress made plans to extend the VRA, which was scheduled to expire that year. New provisions were added including a thirty-day maximum residency requirement for voting in presidential elections and an end to the

After adoption of the Twenty-sixth Amendment, voter registration drives were begun by both the Republican and Democratic parties at high schools and college campuses around the country. By the presidential election of 1972 nearly 65 percent of all college students and 40 percent of eligible high school students were registered to vote.

use of literacy tests nationwide as a precondition to voting. Democratic senators Birch Bayh of Indiana and Edward Kennedy of Massachusetts favored the extension of the Voting Rights Act but also favored lowering the voting age to eighteen. Kennedy and Bayh wanted to attach a rider or an amendment to the VRA extension guaranteeing eighteen-year-old citizens the right to vote. The idea has surfaced each time the United States sends young men to war.

———

If young men are to be drafted at eighteen years of age to fight for their government, they

ought to be entitled to vote at eighteen years of age for the kind of government for which they are best satisfied to fight.

Senator Arthur
Vandenberg, 1942

———

For years, our citizens between the ages of eighteen and twenty-one have, in time of peril, been summoned to fight for America. They should participate in the political process that produces this fateful summons.

President Dwight D.
Eisenhower, 1954

If eighteen-year-olds are eligible for compulsory military service, they should be eligible to vote.

Senator Robert
Kennedy, 1964

———

With the exception of Harry Truman, all presidents from Franklin Roosevelt to Richard Nixon advocated lowering the voting age requirement to eighteen. The eighteen-year-old vote was also supported by the AFL-CIO, civil rights organizations including the NAACP, and 64 percent of the American public. The National Commission on the Causes and Prevention of Violence, a task force studying the underlying causes of the riots in the cities in the 1960s, called for "...draft reforms and a lowering of the minimum voting age to 18 as steps to woo alienated youth back into the mainstream of American society."

Although the idea had wide support, there was disagreement about how the change should occur. President Nixon favored a constitutional amendment because he thought Congress did not have the power to dictate voting requirements for local elections to the individual states. With strong support in Congress, however, lowering the voting age to eighteen was added to the 1970 Voting Rights Act extension, and passed both houses of Congress. President Nixon signed the bill to support the continuation of the VRA, but said he believed the clause lowering the voting age would be ruled unconstitutional for state elections. In *Oregon* v. *Mitchell*, the U.S. Supreme Court ruled that Congress could lower the voting age for federal elections but not for state and local elections.

This decision threatened to create havoc in the forty-seven states that did not allow eighteen-year-olds to vote. Unless each state lowered the voting age for state and local elections by amending its own constitution, individual states would have to hold dual elections in 1972. States would have to maintain one set of registration books, ballots, and voting machines for the national (presidential) election and a second set of books, ballots, and voting machines for state and local races. In addition to confusing the voters, dual elections would be prohibitively expensive. Estimates for dual elections in New York City alone exceeded $5 million in addition to normal election costs. Rigid requirements for amending twenty-two of the state constitutions made it impossible for these states to lower the voting age by the 1972 presidential election.

The Youth Vote

Of all registered voters in the United States, young people between eighteen and twenty years old have had the lowest turn-out in presidential elections. This chart shows the percentage of selected age groups who voted in the last four presidential elections.

Age	1972	1976	1980	1984
18-20 yr	48%	38%	35%	36%
21-24 yr	50	45	43	43
25-34 yr	59	55	54	54
35-44 yr	66	63	64	63
45-64 yr	70	68	69	69
65 yr and over	63	62	65	67

Source: U.S. Bureau of the Census

A Senate subcommittee appointed to study the problem reported that only a U.S. constitutional amendment lowering the voting age for all elections would enable the states to comply with the new law by the 1972 elections. Thus, it was these reasons—the desire to unburden the states from the expense of dual elections and to help them comply with the revised Voting Rights Act of 1970, in addition to the desire to extend the franchise to eighteen-year-old citizens—that prompted Congress to consider a constitutional amendment.

Birch Bayh, Senate floor manager for the bill, said, "Passage of this amendment will challenge young Americans to accept even more responsibility and show that they will participate." There was only token opposition to the bill in the House. Opponents charged that transient students in small college towns might outvote taxpayers and gain control of city government. Other representatives countered the charge by explaining that states could restrict voter registration by imposing strict residency requirements.

The proponents prevailed, and the amendment passed the Senate by a resounding 94 to 0 vote. In the House it was passed by a 401 to 19 vote.

The eighteen-year-old vote amendment easily cleared the first two hurdles. Unlike the women's suffrage amendment of 1920, there was nearly unanimous support in both houses of Congress. Ratification by three-quarters of the states was the final step.

Both Democratic and Republican national committees urged their state leaders to work for ratification of the amendment. On June 30, 1971, Ohio became the thirty-eighth state needed to ratify. The amendment became effective immediately, well before the 1972 elections. Ratification had taken place in record time. Just three months and a week had elapsed since Congress had approved the amendment and sent it to the states for ratification.

Activities

1. Reading Between the Lines

Many of the amendments to the Constitution affect our daily lives. For example, freedom of the press allows us to gather information from a wide variety of sources; voting rights give any citizen over the age of eighteen the ability to participate in our democratic process; and due process grants every citizen the right to legal counsel when being tried in a court of law.

Try to determine which amendments most affect your own life. Carefully read the twenty-six constitutional amendments, writing down those that directly affect you and the rights they grant you. Then choose one and consider how your life would be different if that amendment had never been adopted. How would the loss of the amendment affect those around you?

2. Developing Your Own Perspective

All fifty states have constitutions that outline the duties and responsibilities of the state government. Obtain a copy of your state constitution and compare it with the U.S. Constitution. To help you compare and contrast the two documents, keep the following questions in mind:

- How are the two documents different? How are they alike?

- Does your state constitution include principles found in the U.S. Constitution such as separation of powers and checks and balances?
- Is there a bill of rights in your state constitution? If so, how does it compare with the U.S. Bill of Rights? Do you think it is necessary to have two bills of rights?
- Why do you think state constitutions are needed?

3. Becoming an Active Citizen

The U.S. Constitution grants states the right to establish local governments within their borders. Today, there are over 80,000 units of local government in the United States. Cities, counties, townships, and villages are some examples of the many types of local government. Often, the jurisdictions of different governments overlap. Understanding the complex maze of so many local governments can seem difficult, but knowing where to go to in order to solve a problem or answer a question is one of the first steps toward active citizenship.

To become familiar with the state, county, and other local governments that have jurisdiction in your area, call or write to your city hall and ask for a copy of the charter that established your city government. Familiarize yourself with the basic structure of your city or town government and find out the requirements for office and the responsibilities of your elected officials. Get to know local elected officials, their backgrounds, and their stands on the issues. Attend a city council meeting and watch your local government in action. Remember—their decisions affect you!

★★★★★★★★★★

THE PRESIDENCY

2. The Presidency

In This Chapter

If American politics has a central focus, it is
the president of the United States. Although
elected to head just one of the three branches
of government—the executive branch—the
president is considered the leader of the entire
nation. As the primary shaper of our foreign policy,
the president represents the interests of the United
States to the rest of the world. In the years since our
nation was founded, the presidency has evolved to
become the main force in American government.

Presidential Power

Article II of the Constitution lists the presidential
powers. It grants presidents far fewer explicit
powers than it gives Congress in Article I. The
framers of the Constitution believed that Congress,
because of its close electoral ties to the people, would
dominate the government. Today, it is hard to imagine a president in an inferior position to the
Speaker of the House of Representatives or the
Senate majority leader.

One reason for the growth in presidential
power over the years is the ambiguous language
in the Constitution. The Constitution vests executive power in the president and gives
presidents the power to "take care that the laws
are faithfully executed." This clause enables
presidents to employ the means they think
necessary to ensure compliance with the law. For
example, it allows presidents the use of the armed
forces in times of emergency to protect the
security of the United States. The vague
language in the Constitution permits presidents
to claim certain powers they think necessary to
meet different situations.

The Constitution also gives presidents the
leading role in conducting foreign affairs. As the
nation has become more deeply involved in world
affairs, presidential powers have grown accordingly. Modern technology, including mass com-

munications, has greatly increased the speed with which we learn about world events and react to them. When a quick decision is necessary, a single leader can respond faster than a legislature of 535 members. It is hard to imagine Congress effectively playing a dominant role in U.S. foreign relations, especially in a crisis or negotiations with a foreign leader.

The increased involvement of the government in domestic affairs has also contributed to the growth of presidential power. Government now plays an active role in economic planning, public transportation, environmental protection, the regulation of commerce, and public health. This increased government responsibility has meant the expansion of the federal bureaucracy—a bureaucracy under presidential control.

Yet, considering the powers granted presidents by the Constitution, it seems that, while they are significant, they still do not add up to the formidable role of the president in our political system. Part of this can be explained by the importance of developments in foreign and domestic policy. But much depends on the type of person occupying the presidential office.

Presidential Personality

Depending on their personalities, different presidents have taken very different approaches to their job. Some depended on leadership from Congress and viewed their powers as strictly administrative. They argued that presidents should be limited to those powers expressly granted by the Constitution; otherwise there might be no limit to presidential power. James Buchanan, Calvin Coolidge, and Herbert Hoover are in this category.

Other presidents have been active politicians, often rallying the country behind a cause. Such presidents originated much of the legislation considered by Congress and tried to lead public opinion. They believed that the only limits to their power were those explicitly mentioned in the Constitution. Abraham Lincoln, Franklin Roosevelt, and Lyndon Johnson were all activist presidents.

Still other presidents have avoided political leadership, viewing the job as that of organizer of national consensus in opposition to special interests, which Congress represents. Such presidents believed they should use their veto power liberally to control Congress. Dwight Eisenhower is an example of this type of presidential personality.

Public Expectations

If it seems that presidents have considerable power, it still falls short of what would be needed to meet the expectations most of us have for the office. This is a paradox of the modern presidency; it has become a more powerful office, but relative to public expectations, it is lacking in formal authority. Today, presidents are judged poorly if they do not get their legislative programs enacted; yet under the Constitution, it is Congress and not the president that has legislative power. Similarly, many hold presidents responsible for the performance of the economy; yet the power to manage the economy (insofar as our government can do so) lies with Congress, the Federal Reserve System, and independent regulatory agencies.

Presidents are expected to accomplish much, yet they do not always have the power to command. Rather, they must rely on their power to persuade both Congress and the American people. Because much of the success of presidents rests on their ability to communicate and persuade, our perceptions of a president's capacity to lead changes frequently. At one moment, a president may seem invincible; at another, vulnerable.

Debates Surrounding the Presidency

The paradoxical character of the modern presidency has created two very different perceptions of presidential power. Viewed from inside the White House, the powers of the president usually seem inadequate. Viewed from the outside, the power of the presidency can appear dangerous. These concerns have led to many suggestions for changes in the office of the presidency. Some of the proposed changes frequently raised include restricting the president to a single six-year term of office, Senate confirmation of *all* presidential appointees including personal advisors, and subjecting the president to periodic reviews by Congress. However, even if such changes were adopted, the ability of a president to lead the nation would still be determined by the personality and management skills a person brings to the highest office in the country.

Every day, the president of the United States makes decisions that affect the lives of millions of people. The president commands our armed forces, oversees the bureaucracy, speaks for the United States in world affairs, negotiates treaties, initiates major legislation, and fulfills countless other responsibilities.

Pete Souza/The White House

Courtesy Gerald R. Ford Library

The White House

The White House

34

Thoughts on Presidential Decisionmaking

President Ronald Reagan

Every day the president of the United States is called upon to make decisions that affect millions of people. The size and complexity of the problems that face the nation place enormous pressures on the shoulders of the president, whose job it is to solve them. In this interview, President Ronald Reagan gives valuable insight into the way presidential decisions are made. He explains the significance of some of the many factors that influence his choice of policies and outlines his approach to decisionmaking at the highest level of government.

CLOSE UP: The office of president of the United States brings enormous responsibilities to those who rise to fill it. How difficult did you find it to adapt to the responsibility of the momentous decisions that you, as president, are called upon to make?

President Reagan: As you say, the office is one with enormous and unique responsibilities. While there is no single prior experience that can really train anyone for the presidency, I do think certain kinds of experience are helpful. I think being governor of California, the most populous state in the country, gave me valuable experience for the job. After all, California has about 10 percent of the total U.S. population. As governor, I served as chief executive responsible for leading the state, running a large government, and working with a legislature and other governors.

CLOSE UP: The Oval Office is a focus of advice, information, and even pressure from a variety of sources. Congressional leaders may want one thing, White House staff may want another, members of your Cabinet may want a third. How do you sift through all of this information to make your decisions?

President Reagan: When making decisions, I try to keep in mind overall goals and long-term objectives. If you do not keep an eye on your long-range goals, you are bound to get lost along the way. This approach allows me to evaluate complicated issues and put everything in perspective.

In making specific decisions, I actively seek advice from a variety of sources. I often ask for advice from members of the Cabinet, the White House staff, members of Congress, and individuals outside of government. We have set up a Cabinet Council system that thoroughly analyzes the issues and presents a variety of options for my consideration. Our staffing system at the White House, through which members of the staff provide me with their views, is a major source of information and direction.

One of the things that brings the issues in focus is my opportunity to hear the arguments on all sides firsthand in Cabinet and Cabinet Council meetings as well as in meetings with senators and representatives.

I am satisfied that the process of advising me is both orderly and comprehensive. But I might add, that does not make decisionmaking any easier.

CLOSE UP: It would seem that the private citizen's perspective on issues that confront the nation differs from that which you have as president. Did you find it necessary to alter, once you entered the White House, the policy goals you declared while a candidate?

President Reagan: I have not changed my basic philosophy since I entered the White House. In fact, my years in office have reinforced my conviction that we must reduce the growth of government spending, limit the tax burden, provide relief from unnecessary regulations, return decisionmaking authority to state and local governments, and develop a better partnership between the public and private sectors. In terms of foreign policy, I still believe that the best way for America to maintain strength in the world is by maintaining its own strength. These are the issues on which my campaign was based, and they remain the goals of everyone working for the administration. Certainly, circumstances change, as do one's tactics for achieving goals. But the basic goals of my policy are still the same as when I first took office.

CLOSE UP: It is the responsibility of members of Congress to represent the views of their constituents and to act upon them. In what way do you take into account the fact that Congress might attempt to block a proposal that you make if their constituents are opposed to it?

President Reagan: Of course, I take into account the views of Congress when making any decision or proposal. In fact, I actively consult with members of Congress on a wide range of issues and meet with them on a regular basis. Our system is one of shared power, as the Constitution intended, so it is appropriate that we consider each other's views. In general, we have had a good working relationship. Obviously, we do not agree on everything, but unlike what some have claimed, we have a government that works.

CLOSE UP: To what extent is it necessary for you, Mr. President, to delegate certain decisions to your aides rather than make them yourself? How important to your decisions is the advice of your aides?

President Reagan: There are hundreds, if not thousands, of decisions in government that must be made each day. It is obviously impossible for one person to make every decision or to be an expert in all of those areas. That is why I spent so much time appointing good people to help me run the government. I am confident that the peo-

Ronald Reagan defeated incumbent Jimmy Carter in 1980 to win the presidency and was reelected in 1984 by the largest electoral vote margin in U.S. history. President Reagan says that his two terms as governor of California have helped him fulfill his responsibilities as president.

Michael Evans/The White House

36

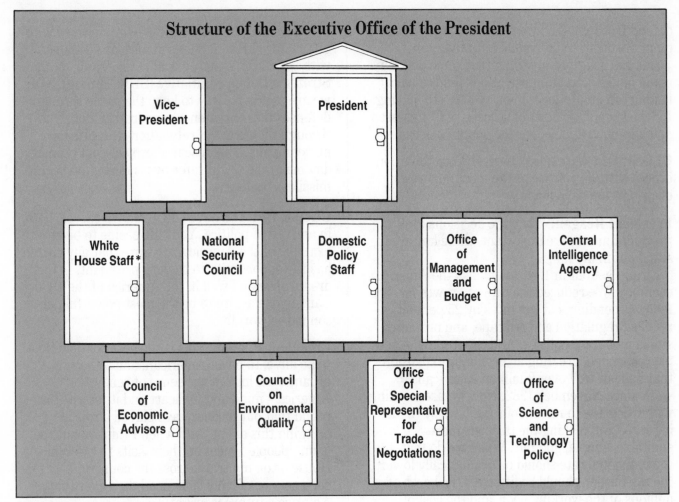

Structure of the Executive Office of the President

- President
- Vice-President
- White House Staff *
- National Security Council
- Domestic Policy Staff
- Office of Management and Budget
- Central Intelligence Agency
- Council of Economic Advisors
- Council on Environmental Quality
- Office of Special Representative for Trade Negotiations
- Office of Science and Technology Policy

*Includes political advisors, press secretary, and speech writers

ple I appointed to the Cabinet and other offices have the expertise, integrity, and wisdom to make the right decisions in their areas.

Those decisions that set major policy direction are the kinds of decisions that I do not delegate. On those, I actively seek information and advice from other people, but I ultimately have to make the final decision. I was elected to lead, so rather than trying to manage every detail, I have tried to focus on major policy issues.

CLOSE UP: Some people prefer that the advice they receive come from people who share their general views, while others like to have a variety of opinions presented to them. Which do you think is the better way to gather information, and why?

President Reagan: I am the kind of person who prefers getting advice on an issue from a variety of points of view. On almost every major issue, there are a large number of factors and opinions supporting different sides of the issue. And I prefer hearing those different views, rather than excluding them. By listening to all sides and get-

ting the best thinking available on an issue, I can sift out the most important factors and make my decision based on all the information available.

CLOSE UP: In a first term, a president is constrained by the decisions made during a previous administration and the pressures of a reelection campaign. Neither is a factor in your second term. Has your decisionmaking changed since your second inaugural?

President Reagan: I have always believed that the people elect their leaders to make decisions that we believe are right and in the best interests of our country. As governor of California, I made it clear that I did not want to hear any advice from my staff on how a given decision might affect future elections. I have enforced the same rule here at the White House. There are no exceptions.

Is my second term shaping up to be especially different than the first? No, I am the same person, with the same basic philosophy I brought to Washington in 1981. I believe that we must keep our country strong to protect the peace and defend freedom. And we must remove government obstacles to individual initiative.

But you are right in saying that some decisions made in previous administrations tend to have lasting effects. Indeed, today we are still paying for the spending habits of successive Congresses and administrations over the past two decades.

CLOSE UP: As you look back on your tenure in office, what do you see as the most important decisions you have made?

President Reagan: While the decisions each president makes are important, three key areas stand out in my mind.

First, I set out in 1981 to unleash the American economy. We reduced the rate of growth in federal spending, cut tax rates by 25 percent, reduced regulation and red tape, and promoted stable monetary policies. And the American people responded, creating an economic expansion that has put well over 9 million Americans to work since November 1982. Now we are working with Congress to reform our tax laws by reducing rates and making the tax code more equitable, simple, and fair. When we do that, the top individual rate should be dramatically lower, the tax burden should be lifted off the backs of millions of the working poor, and the cost of capital should be kept down so the economy can keep growing.

Second, national defense. When I became president, our military was suffering from low morale; ships couldn't sail and planes couldn't fly for lack of experienced crews and spare parts. Crucial strategic weapons programs were behind schedule or had been scrapped altogether. The weapons procurement program was riddled with waste and inefficiency. It was critical that we turn the situation around—and our progress these past five years has been substantial. We reduced the cost growth in major weapons programs from 14 percent to 1 percent, and we are doing even more to ensure that a dollar spent on defense yields a dollar's worth of security. With the addition of the B-1 bomber, the MX "Peacekeeper" missile, and the Trident submarines, we have made the first significant improvement in strategic capability in twenty years. And our recruitment goals are being met with some of the highest-quality men and women our armed forces have ever seen. We have laid the foundation for the most effective military we have ever had in peacetime.

A third crucial decision was to go forward with efforts for real reductions in nuclear weapons with the Soviets, and to conduct research on the Strategic Defense Initiative (SDI). Through SDI, we are seeking a way to keep the peace through defenses that threaten no one, rather than through the threat of retaliation with offensive nuclear arms. This research project could someday make the world safer by rendering nuclear missiles obsolete.

CLOSE UP: You have had an active career, both in and out of politics. Your life seems to be an example of the American dream—that any citizen has the opportunity to become president. Is this dream alive and well in the America of the 1980s? Can anyone aspire to be the most powerful person in the world?

President Reagan: This is the best possible time to be alive, to be an American, and to have a dream. Just look at the sense of renewal of America's mind and its heart and its spirit! I'm proud that our policies have played a role in bringing this about. And when I think about the young people I meet on their visits to the White House or on my trips across the country, I become more firmly convinced than ever that America's future is bright.

America is the land of opportunity, and in this land of opportunity and democracy, anyone the people choose can be elected president.

1. How are decisions made in the Reagan White House?

2. President Reagan states that "...there is no single prior experience that can really train anyone for the presidency [but]...certain kinds of experience are helpful." What kind of experience do you think a person needs in order to be president?

3. President Reagan lists three major accomplishments of his administration. What three things do you think the Reagan years will be most remembered for?

Presidential Power and the Single 6-Year Term

Griffin Bell

Griffin Bell is the cofounder and national chair of the National Committee for a Single Six-Year Presidential Term. He was a circuit court judge for fifteen years before he was appointed as attorney general of the United States during the Carter administration. In this article, Mr. Bell recommends the establishment of a single 6-year presidential term as a way to make our presidents more effective leaders.

In a nation where we as a people embrace many different political beliefs, there is one thing that can be said to be almost universally true—we revere, respect, and uphold that remarkable document of political genius called the Constitution. As a federal judge and attorney general of the United States, I have devoted most of my life to upholding the Constitution. It has served us very well in the two hundred years since it was written. But I also have to agree with Thomas Jefferson who acknowledged that it was not perfect and urged each succeeding generation to "examine it in light of the needs of the times." In these times of swift and often dramatic technological and social change, there are aspects of our government that need to be examined and improved. I believe that a constitutional amendment providing for a single 6-year presidential term is first among them.

The single-term presidency is not a new idea. When our nation's founders wrote the Constitution, the specter of monarchy and excessive power peered over their shoulders. They debated which system would best allow the president of the United States to be a head of state who would be given the respect, but not undue power, that would enable him to do the job that he was elected to do. The question of the length of the presidential term was repeatedly argued at the Constitutional Convention, and many delegates supported a single, non-reelectable term for the president. In the end, they were guided by their expectation that the first president would be George Washington, who believed that official capacities should be limited. Only reluctantly did President Washington run for a second term. In doing so he began a tradition of a maximum of two terms in office that lasted until President Franklin Roosevelt, who was elected to four consecutive terms.

Some years after George Washington left office, the single presidential term was again in the public eye when Andrew Jackson strongly urged the nation to adopt a single six-year term in every one of his inaugural addresses. Sixteen presidents since Jackson have said publicly that they believe a single 6-year presidential term would have allowed them to do a better job.

When we elect a president, we expect him to do his job—to lead the country and make important policy decisions. But these days, it is extremely hard for a president to do a good job in his first term. He comes into office with the budget of his predecessor, and it takes about a year for the president to become fully acquainted with complex foreign and domestic policy matters. He then has about a year to implement his campaign promises and programs before he finds himself involved in a campaign to be reelected. Whether our presidents want to or not, political advisors and public opinion force them to be more concerned with winning a second term in the last two years of a first term than in making the often tough, unpopular decisions that are necessary to lead the nation effectively.

When a president who is in office is running for a second term, a number of factors influence his ability to make long-term decisions. Special interest groups, which often do not represent the general interest, wield a great deal of power, and a president must spend a significant amount of time thinking about these competing interests and calculating how they may affect his chances for reelection. In domestic economic policymaking, short-term decisions that may give the economy a temporary lift are frequently inflationary in the long run. Damaging short-term decisions that create an artificial sense of economic stability—that put money in voters' pockets—are especially popular in a preelection period. Alfred Kahn, former chairman of the

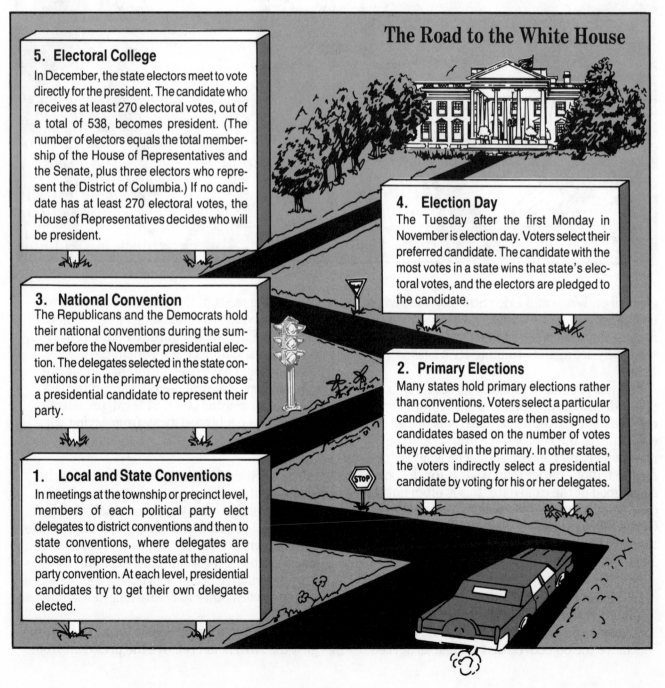

The Road to the White House

5. Electoral College
In December, the state electors meet to vote directly for the president. The candidate who receives at least 270 electoral votes, out of a total of 538, becomes president. (The number of electors equals the total membership of the House of Representatives and the Senate, plus three electors who represent the District of Columbia.) If no candidate has at least 270 electoral votes, the House of Representatives decides who will be president.

4. Election Day
The Tuesday after the first Monday in November is election day. Voters select their preferred candidate. The candidate with the most votes in a state wins that state's electoral votes, and the electors are pledged to the candidate.

3. National Convention
The Republicans and the Democrats hold their national conventions during the summer before the November presidential election. The delegates selected in the state conventions or in the primary elections choose a presidential candidate to represent their party.

2. Primary Elections
Many states hold primary elections rather than conventions. Voters select a particular candidate. Delegates are then assigned to candidates based on the number of votes they received in the primary. In other states, the voters indirectly select a presidential candidate by voting for his or her delegates.

1. Local and State Conventions
In meetings at the township or precinct level, members of each political party elect delegates to district conventions and then to state conventions, where delegates are chosen to represent the state at the national party convention. At each level, presidential candidates try to get their own delegates elected.

Council on Wage and Price Stability, said when he left his post in 1980 that "no successful war against inflation will be waged until a president is resolutely set against running for a second term."

Political pressures similarly affect foreign policy decisions, creating a lack of continuity in our dealings with other nations, which is often confusing to the rest of the world. While the most important concern should be what is good for the nation, rather than what is for the personal good of the candidate, this is often not the case when a president is seeking reelection. Cyrus Vance, former secretary of state and national co-chair of the Committee for a Single Six-Year Presidential Term, points out:

In the last eighteen months of the Carter administration, we lost a great deal of the boldness and drive we originally had to achieve the objectives that we had all agreed

on at the onset of the administration. I am convinced that our handling of affairs in the Middle East, with regard to SALT II in 1979, and the situations that arose in the Caribbean would have been different had we not been in an electoral period. During the last eighteen months of a first term, presidents sadly are frightened away from saying what they think.

The Carter administration was not alone in changing its political course before an election. Many presidents delay making tough decisions until they are reassured of a second term. If the second term does not come, as it often does not, the short-term decisions and delays can create a very destructive cycle. Short-term solutions pile on top of each other to create long-term national problems.

In proposing a single 6-year term, I do not suggest that we should remove the president from politics or insulate him in any way from public opinion. Our system of divided powers ensures that every president will need to take his policies to Congress and the people to win support. In its best sense, politics does not involve the manipulation and evasion required in running for reelection. It does involve managing the nation's business with a realistic long-term perspective in mind and providing leadership for one's political party in doing so.

As an issue, the single 6-year term is supported by people with a variety of political persuasions. Among its supporters are Cabinet members from every presidential administration since Franklin Roosevelt and both democratic and republican members of the United States Senate and House of Representatives. Single 6-year term supporters are, like most Americans, deeply grateful that the nation's founders made the task of amending the Constitution a difficult one, but are also strongly persuaded that we cannot continue going in the direction that two years of presidential electioneering in a first term inevitably takes us. The country suffers when our presidents and their staffs become more concerned with winning an election than with the task of leading the nation, and it will continue to suffer until the diversion of a second term is removed.

With the two-hundredth anniversary of the drafting of the Constitution, I think now more than ever we need to respond to Thomas Jefferson's plea that we take a hard look at what is working and what isn't working in the structure of our government. It seems clear to me that the executive branch is not working as effectively as it should. A constitutional amendment providing a single 6-year term seems to be the logical first step toward allowing our presidents to do their job from the day they are sworn in until the day they leave office.

Of recent presidents, perhaps Lyndon Johnson put it best when he wrote, after leaving office, "if a fellow knew...that he had a definite limitation and the bell's going to ring at a certain time, he might be able to tackle some of the problems he's inclined to postpone."

Questions to Consider

1. What are some of the advantages cited by the author of the single 6-year presidential term?

2. What are some of the limits on presidential power and decisionmaking that are caused by the current 4-year term? Do you think our country is helped or hampered by these limits?

3. The Twenty-second Amendment to the Constitution prevents a president from serving more than two terms. Why do you think this amendment was adopted? Do you think this restriction on presidential terms is good for the country? Why or why not?

Public Expectations of the President

Edward C. Smith

Edward C. Smith is currently a professor at the American University in Washington, D.C. From 1977 to 1978, he served in the Carter administration as the associate director to the assistant to the president for public liaison. In this article, Mr. Smith describes the challenge that faces every president—to be both president and presidential.

Every four years, the American people elect a president to preside over the nation. During the campaign, the candidates' media advisors try to market to the masses the image of a deliberate, decisive, compassionate, and controlled man. They promise that—once in office—their candidate will personally run the government, through the force of his character and charisma, and that he will indeed be both *president* and *presidential*. Yet, after only a few months in office, the nation quickly witnesses the limitations of presidential power. The president's "honeymoon" with the American electorate is invariably short-lived. For most of his administration, a president will be challenged by nearly every sector of public opinion, either for retreating from earlier campaign promises or for not advancing others. The persistence of such criticism can steadily chisel away at the president's stature among foreign and domestic leaders. Such criticism can also seriously limit his ability to govern by reducing the influence of his endorsement of any given set of issues.

America gained its independence through a revolutionary war against royalty. Indeed, the formation of our new nation was made possible by a rare combination of leaders with uncommon skill and tenacity. Our nation's founders were able to arouse a spirit of admiration and allegiance, sacrifice, and service from the citizens who followed them. However, although we honor the common man, we also covet "royalty" (as evidenced by the homage we pay to celebrities in every walk of life from athletes to academics and most especially in our deferential treatment toward foreign royalty). This acceptance and promotion of the celebrity influences our attitude toward the president; we want him to be one of us and above us at the same time.

A key factor contributing to a president's popularity is his ability to inspire the nation. This is particularly important since, for the past twenty years, the political process in America has become a form of "theater": Washington, D.C., serves as center stage, and the rest of the nation, even the rest of the world, serves as the audience. Thus, the president is elected not only to lead the nation, but he is also expected to play the role of the nation's "leading man."

In addition to being the nation's capital, where all of the major departments and agencies of the federal government are housed, Washington, D.C., is also the host city for foreign embassies

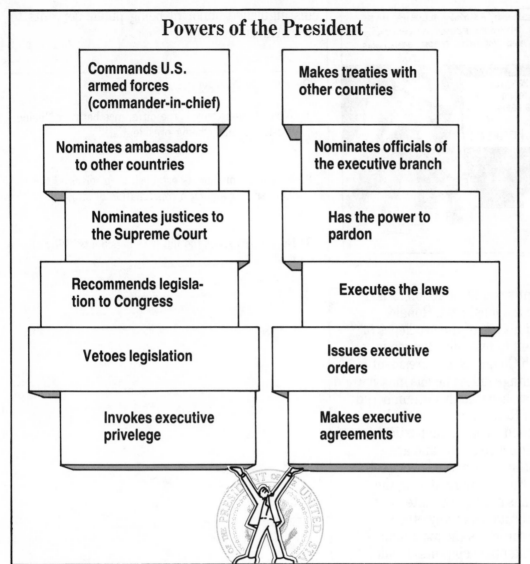

Powers of the President

Commands U.S. armed forces (commander-in-chief)

Makes treaties with other countries

Nominates ambassadors to other countries

Nominates officials of the executive branch

Nominates justices to the Supreme Court

Has the power to pardon

Recommends legislation to Congress

Executes the laws

Vetoes legislation

Issues executive orders

Invokes executive privelege

Makes executive agreements

Article II of the Constitution details the powers of the president. Throughout our country's history, changing social, political, economic, and international conditions have led different presidents to interpret these powers in different ways.

and legations and for the international press corps. In addition, within the past few decades, Washington has become an oasis for public interest, corporate, and diplomatic lobbyists, as well as attorneys, management consultants, and brokers for narrower interests. Most, if not all, of these individuals at one time or another deal directly or indirectly with the federal government. The success of these ambassadors, who represent a wide array of domestic and global concerns, is measured largely by how effectively they serve as the link between the federal bureaucracy and the people they represent.

In this setting, the president must assert himself as the stellar star among a constellation of stars. He must establish himself as a leader, not a manager. He is expected to be on a "hill" examining the vast panorama of national and global problems, not in the trenches exhausting himself by going one-on-one with individual issues. Furthermore, a president strives to be identified with certain national themes, which, if not unique, are at least unifying. Above all else, it is the president who—through his manner, conduct, vision, and selection of principal staff—establishes the tone of the nation.

A president's success is largely determined by how well he deals with Congress, the press, foreign leaders, career civil servants, and public interest and corporate lobbying groups. Consequently, to cope with the ever-increasing and diverse demands of each group, the president must employ all of the resources and perquisites of his office (e.g., invitations to the White House, Camp David, Air Force One, etc.) in order to inform, educate, and influence the nation. If he shuns using presidential perquisites, as Jimmy Carter did, or overindulges in them, as Richard

Since this "great president," as you call him has been in office, he's invaded four countries including Australia and imposed trade sanctions on Rhode Island...

Hey, you can't expect a president to be perfect.

distinguished honor of being public servants to the American people.

Questions to Consider

1. What do you think is the difference between "being president" and "being presidential?"

2. Why must presidents establish themselves as the "stellar star among a constellation of stars?"

3. Do voters expect too much of presidents? Why or why not?

Nixon did, a president's course of action is likely to end in failure. For the most part, Ronald Reagan has balanced his use of the privileges of his office to the pursuit of his political agenda.

In his dealings with Congress, the president is at a decided disadvantage unless he has massive popular support. First, he is vastly outnumbered (Senate and House of Representatives combined) by over 500 to 1. Second, senators in particular are members of an elite club of 100 and are elected to terms of office that exceed the president's by two years. Furthermore, during the past twenty years it has been the Senate—not the universities, corporations, or any other institution—that has served as the most important nursery for presidential aspirants. In addition, a chairman of an influential Senate committee (such as appropriations or foreign affairs) can wield enormous political power by preventing the president's proposals from ever getting to the Senate floor for a final vote. Finally, although the president works and resides in the splendor of the White House, the architectural grandeur of the Capitol is equally imposing. It instills a sense of power in the people who work there and helps to bring the prestige of Congress up to that of the president.

In closing, we extend to the president the authority to execute a limited amount of power. However, let it be understood that through this authority we entrust to him the responsibility for galvanizing the necessary resources and talent to advance the political agenda that he was elected to achieve. Our president is not and never will be a prince; rather, he is the first among all other elected and appointed officials who share the

A Field Watcher's Guide to the Presidency

Lee White

Lee White is currently a lawyer in the Washington, D.C., law firm of White, Fine, and Verville. He served as assistant special counsel to President John F. Kennedy and as special counsel to President Lyndon Johnson. In 1966, he became chair of the Federal Power Commission, a post he held until 1969 when he returned to private law practice. In this article, Mr. White discusses his guidelines for rating a president's performance in office.

The office of president of the United States, aside from its importance to the well-being of this country and indeed to the security and quality of life on the entire planet, provides an occasion for one of the nation's outstanding indoor sports. Somewhat like the Super Bowl, it affords everyone—from the most sophisticated observers and critics to the average citizens across the country—the opportunity to engage in observing, characterizing, criticizing, evaluating, and talking about whoever happens to be the president at any particular time. Because of the magnitude of the position and, most particularly, because of the electronic age in which we live, each of us can comment on the president's policies, personality, intelligence, and family—even the president's hairstyle. And with so many politicians expending nearly all their efforts to wind up in the Oval Office, it is worth taking a careful look at the position and at some of those who have occupied it recently.

The presidency is not a suit of clothes passed on from one occupant to another. Rather, it is an office that gives its occupant an enormous opportunity to shape the assignment to fit his own personal style and his personal view of what should be accomplished during his administration.

The U.S. Constitution confers a range of responsibilities and authorities upon the president. The president is the chief implementor of the laws of the land, the commander-in-chief of the armed forces, and the principal architect of U.S. foreign policy. He appoints individuals to serve in the executive branch and on federal courts, including the U.S. Supreme Court. He can also veto legislation sent to him by Congress (although that veto can be overridden by a two-thirds vote of both the House and Senate). Additionally, the president has responsibilities that, although not spelled out in the Constitution, are accepted as part of the job. The president is head of a national political party and has the opportunity to address American citizens (and, of course, the world) in a manner that ensures that his ideas, thoughts, and recommendations will be heard. All of these duties and responsibilities are passed from one president to another. But the appeal of president-watching is to see how different occupants of the office use their presidential powers.

Because presidential powers are so visible, there is a tendency to characterize presidents as powerful (the Roosevelts) or weak (Hoover and Carter); as usurpers of power (Nixon); or as abusers of power (Johnson). However, a more useful standard is to ask how effectively the president uses his power. In the short term, one may look at how well the president persuades Congress to adopt his programs, how he is perceived by the electorate, and how successful his party is at the election polls. In the long term, one must look at how wise and effective his policies were and whether he left the country more secure, more prosperous, and better educated than when he took office.

Each president brings his or her own personal working style to the office. Some, like Jimmy Carter, find it extremely difficult to delegate responsibilities, even to their own appointees. Others, like Ronald Reagan, appear to be concerned only with the broadest and most basic policy issues, leaving the details to others. There is no particularly right way or wrong way to be president; rather, it is the personality and operating style of a president that determine how he or she will handle the job.

Undoubtedly one of the most important decisions made by the president is the selection of the team of political appointees to serve in the administration. Even the most energetic, vigorous, and hardworking president requires a strong, talented, and experienced White House staff. Similarly, the department and agency heads who will lead vast bureaucracies are crucial to how effective a president will be. When the president is a very generous delegator of responsibility and authority, the choice of those who make up his executive branch team becomes even more important. Thus, examining the backgrounds of both the visible and the nearly "invisible" 200 to 250 appointees who really run the government can provide insight into how the president is going to do his job.

How the president communicates with Congress, with the American people, and with the world is also of crucial importance. Almost by definition, presidential candidates have to demonstrate skill in this particular area if they are to wind up in the Oval Office. Franklin Roosevelt demonstrated a mastery of radio that made possible so many of the accomplishments of the New Deal era. John F. Kennedy was a natural in using the medium of television effectively. On the other hand, Lyndon Johnson was extremely uncomfortable in front of the television camera. His forte was the small, intimate gathering where his considerable powers of personal persuasion could be put to effective use. The point is that the ability to communicate is increasingly important in terms of how effective a president will be.

Although television affords us an opportunity to develop our perception of the character of the president, our perceptions are also influenced by the opinions of others, such as members of Congress and journalists. The cumulative effect of their commentary is a significant factor in how a president is perceived by the people of the United States. Regardless of what one might think of his policies and programs, President Reagan has a wonderful ability to demonstrate on television that he is not a mean or vindictive soul. He possesses an easy and relaxed style that is generally pleasing to Americans. Over a period of time, the president's dominant characteristics will be evident even to the most casual follower of the political scene. Press conferences are especially insightful, since the president is required to respond to questions that he may not have thought out in advance.

The White House

The White House was designed by James Hoban in 1792. Construction began that same year; but labor, money, and transportation problems delayed completion of the "president's house" for eight years. The building was still unfinished in 1800 when John Adams moved in.

During the War of 1812, British soldiers set fire to the White House, destroying everything but the walls. Using most of the original walls, Hoban rebuilt the "president's house" and painted the walls white in 1817. Although many people believe that the white paint inspired the name "White House," the building had been known as the "White House" before the fire. Historians speculate that the name may have come from either the white sandstone used in the walls, the use of white paint before the War of 1812, or the southern tradition of calling the main house of a plantation— which the president's house resembled—a "white house." In 1818, James Madison officially named his residence the "Executive Mansion." This title remained until 1902, when Theodore Roosevelt and Congress elevated the more popular title of the "White House" to official use.

The press conference can demonstrate the familiarity of the president with what is going on in the world and in American government.

Nearly all presidents want to be reelected for a second term, and certainly all presidents want to be regarded as having been effective leaders during their administrations. With common goals and objectives motivating each president and with the multitude of pressures, there is a broad range of responses to those pressures. How each president responds helps shape our image of a particular president.

Two other basic principles are worth noting. First, each president in the short run is most sharply contrasted with his immediate predecessor. This simply means that President Y will be measured against all other presidents in the long run, but, in the short run, most sharply with President X. Thus, every president has to hope he has "an easy act to follow." Second, in the long run, it is by and large outside circumstances—many of which are completely beyond the control of the president—that form the most significant factor in the evaluation of a president's conduct of the office. For example, our view of Harry Truman has changed remarkably during the thirty years following his administration, mostly for the better. With the passage of time, some small, insignificant, and petty deficiencies of his administration are seen as just that, and the larger, lasting, positive accomplishments are recognized as a great contribution to the post–World War II era. Similarly, Dwight Eisenhower's administration appears to be undergoing a reexamination with some comparable upgrading.

Journalists and other observers of the national scene are fond of describing the tremendous power of the president. There can be no dispute with that observation, but clearly it is an office that reflects the personality, the operating style, and the personal qualities of its occupants.

Questions to Consider

1. According to the author, what are the guidelines to follow when attempting to rate the performance of a president?

2. How important are public speaking and other communication skills to public opinion of the president?

3. In evaluating a president, do you think it is fair to compare him to his predecessors? Why or why not?

Presidential Power and U.S. Foreign Policy in Nicaragua

Foreign policy, in simplest terms, is the way in which a government of a country maintains national security, protecting its citizens from foreign threats, and advances the country's economic interests. It encompasses the countless day-to-day actions taken to build a peaceful, stable world in which the nation is secure and its economic needs fulfilled as well as the decisions made during wars and major crises.

The making of foreign policy is a complex and never-ending task. In the United States, it is the president, more than any other person, who shapes foreign policy. He is assisted by many departments and agencies of the federal government, in both the executive and legislative branches, that cooperate—and compete—in helping to formulate and execute foreign policy. Private citizens, special interest groups, and the media also work to influence the outcome of the process.

Because the United States was not a world power in the 1780s, the Constitution says little about foreign policy. The president has the powers of acting as commander-in-chief of the military, of appointing ambassadors, and of being the chief public official elected by all the American people. He is the chief of state who speaks for the entire country and acts as the principal decisionmaker in foreign affairs.

The president exercises these powers through his ability to appoint key officials such as the secretary of state and the secretary of defense, heads of the military services, director of the Central Intelligence Agency (CIA), all ambassadors, and the president's own increasingly influential personal staff. Moreover, it is the president who proposes the annual budget for defense, diplomacy, and foreign aid and directs the negotiations that produce international treaties.

The Importance of the State Department

The Department of State plays a dominant role in foreign policy, and, in principle, the secretary of state is the president's preeminent foreign policy advisor. The department is responsible for conducting relations with all other countries. In Washington, it employs specialists who analyze international events, plan U.S. responses, and carry on day-to-day communications with other nations and international organizations. Abroad, its highly trained foreign service officers work in American embassies in 150 foreign countries. The department also has the responsibility to explain international relations to the American people.

Other Departments Help Shape Foreign Policy

Many other departments and agencies are also involved in foreign policy. The Defense Department maintains U.S. military forces and facilities to secure world peace. Military cooperation with allies and arrangements to protect trade routes and other U.S. interests around the world give the Pentagon a major role in making foreign policy. The Department of Commerce and the Department of the Treasury conduct trade relations to guarantee markets for American exports and a steady supply of imports. The Department of Agriculture sells and helps arrange sales and gifts of farm products to other nations. The CIA gathers and analyzes information essential to effective decisionmaking in Washington. The CIA also carries out covert operations—i.e., secret activities to support national foreign policy objectives. Because these departments and agencies of the executive branch often disagree on policy priorities and sometimes compete for both money and influence, the president often has to settle disputes among the members of the foreign policy team.

National Security Council: Coordinating Foreign Policy

To manage all of these actors and to help the president coordinate U.S. activities abroad, the National Security Council (NSC) was established in 1947. On the NSC are the president, the vice-president, the secretary of state, and the secretary of defense. The director of the CIA and the chair of the Joint Chiefs of Staff are permanent advisors. The secretary of the treasury regularly attends NSC meetings, as does the assistant to the president for national security, who is also the director of the 100-person NSC staff that supports the work of the council. The NSC system is the primary mechanism for assisting the president in making decisions and overseeing the implementation of foreign policies. The members of the NSC are the president's top advisors, who also have responsibility for carrying the president's decisions back to their individual departments.

Whenever the president wants to review existing policy or when new problems require a response, the NSC undertakes a major study to develop alternatives and make recommendations to the president. The actual study is conducted by a working group made up of experts from the State Department, the

How U.S. Foreign Policy Is Made

President
Makes foreign policy decisions
Serves as commander-in-chief of military
Makes executive agreements

Department of Defense
Advises president
Implements policy decisions and military orders
Maintains nation's armed forces
Oversees military aid to other countries

National Security Council
Advises president
Coordinates policymaking and implementation
Conducts major policy studies

Department of State
Advises president and acts as nation's chief diplomat
Implements policy decisions
Conducts relations with other countries
Administers foreign aid

Central Intelligence Agency (CIA)
Advises president and National Security Council
Gathers and analyzes information
Carries out special covert operations

Other Executive Departments and Independent Agencies
Other executive departments and independent agencies also advise the president on foreign policy issues. These include: Department of Agriculture (overseas grain sales); Department of Commerce (trade agreements); Department of the Treasury (value of the dollar); Arms Control and Disarmament Agency (arms control treaties); U.S. Information Agency (Voice of America).

Pentagon, the CIA, and other executive branch agencies. Generally, the State Department's representative chairs the working group.

Once completed (sometimes large or difficult studies will take a full year and hundreds of pages), the study is reviewed by the NSC Policy Review Committee. After the committee has refined the policy recommendations, NSC staff prepares a decision paper for the president, which spells out the pros, cons, and costs of each alternative. Before making a final decision, the president may also consult with the full National Security Council and other key advisors, members of Congress, academic experts, and sometimes the leaders of our allies. While all of these individuals act as advisors and can make recommendations, the decision is ultimately made by the president. When the president makes a decision, the NSC writes a Presidential Decision Memorandum, which then serves as a guide to all agencies involved in carrying out the new policy.

Congress: Checking the President
The Constitution gives Congress important powers regarding our international relations. Among these powers are the control of all federal spending (most importantly, the funds for the defense and foreign aid budgets), the power to set tariffs regulating foreign trade, and the requirement that the Senate approve all treaties by a two-thirds majority before they can become law. The Senate also confirms the top appointments to executive departments and agencies as well as ambassadors.

For most of our nation's history, Congress played a minor role in the design and conduct of U.S. foreign policy. However, the bitter divisions of the Vietnam War led Congress to claim a more direct role in setting foreign policy, in the belief that this would give the American people a stronger voice in issues that vitally affect the lives of every citizen. Accordingly, in the past few years, Congress has voted itself increased powers to become more involved in foreign policy issues. For example, Congress now has the power to block major weapon sales to foreign nations, to review intelligence activities, and to remove U.S. troops from foreign combat zones.

However, these congressional checks over executive branch actions have raised questions about the constitutional separation of powers and frequently cause considerable conflict between the executive branch and the legislative branch. A basic question is how a body of 535 members can be most effective in a process that requires close attention, expert knowledge, confidentiality, and quick and decisive action.

Impact of Interest Groups, the Public, and the Media

In the United States, private citizens and the media also have an influence on the nation's foreign policy. People write letters to members of Congress and the president and give expert testimony before Congress. Prominent citizens give speeches enunciating their views. Special interest groups lobby on behalf of particular causes. Experts write influential articles and books. The media report world events and the reactions of the public. All of these forces combine to influence the thinking of those making foreign policy.

U.S. Foreign Policy in Nicaragua

Since World War II a major theme of U.S. foreign policy has been containment of the international influence and activities of the Soviet Union. Since he became president in 1981, Ronald Reagan has strengthened this theme, stressing the need to take a tougher stance with the Soviet Union. In Central America, U.S. foreign policy shifted in tune with this emphasis, particularly in Nicaragua where President Reagan and his advisors saw the newly installed Soviet and Cuban-assisted Marxist government as a threat to the national security of the United States.

Another important theme in U.S. foreign policy for Central America is built on the Monroe Doctrine. When President James Monroe first pronounced it in 1823, the Monroe Doctrine was focused on keeping European nations out of the Americas and on allowing Americans "to decide their own destiny." After the Spanish-American War in the early 1900s, President Theodore Roosevelt expanded the focus of the Monroe Doctrine to encompass all kinds of U.S. intervention in the affairs of the Americas as deemed necessary to protect U.S. national security and economic interests. Today, under the Monroe Doctrine, our foreign policy continues to regard all of Central America as being in our "backyard," or sphere of influence.

Nicaragua is the largest country in Central America. In size and population, Nicaragua is approximately equivalent to the state of Iowa. Honduras borders the country on the north, Costa Rica on the south. Nearly half of Nicaragua is taken up by the Caribbean lowlands—hot, humid, and tropical.

The central highlands have a temperate climate and a rich soil ideal for growing coffee. The principal cities and most of the population are in the western lowlands, which have a chain of volcanoes, two large lakes, and a climate suitable for growing rice, cotton, and sugar. The capital, Managua, is approximately 1,700 miles overland from Brownsville, Texas, and more than 1,100 miles by sea from Florida.

The United States first became intensely interested in Nicaragua in the 1840s when faster routes to the West were needed because of U.S. expansion to the Pacific coast and the discovery of gold in California. Travel mostly by water between the Atlantic and Pacific oceans was possible across Nicaragua, up the San Juan River, then through Lake Managua and Lake Nicaragua—a route that minimized the considerable hazards of travel on land through Central American tropical forests.

Interest waned with the completion of a railroad across the Isthmus of Panama in 1855 (at the same time that American William Walker acted briefly as dictator in Nicaragua). Interest further lessened when the United States

Created by Congress in 1947 to direct U.S. foreign policy, the National Security Council has four statutory members: the president, the vice-president, the secretary of state, and the secretary of defense. Here, President Ronald Reagan makes a point while Secretary of State George Shultz (left) and Secretary of Defense Caspar Weinberger look on.

Congress created the Central Intelligence Agency (CIA) in 1947 to coordinate the intelligence activities of the United States. The CIA analyzes information gathered from around the world and advises the National Security Council on foreign policy matters.

UPI/Bettman Newsphotos

decided to build a canal across Panama, finally starting the project in 1909. Nevertheless, the United States continued to monitor events in Nicaragua. Nicaragua was close to the Panama Canal, which was of vital importance to the U.S. Navy and our national defense. When Nicaraguan head of government Jose Zelaya began negotiating with other foreign powers to build a second canal, the United States was gravely alarmed, and in 1912 landed a force of U.S. Marines to protect American interests. Zelaya went into exile. The next leader, Benjamin Zeladon, was killed in the confusion and interregional warfare that followed. Legend has it that present as a witness to Zeladon's death was a young man named Augusto Sandino, who became a focal point for Nicaraguan opposition to the United States both through his own actions and later as an inspiration to the revolutionary Sandinistas.

U.S. concerns over the safety of the all-important Panama Canal kept U.S. troops stationed in Nicaragua until 1925 and again from 1926 to 1933. During the U.S. military occupation of Nicaragua, a treaty was signed giving the United States exclusive rights forever to

build a canal across Nicaragua. The U.S. military presence also set the stage for the establishment of the Somoza governments and for what Augusto Sandino came to see as a war for liberation from foreign interference and puppet governments. Sandino developed effective guerilla tactics, involving the U.S. Marines in what would later be called a Vietnam-style war.

When the U.S. Marines left in 1933, the war against Sandino's guerillas was carried on by the National Guard, a military force that the United States had helped develop to maintain a stable environment. The commander of the National Guard was Anastasio Somoza Garcia—intelligent, ambitious, and educated in the United States. The National Guard captured and executed Sandino in 1934. Somoza further consolidated his control and ruled Nicaragua from 1937 to 1956 either directly as president or through a stand-in.

Somoza was a staunch supporter of the United States. He opposed communism, and even offered to send his National Guard to fight in the Korean War in the 1950s. In 1954, Nicaragua served as a training area and launching point for the CIA-organized ouster of leftist

Guatemalan president Jacobo Arbenz. When Somoza was assassinated in 1956, his oldest son, Luis, assumed the presidency and continued to give Nicaragua's full support to the United States. Nicaragua served as launch site for President John F. Kennedy's Bay of Pigs attempt to invade Cuba in 1961. National Guard troops teamed up with U.S. forces to occupy the Dominican Republic in 1965 in accord with the foreign policy of President Lyndon B. Johnson.

The younger of Somoza's sons, Anastasio, took over in 1967 when Luis died of a heart attack. Although Luis had kept a low profile and ruled through stand-ins as his father had, the younger son did not. Discontent within the country grew. In 1972, a devastating earthquake struck Managua, and Anastasio channeled international relief funds and materials provided for quake victims into his and his associates' pockets by controlling reconstruction contracts and by purchasing businesses and lands targeted for reconstruction. More and more people joined the Sandinist Front of National Liberation (FSLN), which had been founded in 1962 and named after Augusto Sandino. Atrocities committed by the

National Guard units pursuing FSLN members were witnessed by Catholic missionaries. The disregard of human rights brought denunciations by church groups and, in 1978, by President Jimmy Carter, who placed human rights at the center of his foreign policy. By the summer of 1978, international condemnation of Anastasio's dictatorship was nearly universal, and opposition forces within the country united.

U.S. alarm that Nicaragua might turn into another Cuba—that a loyal American ally might be overthrown by Communists—grew. The United States saw a major threat to its national security interests and the Panama Canal—still important despite post-World War II developments in air power.

Mediation efforts failed, and the revolutionary Sandinistas proclaimed triumph on July 17, 1979. The United States faced difficult problems in its foreign policy. Would Nicaragua, located strategically close to the Panama Canal, remain a strong anti-communist ally? The new leftist government was not only reestablishing diplomatic relations with European countries, but was also setting up new relationships with Third World and socialist countries. Many saw the Sandinistas' foreign relations as a dangerous drift toward communism and the Communist bloc.

President Jimmy Carter, supported by his advisors in the State Department, decided that U.S. economic aid and normal diplomatic relations with Nicaragua's new government would "save" Nicaragua from becoming a Cuban or Soviet satellite. However, some advisors in the CIA and the Pentagon argued that Nicaragua had already become a member of the Communist bloc.

Ronald Reagan campaigned and came into office in 1980 on a platform "abhorring the Marxist-Sandinista takeover." The alignment of Nicaragua with the Socialist bloc was a direct security threat to

From 1933 to 1979, the Somoza family ruled Nicaragua. The last member of the Somoza family, Anastasio Somoza Debayle (shown here) was overthrown in 1979 in a revolt by the Nicaraguan people.

UPI/Bettmann Newsphotos

the United States and to the stability of Central America. It was clear to President Reagan that the new government in Nicaragua would suppress domestic opposition, violate the human rights of its citizens, export terrorism and weapons to other Central American countries, and pose a serious threat to U.S. communications lanes unless action was taken. Therefore, Reagan reversed President Carter's policy of "friendly cooperation" and cut off aid to Nicaragua.

New Directions
With this tougher stance, relations between the United States and Nicaragua deteriorated steadily over the summer of 1981, reaching a low point when the United States undertook routine naval exercises near the Nicaragua coast. However, Congress remained undecided about the political direction of the Sandinista government and continued debating the issue of aid to the Nicaraguans. The State Department

maintained normal relations, undertaking various diplomatic initiatives to promote stability in Nicaragua.

During the summer, secret intelligence findings—particularly reconnaissance photographs—indicated that the Sandinistas were supplying weapons to communist guerillas in El Salvador. The White House staff asked the CIA to outline for President Reagan what covert, or secret, activities the United States could use to deal with the situation.

Since 1974, the president is required by law to justify each covert action as being in the national interest by releasing a Presidential Finding to Congress. In practice, this means that the relevant congressional committees—the House and Senate Intelligence, Armed Services, Appropriations, and Foreign Affairs/Foreign Relations committees—must be informed, although not necessarily before the action is taken. The law requiring the president to justify such activities was passed in reaction to

Presidents often appeal directly to the public for support of their policies and programs. Here, President Reagan speaks on behalf of the *contras* fighting against the Sandinista government in Nicaragua. Reagan's appeals helped pressure Congress into approving funding for the *contras*.

Carcel Modelo Prison
Tipitapa, Nicaragua

disclosure of abuses of the covert activity option in the early 1970s during the Vietnam War.

In November 1981, the National Security Council met to consider the options proposed by the CIA. These ranged from economic pressure (e.g., cutting off trade) to overthrow of the government (e.g., backing a local paramilitary force against the Sandinistas). The paramilitary options were rejected, although returned to the NSC for study, on November 19 and again on November 26. One reason that the United States was reluctant to support a local military force was that former Somoza National Guard members had infiltrated anti-Sandinist groups. Support of such opposition forces would have once again seemed to equate U.S. foreign policy with the corruption and brutality of the last Somoza regime. Another reason was that Secretary of Defense Caspar Weinberger and the defense establishment as a whole vigorously opposed any sort of military operation that would arouse strong reactions and objections in the United States. They felt that the American public was so opposed to any level of American military action in Nicaragua that their involvement was impossible. As high Pentagon officials put it later in testimony before the House and Senate Intelligence committees, "One of the lessons of Vietnam is

55

Jorge G. Castaneda

Central America: Time for a New Approach

INTERNATIONAL

Contadora doggedly pursues Central American peace

mbers split on questions reduction, maneuvers

Reagan Intensifies Contra Plea

Democracy in Nicaragua Doomed Unless U.S. Helps, President Says

Guatemala's Unspoken Bargain

Civilian Rulers Block Prosecution of Rights Abuses by Military

Costa Rica divided over presence of 'contras' and US aid to them

Contadora Peace Efforts Revived

5 Central Americans Plan Summit, Consider Regional Assembly

House Reverses Vote, Backs Reagan's Contra Aid Plan

Guatemala inches forward

Shadows of history dim hopes for quick change

Sandinistas seek strategy

Brace for impact of renewed US funding to rebels

Nicaragua Tries to Put It in Writing

By STEPHEN KINZER

Waiting in Honduras

Nicaraguans Fleeing War and Draft Form Support Base for Guerrillas

By Robert J. McCartney

---

that we can't engage in a war that is not supported by American public opinion."

Covert Activity in Nicaragua

The option that President Reagan did approve was the option for secret financing of non-Sandinist leaders within Nicaragua, with the goal of strengthening private economic and political institutions within the country. A total of almost $20 million was provided to bolster membership drives and publicity campaigns designed to encourage shifts in allegiance away from the Sandinistas to non-Sandinist political parties, unions, and businesses. Although this option specifically excluded paramilitary operations designed to undermine the Sandinistas, the CIA was, as a defensive measure, authorized to begin funding a counterrevolutionary—or "contra"—force. The contras would operate in Nicaragua

to intercept weapons being sent to Salvadoran guerillas.

In the next months, however, the CIA's support of the contras was expanded to include both money and equipment for training paramilitary groups operating both in Honduras and Nicaragua. President Reagan signed a Presidential Finding to Congress, justifying that this covert action was in the national interest, although the finding was not released until later. Among those who knew of the secret military support, support of the contra group fueled disagreement. Then Secretary of State Alexander Haig and Assistant Secretary of State for Inter-American Affairs Thomas Enders said that the support was an attempt to strengthen Nicaragua's existing democratic institutions. Some senior officials—remembering the damage to intelligence-gathering capabilities in the early 1970s when the CIA underwent

public scrutiny after directives to develop assassination plots and to topple governments were revealed—were convinced that covert action against the Sandinistas should be used only as a last resort. Others felt that direct covert paramilitary operations could sustain a viable anti-Sandinist movement. Many, including CIA director William Casey, felt that the United States should take advantage of this opportunity to fight communism and that covert action was the way to get around the American public's lack of support for military action to do so.

Those who were not aware of the secret military support—including many members of Congress and the American public—continued to believe that the United States was negotiating with Nicaragua to resume aid if certain political conditions were met (for example, if no more weapons were supplied to guerillas in El Salvador). In March 1982, the story of covert action in Nicaragua leaked. The *Washington Post* and the *New York Times* published reports on the ambitious paramilitary and political operations, on the large staff of field advisors and on the funds, training, and military equipment being provided to groups aiming to overthrow the Sandinist government. The covert war became overt.

Officials at the State and Defense Departments saw their diplomatic efforts to bring stability through negotiations undermined. Some members of Congress reacted strongly. Senator Paul Tsongas (D-Mass.) and Senator Christopher Dodd (D-Conn.) introduced bills requiring prior congressional approval before covert activities could be undertaken in Central America. Representative Michael Barnes (D-Md.) took the same initiative in the House. The House voted 411-0 to prohibit CIA funding of anti-Sandinist groups.

The Debate Continues

President Reagan's plans for Central America have since been scaled back, and our policy in the region has remained controversial. An even larger debate has developed over how the United States should fight communism, whether the nations of Central America truly are sovereign, and how U.S. foreign policy should be developed.

In using covert action in Nicaragua, Reagan bypassed some of the usual contributors to foreign policy (in this instance, members of Congress and the public). In defense of the president's policy toward Nicaragua, some have argued that some situations are so delicate that only the president can handle them; interference must be kept to a minimum. But others say that the rest of the nation has a right to know what our country is doing; a president cannot act without first getting approval from the American people.

Activities

1. Reading Between the Lines

In this chapter, Griffin Bell argues that our presidents could do a better job if they were limited to a single, 6-year term. Do you agree with this view? Do some research on this topic before you make a decision. Is the president really hampered by a 4-year term? What are the advantages of having a president face the voters every four years? Be sure you examine both sides of the issue before you reach a decision.

2. Developing Your Own Perspective

Everyone has an image of what they would like to see in their president. Besides physical characteristics, most people believe that a president needs to possess certain personal qualities in order to govern the nation properly. What do you think it takes to be president? For example, what kind of education should a president have? What skills should he or she possess? What other characteristics—such as age, marital status, or religion—would your "ideal president" have? Finally, which characteristics do you think are most important? Least important? Why?

3. Becoming an Active Citizen

Before anyone can occupy the Oval Office, they must first conduct a presidential campaign. Running a political campaign is both hectic and exciting, and all candidates need volunteers. Take a look at the positions of several presidential hopefuls to find out which one you might support. Then see if the candidate of your choice has an office in your town. If so, see if you can help out after school or on weekends. If your candidate does not have an office in your town, contact your state Democratic or Republican party to see what you could do locally to help get your candidate elected. It's a great way to become involved in presidential politics on a local level!

★★★★★★★★★★

THE CONGRESS

3. Congress

In This Chapter

The framers of the Constitution intended the legislature to be the strongest branch of the new government. They considered it the most important branch because, in their view, representative democracy could only exist with an independent legislature that was accountable to the people. By giving the people a voice in their government, Congress plays a crucial role in our representative democracy.

Congress and Representation

Congress, the lawmaking body of our government, is an assembly of elected individuals who are expected to give voice to—that is, to re-present—the attitudes and interests of the people. The combination of lawmaking and representation into one body is supposed to assure that the laws passed will conform to popular will. But there are many questions about what the role of members of Congress should be:

■ Should members of Congress do only what their constituents want, or should they follow their own judgment about what is best?

■ What should members of Congress do when the interests of their districts conflict with the needs of the nation as a whole?

■ Should members of Congress recognize a "common good" beyond the boundaries of their districts?

One reason for these questions is that senators and representatives are both national and local representatives. They are national in that they make up one branch of the national government, are employed by the federal government, and are required to support and defend the interests of the entire nation. Yet, they are elected by local districts or states. In running for election,

The House of Representatives and the Senate comprise the legislative branch of government, the Congress. Congress makes the laws that govern our nation.

Office of Photography/U.S. House of Representatives

members of Congress must assure local constituents that they are looking out for local as well as national interests. In areas like budget-cutting, however, the representative's view of the national interest may be quite different from local popular opinion.

Congress and Constituents

Serving constituents is an important part of every legislator's job. Members of Congress pay close attention to their constituents' needs, desires, and opinions on the issues. They develop particular styles of keeping in touch with the people back home. For example, many senators and representatives frequently travel back to their districts to meet with constituents, keep offices in their districts so people can have immediate contact with them, and mail newsletters and issue questionnaires to get a sense of their constituents' opinions on particular issues. Although constituents comprise the largest group that demands representation of their interests, they are just one group to which members of Congress must respond.

Congress and the President

Relations between Congress and the president vary greatly from administration to administration. Some presidents have smooth relations with Congress, while others are in almost constant conflict. As a rule, the two branches get along

better when the president makes minimal demands on Congress. Presidents who insist that Congress enact their entire legislative program and who try to mobilize popular support for its passage usually meet with congressional opposition, particularly if those presidents' proposals are unpopular with the constituents of members of Congress.

The foundation for the conflict is the system of separation of powers and checks and balances. The Constitution not only makes the branches independent of each other, but also provides for them to share functions and powers. This governmental arrangement is an invitation for the two branches to disagree as each may have a different idea of what is good for the public.

Most presidents are reluctant to confine themselves to administering the laws passed by Congress, preferring instead to initiate policy proposals and act as chief legislator. On the other hand, Congress sees itself as the principal lawmaking body and is seldom satisfied to simply approve legislative proposals coming from the executive branch. Still, there can be no doubt

that presidents have a powerful influence on Congress. The success of presidents in getting a program passed by Congress is likely to depend on the number of representatives who support the proposal, the vigor and skill with which presidents pursue their initiatives, their ability to get bipartisan support, and public approval.

Congress and Political Parties
Political parties play important administrative and ideological roles in Congress. The majority party of each house of Congress—the party with the most members—has tremendous administrative powers. The majority party makes key committee appointments and assigns its members to the leadership positions, including Speaker of the House and Senate Majority Leader. Whether democratic or republican, the House of Representatives or the Senate, the party with the most members controls that session's legislative agenda. And while individual members of Congress may not agree with their party's position on every issue, most members vote with their party about two-thirds of the time.

Congressional Staff

The increase in the amount of work performed by Congress—last year nearly 8,500 pieces of legislation were introduced—has caused a rapid growth in the number of people working on congressional staffs. Over the past twenty-five years, the number of people working for the legislative branch of government has almost doubled, from 23,000 in 1960 to more than 40,000 in 1985. Some of these people perform clerical duties, some help constituents deal with federal agencies, but many take a direct role in the legislative process, including drafting legislation, scheduling witnesses for committee hearings, developing strategies for getting legislation passed, and advising senators and representatives on upcoming votes. Some policymakers have argued that, with thousands of nonelected staff members making their mark on legislation, congressional lawmaking may no longer truly reflect the will of the people. However, most staffers see themselves in a supportive role to the member of Congress who employs them. They work as a team to see that the views of their boss—and their boss's boss, the people in the home district—are properly represented.

By combining lawmaking and representation into one body, the framers of the Constitution sought to create a government that produced laws to represent the will of the people. Today, however, lawmakers must balance a variety of concerns—from constituents, interest groups, the president, the party, the media, and even the federal bureaucracy.

Representation and the Legislative Process

David Michael Staton

David Michael Staton of West Virginia served as a member of the House of Representatives from 1981 to 1983. He is currently manager of Political Action Programs for the United States Chamber of Commerce and executive director and treasurer of its political action committee. Drawing on his perspective as both a member of Congress and a lobbyist, Mr. Staton shares his view of how the legislative process works.

Traditionally, the conduct of congressional campaigns was largely dictated by the party. Campaign themes, issues, and slogans were controlled by a central national or state organization. In recent years, however, there has been a move away from this form of campaigning. Today, congressional candidates plan campaigns characterized by high visibility of the candidate and a one-on-one candidate-to-voter relationship. This change has produced two significant results. The first is that political parties have become less important. The second is that the elected official has removed the aura of inaccessibility that used to surround senators and representatives.

By campaigning aggressively on a personal level—such as door-to-door and at plant gates, rallies, and parades—a candidate hopes to forge a bond between himself and the voter. The sometimes "homey" nature of a candidate's television advertisements reinforces that relationship. When the candidate becomes an officeholder, it is certainly reasonable to think that this link still holds.

Therefore, when the voters, workers, and financial supporters of the officeholder call or write on legislative matters, they can usually expect to be heard. The press, the Washington lobbying corps, Congress, and the president are all aware of this, also. Thus, the evolution of grassroots lobbying—groups of people organized at the local level—was only a matter of time. As Robert Keith Gray, one of Washington's top lobbyists, once said, "Effective lobbyists make sure the grassroots are heard. They recognize that in our great participatory democracy neither Congress nor presidents can move very far from the will of the people."

There is no question that constituents compete with other sources of pressure. But in most cases, especially when the voice of the people is strong and consistent, the people can expect to win. An example of this occurred in March 1986. A freshman Republican from a midwestern farm state was elected to a seat previously occupied by a more liberal member of the other party. This particular district had been hurt badly by the farm crisis and had been doubly troubled by the administration's unwillingness to release funds for farm needs.

One of the most intense conflicts over representation that the new member faced was a bill authorizing $100 million in aid to rebels fighting the Marxist government in Nicaragua. The measure had captured headlines across the country, and some spokesmen from the administration had even made the vote into a test of patriotism. The president himself had become deeply involved in lobbying undecided members of Congress. In a highly charged situation such as this—with press attention, pressure from the party leadership, and considerable presidential arm-twisting—a new member could be forgiven for voting with his party or his president. But when the vote was taken, this particular member looked homeward and voted the sentiments of his district. His constituents said that if money was not available for their farm needs, then it certainly was not available to be shipped out of the country. The people's argument prevailed.

As visible and dramatic as voting on a piece of legislation is, it is only one means by which representation takes place in Congress. Another method frequently used by members of Congress to represent a view is to introduce bills or to offer amendments to current public law or other pending legislation. The number of new bills introduced into each Congress bears witness to the popularity of this particular means.

Ideas for new legislation come from a variety of sources. For example, as a campaign develops, there also frequently develops a set of issues that are unique to a particular state or district. During the campaign, candidates discuss the types of legislative proposals they would develop to remedy a specific problem. For instance, the voters in my home state of West Virginia were very interested in whatever legislative solutions I might have offered during the campaign to deal with the faster shipment of coal from our seaports.

While election campaigns provide one type of inspiration for legislation, the officeholder's own personal agenda is also very important. Proposed legislation might come from a member's committee assignments or be an outgrowth from the suggestions of his staff. And some members will amend bills in committee or on the floor to benefit their constituents or an industry in their district.

Certainly one aspect of Washington life that is vastly misunderstood is the relationship between members of Congress and the various industry and association representatives—the lobbyists. When I was first elected, I probably received more warnings about lobbyists than anything else. Having had no previous legislative experience, I did not know what to expect. I must say that I was pleasantly surprised.

How a Bill Becomes a Law

Bill Introduced and Assigned to Committee
Any member of Congress may introduce, or sponsor, a bill. Other members may sign on as cosponsors. If the president wants a bill introduced, he or she must get a member to sponsor the bill. The bill is numbered and assigned to the appropriate standing committee. The committee chair then assigns the bill to a subcommittee.

Subcommittee Action
The subcommittee holds hearings. Witnesses testify on the bill and answer questions from subcommittee members. Witnesses may include government officials, members of Congress, lobbyists, and concerned citizens. Next, markup sessions are held, in which the bill can be rewritten. Subcommittee members then vote on the bill and any proposed amendments. If passed, the bill is sent to the full committee.

Committee Action
The full committee may hold additional hearings, markup, and debate, or it may vote immediately on the bill. If the bill has many amendments, the committee may introduce a new, clean bill. If the full committee approves the bill, it must write a report explaining the bill and any minority views. The bill is then sent on to the Rules Committee in the House of Representatives or to the floor of the Senate.

Rules Committee
(only in the House)
In the House, every bill must go to the Rules Committee before reaching the floor. This committee determines how much time will be allowed for debate and whether or not members can propose amendments to the bill. The "rules" given a bill can have a major impact on its chances of passing.

Floor Action
Once a bill reaches the floor, all members can debate and vote on the bill. In the Senate, debate is unlimited unless cloture, a vote to limit debate, is approved by at least 60 senators. In the House, debate is limited by the Rules Committee, and there may be strict rules regarding amendments. In both houses, amendments to a bill can be voted on separately before the whole bill is put to a vote.

Conference Committee
If the House and Senate pass different versions of the same bill, members from each house meet to work out the differences. After the conference, the House and the Senate vote on the new bill.

Sent to the President
If the House and Senate pass the same bill, it is sent to the president to sign into law. If the president takes no action within ten days, the bill becomes law. If the president vetoes the bill, it returns to Congress for another vote. If two-thirds of the members of both houses vote for the bill, it becomes law over the president's veto. If either house falls short of a two-thirds majority, the bill is defeated.

It may seem unlikely, but there are many bills on which the member receives very little correspondence from home. Either the issue has not captured the attention of the press, or it is simply too esoteric to be widely understood. In cases such as this, and at other times too, lobbyists provide a member of Congress with valuable information upon which to make a sound decision. Most lobbyists who visited me were articulate and scrupulously honest. A lobbyist lives on his ability to tell his story to members of Congress. One deliberate misrepresentation of the facts can put that person out of business—permanently. As odd as it may seem, a vast majority of lobbyists told me both sides of the issue. It was interesting to find that lobbyists on opposing sides of an issue nearly always said the same thing about a particular bill. Seldom is a high-pressure tactic ever used, and even more seldom is it successful.

Another group that has considerable impact on a member is his colleagues. Members are under tremendous pressure from their peers. In the great legislative battles in the House and Senate, where the course of the nation rides on the vote of one member, knowing that your friends want you to vote a certain way on a bill places an enormous burden on that member. If a member votes against his peers, he may feel he has let them down and that can be painful indeed.

The best lobbyist in Washington lives at 1600 Pennsylvania Avenue. Even a president who is not considered particularly persuasive has an unbelievable arsenal at his fingertips. I have had the pleasure of visiting with the president in the

Oval Office, and I must say it is easy to feel over-whelmed. When the attention of the most important person in the free world is focused on you, even for a short while, it can weaken one's defenses.

Now that I work on the other side of the fence, as a lobbyist, I find that my job is made much easier if my organization can convince the president to support our bill. Having the president on your side is an added bonus that often signals victory.

The job of representing a state or congressional district in Congress is a challenging, tiring, and yet intensely rewarding job. I cannot think of any vocation that brings as much satisfaction. Most members I know feel the same way. Their overriding concern is to protect and preserve our American way of life and to be faithful to the voters who placed their trust in that member.

Who then is really represented in the legislative process? Through all the partisan fights, the committee squabbles over jurisdiction, the parochial interests of the members themselves, and all the conflicting pressures and counterpressures, America itself is represented. Before I was elected to Congress, Lew McManus, former Speaker of the House of Delegates in West Virginia, told me he promised his constituents only one thing. He said he would use his time to gather information, listen to all sides, and then vote according to what he felt was best. This is true representative government: a melding of the will of the people with the leadership of those selected to execute that will.

Questions to Consider

1. According to the author, why must lobbyists be "scrupulously honest" in their dealings with Congress? Do you believe the author when he says that high-pressure tactics are seldom used?

2. Why do you think it is important for lobbyists to have presidential support in their dealings with Congress?

3. If you were a member of Congress, would you listen primarily to your constituents or your conscience? Do you think there would be a difference between the two?

Congress and the Presidency

Senator Robert Dole

Senate Minority Leader Robert Dole (R-Kans.) was first elected to the Senate in 1968. He was the Republican nominee for Vice-President in 1976, and he chaired the Republican National Committee from 1971 to 1973. In this article, Senator Dole describes the give-and-take relationship that exists between Congress and the president.

In many ways the relationship between Congress and the president is like that of a husband and wife. The two depend on one another for support and guidance. They sometimes disagree. But in most instances, they usually find a middle ground—a compromise both can live with.

That is the way the nation's founders designed our government—a system of checks and balances that guarantees that no one branch of government gains too much power.

In theory, it is the president who proposes and Congress that disposes. But that is not always the case. Sometimes Congress takes the initiative, developing legislation without help or approval from the White House. And there are other times when the president vetoes legislation that he has proposed that Congress has altered in an unacceptable way.

Why do certain pieces of legislation receive attention and others barely see the light of day? Certainly, when the president decides to make a major push for a program—such as President Reagan did with tax reform—it is hard for members of Congress to ignore.

But the success or failure of many initiatives—whether they originate in the White House or on Capitol Hill—often stems from parochial concerns. Whether it is the plight of the American farmer, the distressed steel or textile industry, tax reform measures that affect business investment, or the closing of a military base, nearly every piece of legislation that Congress considers is influenced by regional or special interests.

The president is elected by all the people—his base of support is wide and diverse. He is concerned with the welfare of all Americans, thus his policymaking is less susceptible to the vagaries of geography.

Congress, on the other hand, is elected by the voters of a particular district or state. Individual members of Congress have as their base of support only those people who elected them to office. Thus, members of Congress must be much more responsive to the concerns of their own constituents.

Naturally, this difference in the scope of representation results in some tension between the two branches of government. And this delicately balanced relationship can be even further strained if the White House is controlled by one political party, and one or both houses of Congress by the other.

Members of Congress often meet with the president to discuss important domestic and foreign policy matters. The meetings increase cooperation between the executive and legislative branches.

Most of the time, the three institutions involved in the legislative process—the House of Representatives, the Senate, and the White House—are not controlled by the same political party. This makes the job of lawmaking more difficult. Compromises must be worked out. Naturally, a president would like to have both houses of Congress controlled by his political party. However, even when this is the case, it is no guarantee that Congress will give a president everything he asks for—but he certainly has a more receptive audience.

In no policy area does the president hold more sway than foreign affairs. Foreign policy initiatives almost always come from the White House. With few exceptions, decisions involving international relations are free from the kinds of parochial concerns that influence domestic issues. And while there are always partisan differences regarding foreign relations, there is a general feeling that, where and when possible, the best foreign policy is a bipartisan one.

There are many recent examples that illustrate this point. For example, our Middle East policy, the role of the United States in the Philippines, and our response to the terrorist takeover of the Italian ocean liner *Achille Lauro*, with few exceptions were supported by a majority of members from both political parties.

But there are other foreign policy initiatives that are extremely controversial. One example is President Reagan's policies in Central America. The president's recent campaign to convince Congress of the rightness of his policies is a good example of the power and the limits of presidential persuasion.

To gain support for his policies, the president staged an extensive lobbying effort. He met face to face with representatives and senators and talked to many others by telephone. He took his case directly to the American people, by making a nationally televised speech and addressing the issue in his weekly radio talks. He sent his emissaries—from the Secretary of State and Secretary of Defense to the head of the National Security Council—to Congress to lobby personally for his policies. Yet he still had difficulty getting Congress to authorize funding for his proposals.

The point is that even though the president of the United States has considerable skills as the "Great Communicator" and all the powers of the presidency at his disposal, if there is no consensus among the public on an issue, then there is unlikely to be one in Congress. On this issue, as with many others, the president had to give in some, and so did Congress.

The tension between Congress and the presidency—and the constant give and take between them—is all part of our democratic system. It can get pretty messy and time-consuming. But ultimately, the symbiotic relationship between the president and Congress produces policies that most fully reflect the will of the American people. And that is what representative democracy is all about.

Questions to Consider

1. Do you think the existence of tension or a difference of opinion between the president and Congress is a good or bad thing for the country? Why?

2. Explain what you think Senator Dole means by the statement, "the best foreign policy is a bipartisan one."

3. Explain how the relationship between the president and Congress might be affected in each of these situations: (1) The White House is controlled by one political party, and both houses of Congress are controlled by the other; (2) The White House and both houses of Congress are controlled by the same political party; and (3) The White House and only one house of Congress are controlled by the same political party.

Who's Who in Congress

Each session of Congress brings change in the leadership of both the Senate and the House of Representatives. Competition for committee assignments is intense. Both parties want to place their members in powerful committee chairs so that they have better control over the legislative process. Who's who in Congress? For each of the key positions listed below, fill in the name of the senator or representative as well as his or her party affiliation and state.

Senate

President Pro Tempore

Majority Leader

Majority Whip

Minority Leader

Minority Whip

Key Committee Chairs

Agriculture, Nutrition, and Forestry

Appropriations

Armed Services

Budget

Energy and Natural Resources

Environment and Public Works

Foreign Relations

Intelligence

Judiciary

Rules and Administration

House of Representatives

Speaker of the House

Majority Leader

Majority Whip

Minority Leader

Minority Whip

Key Committee Chairs

Agriculture

Appropriations

Armed Services

Budget

Education and Labor

Energy and Commerce

Foreign Affairs

Intelligence

Judiciary

Rules

71

Party Politics and Congress

Representative Tony Coelho

Tony Coelho (D-Calif.), House Majority Whip, was elected to the House of Representatives in 1978. He chaired the Democratic Congressional Campaign Committee from 1981 to 1986. In his article, Representative Coelho explains the role that political parties play in Congress.

A political party is a collection of people who share, in some measure, common values and policy orientations. In the broadest sense, the mission of the party is to identify national problems and priorities, and to work for their settlement or achievement. In a narrower sense, the task is to consolidate and fulfill promises made to the electorate during the campaign.

The party leadership is critical to the functioning of the legislative process. Party leaders in Congress help to organize orderly consideration of legislative proposals, try to line up party support for or against legislation, attempt to reconcile differences that threaten to disrupt the chamber, and plan strategy in important legislation.

In the House of Representatives, the formal leadership consists of the Speaker of the House, who is both the chamber's presiding officer and the majority party's overall leader; the majority and minority leaders; whips from each party (members who enforce party discipline and insure attendance); assistants to the whips; and various party committees that develop party strategy, schedule legislation, and assign party members to legislative committees.

Congressional party leaders perform a number of functions. First, they organize the party to conduct business. In the House, the Democratic Steering and Policy Committee makes the committee assignments for all Democratic members. The Steering and Policy Committee is comprised of the House Democratic leadership, members appointed by the Speaker of the House, and members elected to the committee on a regional basis.

Second, congressional party leaders perform scheduled business on the House floor. The Speaker of the House and the majority leader make these decisions. A number of factors influence their decisions, including the pressure of national and international events, House rules, and the substance of bills.

Third, party leaders are responsible for promoting attendance on the floor of the House. The Democrats in the House do this primarily through the whip, who is responsible for informing all party members that a critical vote is at hand and their presence on the floor is required.

Fourth, party leaders are constantly collecting and distributing information. In the House, the Democratic whip serves as the focal point for this

Congress and Its Committees*

U.S. Senate

Standing Committees
Agriculture, Nutrition, and Forestry (6)
Appropriations (13)
Armed Services (6)
Banking, Housing, and Urban Affairs (5)
Budget
Commerce, Science, and Transportation (8)
Energy and Natural Resources (5)
Environment and Public Works (6)
Finance (8)
Foreign Relations (6)
Government Affairs (6)
Judiciary (8)
Labor and Human Resources (6)
Rules and Administration
Small Business (7)
Veterans Affairs

Special and Select Committees
Aging
Ethics
Indian Affairs
Intelligence

Joint Committees
Economic (6)
Library
Printing
Taxation

U.S. House of Representatives

Standing Committees
Agriculture (8)
Appropriations (13)
Armed Services (7)
Banking, Finance, and Urban Affairs (8)
Budget
District of Columbia (3)
Education and Labor (8)
Energy and Commerce (6)
Foreign Affairs (8)
Government Operations (7)
House Administration (6)
Interior and Insular Affairs (6)
Judiciary (7)
Merchant Marine and Fisheries (6)
Post Office and Civil Service (7)
Public Works and Transportation (6)
Rules (2)
Science and Technology (7)
Small Business (6)
Standards of Official Conduct
Veterans' Affairs (5)
Ways and Means (6)

Select Committees
Aging (4)
Children, Youth, and Families
Hunger
Intelligence (3)
Narcotics Abuse and Control

Joint Committees
Same as U.S. Senate

*For each committee, the number of subcommittees is indicated in parentheses.

function. The whip solicits members' attitudes on selected upcoming bills and disseminates the leaders' preferences to party members. All of these functions are performed in such a way so as to enhance the possibility of attaining specific desired policies and programs.

Political parties play a major role in every step of the legislative process. No other group is as influential in Congress as is the political party. Committee and subcommittee members organize as Democrats and Republicans. Members get their committee assignments from their respective parties. They caucus with each other and sit together in the committee rooms.

Committee leaders must rely on the party leaders for scheduling business on the floor and working for its passage or defeat; for communicating information about noncommittee members' preference to the committee; and for communicating committee opinions to noncommittee members.

Once a bill has been reported out of committee, it is usually brought before the Committee on Rules to be scheduled for floor debate. The Rules

Committee establishes the conditions under which most bills are debated and amended. Rules determine the length of introductory debate and permit or prohibit amendments. In the House, the majority party is able to exert more control over the Rules Committee because the Speaker of the House can appoint loyal members of his party to the Rules Committee.

Political parties play an important, centralizing role in helping Congress to carry out its lawmaking duties. In the House, the Democrats and Republicans sit on separate sides of the chamber, have separate conference rooms and cloakrooms, and have equal time in debating legislation. However, the work of the political party outside committees and subcommittees shows up primarily in the policy committees, the caucus, and the whip system. Discussions are held on whether to take a party position on a particular bill, with the degree of party unity obviously the most important factor. If the policy committee decides to take a position, this position is then transmitted to the membership. The policy committee also forwards particular issues to the

party caucuses for debate. Majority party leaders also must determine when to schedule legislation as well as crucial votes.

Public policy questions regularly produce conflicts between the two parties. Today the nation faces three grave threats: uncontrolled massive federal budget deficits, faltering competitiveness in markets at home and abroad, and the escalating nuclear arms race. I believe very strongly in my own party, the Democratic party, and that we have a long and successful tradition of responding forcefully when the nation faces such serious and demanding challenges. We stand ready again to supply the leadership America needs to meet these challenges.

Questions to Consider

1. What is the role of political parties in the legislative process?

2. Do you think individual members of Congress are more likely to vote with their party or with their conscience? Why?

3. Do you agree with the author that "no other group is as influential in Congress as the political party"? Why or why not?

Representatives and Their Constituents

Representative Barbara Boxer

Representative Barbara Boxer (D-Calif.) was elected to the House of Representatives in 1982 after serving as a member of the Marin County Board of Supervisors and an aide to U.S. Representative John Burton. In her article, Representative Boxer describes how she performs one of the most important aspects of her job—staying in touch with her constituents.

I feel fortunate to represent the diverse Sixth District of California, which includes urban metropolitan neighborhoods in San Francisco, rural farmlands in the Sonoma Valley, and suburban communities and small towns in Marin County and Sonoma County, as well as the city of Vallejo—which boasts one of the seven naval shipyards in the country. My constituency includes people who make their living in all kinds of jobs—shipworkers, ranchers, corporate executives, teachers, storekeepers, nurses, construction workers, pilots, stockbrokers, artists, computer programmers, letter carriers, and virtually every other occupation one could name.

Some are Democrats, some are Republicans, some are independents, and some are active in smaller political parties. They differ in ethnic background, religion, and lifestyle. They range from those in deep poverty to the middle class and the very affluent. The 526,000 people in my congressional district reflect a wide range of interests, with concerns that span every issue affected by the federal government. In essence, my district is a mini-America.

It might seem that this diversity would make my district difficult to represent in Congress. Not so! In fact, the diversity helps me to understand the implications of the legislation we consider and to relate to the concerns that other members of Congress must address on behalf of their constituents. My district has something in common with every district in the country. This makes me more sensitive to the problems of our country as a whole and increases my ability to work effectively with other members of Congress.

My district is further in distance from Washington, D.C., than almost any other— except Hawaii and Alaska, of course. I come home to work in the district at least three times a month, usually arriving late Thursday night. The House of Representatives normally votes on Tuesdays, Wednesdays, and Thursdays. I use Fridays and Saturdays for meetings with constituents and participating in community functions; Sundays are for my family, and then it's back to Washington on Monday.

While I am in the district, I have a very full schedule, which begins with breakfast meetings and goes through the evening hours. I schedule office hours with individuals and groups who want to discuss a particular problem or a specific

Representatives and senators try to meet regularly with their constituents. Voters "back home" expect members of Congress to look after their interests in Washington.

bill pending in Congress. I also save time to go over current legislative priorities with my district office staff, so that they can respond to constituents' questions about issues that are going to be voted upon in Washington. In addition, I receive many invitations to speak at local high schools, community service organizations, business conferences, senior citizen clubs, etc. I feel honored that such groups want to hear about the work I'm doing as a member of Congress.

Generally, the people who live in my district are well informed, articulate, and quite sophisticated about government. They are concerned about world peace, the environment, the federal deficit, and dozens of other issues, and they communicate their concerns to me. I place a lot of importance on the quality of service offered to my constituents and reach out to open channels of communication. They respond with vigorous, intelligent comments and ideas. In fact, one of my newsletters—which included a constituent questionnaire—brought more than 25,000 responses!

With more than half a million people in my district, there is simply no way to meet each one personally, so I hold regularly-scheduled community meetings in various parts of my district, where every resident is invited to hear what I've been doing in Washington and to ask questions

or offer comments about issues of concern. Even with a crowd of a hundred or more at a community meeting, we can have energetic dialogue about tax reform, offshore oil drilling, military procurement, or other issues. I value these sessions for the direct two-way communication with my constituents, and the message I get back is that the sessions are appreciated by those who participate.

Because I am in Washington most of the time, the problems that my constituents may be having with agencies of the federal government are almost always handled by my district office staff. Caseworkers with experience in untangling knots of red tape help thousands of constituents each year. Many of the problems are brought to my office because people have encountered roadblocks in their efforts to work within the bureaucracies of the Internal Revenue Service, Veterans Administration, Social Security, Immigration and Naturalization Service, etc. My staff opens up lines of communication and gets problems resolved in the proper way.

More than half of my employees are based in the district offices, providing constituent services by telephone, letter, or in person. Up to 100 people per day call my San Rafael district office, asking for information, giving opinions, ordering documents, or seeking assistance. In two days,

Tips on Writing Your Senator or Representative

Why Write Your Senator or Representative?

- To state your position on an issue or bill being considered by Congress;
- To ask his or her position on an issue or bill;
- To inquire about his or her votes and other activities;
- To resolve a personal problem involving the government with which the office might be able to assist you.

How to Address Your Letter:

The Honorable Mary Smith
U.S. House of Representatives
Washington, D.C. 20515
Dear Representative Smith:

The Honorable John Smith
U.S. Senate
Washington, D.C. 20510
Dear Senator Smith:

Points to Remember:

- Present your views rationally. If you disagree with the member of Congress, do so without being disagreeable. Threatening or impolite letters have much less effect than do well-reasoned and sincere arguments. Personal letters are more influential than form letters.

- If possible, identify by number the bill that concerns you. Be brief, and explain why you are concerned with this issue or bill.

- Try to time your letter so that it reaches your representative or senators before they vote on the bill in question.

- If you are concerned about a particular issue, also write to the chair and the members of the appropriate committee.

- If your letter concerns a personal or family problem involving the government, follow up the letter with a telephone call to the office of your senator or representative.

- Ask for a response, and include your return address. Keep in mind that your letter will probably be read and answered by a congressional aide. A senator or representative receives thousands of letters each month and cannot personally respond to each.

my staff handled more than 1,000 calls on the *contra* aid bill (a controversial measure to give U.S. foreign aid to anti-government forces fighting in Nicaragua).

I receive about 100 letters each week, and every one is answered either in Washington or in the district offices. Most of the correspondence dealing with legislation goes to my Washington office. There, a legislative correspondent confers with me to draft responses that reflect my thinking on the issue in question. My Washington office has at least five interns working without cost to taxpayers. I couldn't keep up with the mail volume without them. I review all the correspondence that goes out of my office. This is the kind of work I bring with me on the airplane between Washington and San Francisco, for the relative peace and quiet of the 5-hour flight allows me to get a lot of reading and writing accomplished.

There have been only a few instances where my positions on a national issue were seen by some of my supporters to be detrimental to interests within my district. For example, I voted for the textile import bill (which limited the amount of textile products that could be imported from some Asian countries) because I felt strongly that the overall impact of massive imports from countries with high tariffs against our exports should not remain unchecked when so many American jobs are being lost as a result. I certainly heard from a lot of Bay Area importers about that vote, but I explained to them that, in the long run, reciprocity in trade will help everyone.

My efforts in Congress are sustained by my deep personal convictions about justice and democracy. I have a strong sense about what America should be about, and I have a deep commitment to live up to the principles that our founders built into the Constitution. I also believe that no matter what social or economic class people are in, they all want the same thing—a peaceful and secure world that is environmentally sound, where their children can grow up with both opportunity and hope.

1. Why does Representative Boxer believe that diversity makes her district easier, rather than harder, to represent?

2. Do you think Representative Boxer made the right decision in voting for the textile import bill, even though many of her constituents did not favor the legislation? Why or why not?

3. Even though it is not stated in the Constitution, many members of Congress feel it is their duty to help constituents who are experiencing problems with a federal agency. Why do you think most representatives perform this task? After reading about Representative Boxer's busy schedule, do you think constituents demand too much of their representatives?

A Day in the Life of a Member of Congress

For many members of Congress, the workday starts early in the morning and ends late in the evening. Representatives often must choose among several different meetings or events that are scheduled at the same time. Representative Lindy Boggs (D-La.) is no exception. Her appointment schedule for Tuesday, February 25, 1986, is reprinted here as an example of the amount of work that faces a member of Congress each day.

House Meets at Noon

8:00 a.m.	B339 Rayburn Building	Breakfast meeting of the Association of Community College Trustees
9:30 a.m.	2237 Rayburn Building	Hearing of the Select Committee on Children, Youth & Families concerning the diversity and strength of American families
10:00 a.m.	2362 Rayburn Building	Hearing of the Energy & Water Development Subcommittee concerning the Army Corps of Engineers: Lower Mississippi Valley Division, North Atlantic Division, New England Division
10:00 a.m.	H143 Capitol	Hearing of the HUD—Independent Agencies Subcommittee concerning the Selective Service System
12:30–1:30 p.m.	2167 Rayburn Building	Annual luncheon of the Congressional Arts Caucus with guests Peter, Paul, and Mary (stop by only).
1:00 p.m.	2360 Rayburn Building	Meeting of the Appropriations Committee to consider the views and estimates report for fiscal year 1987
2:00–4:00 p.m. (FYI)	2141 Rayburn Building	Special meeting of the Democratic Caucus to review recent Democratic National Committee poll
2:00 p.m.	H143 Capitol	Hearing of the HUD—Independent Agencies Subcommittee concerning the Neighborhood Reinvestment Corporation
3:00 p.m.	H301 Capitol	Hearing of the Legislative Branch Subcommittee concerning the Railroad Accounting Principles Board
4:00 p.m.	office	Meeting with the principals regarding the South Point Development in the New Orleans East area
5:00 p.m.	office	Meeting with representatives of the Louisiana Credit Union League
5:30 p.m.	office	Meeting with P. Landrieu of New Orleans concerning health care facilities
6:15–7:00 p.m.	B338 Rayburn Building	Reception of the American Legion
7:30 p.m.	L'Enfant Plaza Hotel	Reception of the National Association of Letter Carriers
7:30–9:00 p.m.	National Gallery of Art	Reception and viewing of new art exhibit sponsored by AT&T

The Role of Congressional Staff: A Roundtable Discussion

In the past two decades, the number of congressional staff members has more than doubled. CLOSE UP held a roundtable discussion with three congressional staffers to discuss their jobs on Capitol Hill and how much influence they have on the policymaking process.

Ellen Boyle

Ellen Boyle is press secretary for Representative Mickey Leland (D-Texas). Ms. Boyle also served as press assistant to former Speaker of the House Thomas P. ("Tip") O'Neill.

David Gribbin

David Gribbin, currently executive director of the House Republican Policy Committee, was an administrative aide for Representative Dick Cheney (R-Wyo.) for seven years.

Cedric Hendricks

Cedric Hendricks is a legislative aide to Representative John Conyers (D-Mich.). A graduate of Howard University Law School, Mr. Hendricks also worked as a probation officer for five years.

CLOSE UP: The term "congressional staff" is an expression that covers a number of job descriptions. Each of you does a different type of job for your member of Congress. Could you describe the work you do?

Mr. Gribbin: Generally, the job of administrative assistant (AA) is divided into three functions. The first is to act as chief of staff. In that capacity, I make sure that everything in the office runs smoothly. That involves everything from taking care of mundane personnel matters, to devising systems to ensure that information flows to the congressman the way he wants it to, to making sure that constituents are being adequately taken care of.

A second aspect of the job is political. For example, some AAs actually go off the government payroll for periods of time to work in the congressman's reelection campaign.

Third, many AAs get involved with legislative issues. In my case, that was almost strictly confined to issues of particular concern to constituents in Wyoming.

Ms. Boyle: As a press secretary, my responsibility is to work with the press—always keeping in mind, of course, that the press is a conduit to the public, and that what I'm really trying to do is to let the public know where my boss stands on issues and what actions he's taking to represent the Houston community. My work involves everything from scheduling interviews, to responding to requests for information, to going out and generating coverage of a particular issue.

Mr. Hendricks: My job as a legislative assistant involves actually developing legislation. Sometimes the congressman will come into the office in the morning with a new idea for a bill. I would then work with the Office of Legislative Counsel to develop the language for the bill. I might try to generate support for the proposal among other members of Congress. For example, it may be in our interest to bring them on board as original sponsors to show bipartisan support for the bill. I would also work out a strategy for getting the bill referred to a committee that would move our bill as quickly as possible through the committee process.

At the same time, I would also be monitoring legislation coming up on the floor and advising the congressman on how he ought to handle any votes. If there were any lobbyists who wanted to express a particular point of view on the legislation, I would meet with them, and if it was appropriate for them to meet with the congressman, I would set up an appointment.

Sometimes a personal interest of the congressman takes on a legislative twist. For example, we sponsored a jazz workshop last year during the Congressional Black Caucus weekend. Now we're working on getting a House concurrent resolution passed, which will proclaim jazz an American national treasure. We're working with a number of community groups to develop the language for the resolution and to get their help in building congressional support for the project.

CLOSE UP: The number of staff people on Capitol Hill has more than doubled since the 1960s. Do you think that members of Congress have too many staff members?

Mr. Hendricks: Because of federally mandated budget cuts, the size of our staff has actually decreased. This situation has caused us to work with outside groups that can provide us with volunteers. We had a hearing yesterday on a bill that the congressman introduced, and I had a student distribute our press releases to some of the local college campuses.

Ms. Boyle: My situation is a little different. The congressman that I work for has a couple of different staffs because he chairs a couple of different committees. I think our office is very lucky to have all those people and resources available to us. My congressman is involved in so many issues that it would be next to impossible for three or four people to keep track of everything.

Mr. Gribbin: The growth of staff has been a direct result of the growth of government. Back in the 1930s, the Roosevelt administration began very actively involving itself in the lives of the citizens, and with every succeeding presidency, that involvement has increased. You put that together with the huge amount of mail we get from constituents every day, and government has a tremendous responsibility to respond to its

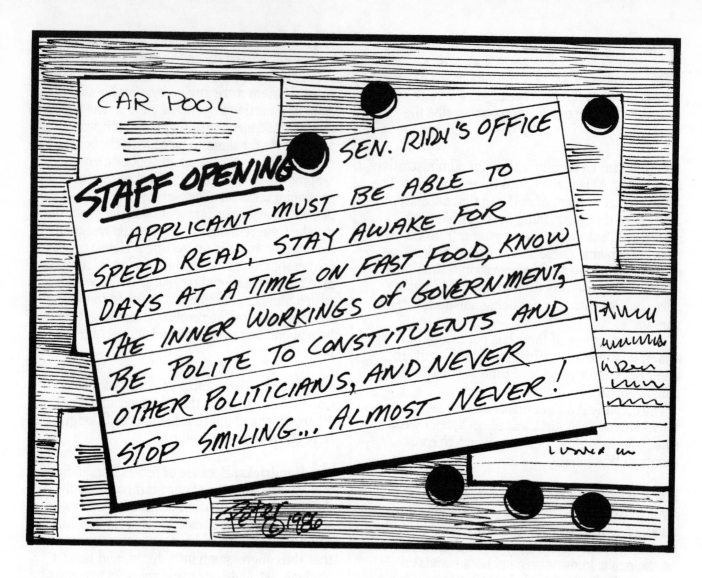

citizens. Over the years, the workload on Capitol Hill has increased, and that has led to the increase of congressional staff.

CLOSE UP: How much do congressional staff affect public policy?

Mr. Gribbin: As an AA, I had very little direct personal influence on the development of policy. And I would venture to say that few AAs in the House have much influence on the development of policy.

Ms. Boyle: I'm a press secretary dealing with the public side of an issue. I'm not involved in specific planning of public policy, but in educating the public by communicating that policy.

Mr. Hendricks: Legislative assistants are in a good position to influence policy. Certainly we are in a position to develop ideas on our own as a result of our interaction with a wide range of people—lobbyists, academics, even personal friends. And we can take our ideas to the congressman and discuss them with him or her. If he likes the idea, we would then be free to develop legislative proposals or positions on legislation. So legislative assistants can play a fairly substantial role in policymaking.

CLOSE UP: Some people argue that staff members have too much power in American politics. Does this raise a question in your minds about representation in Congress—in the sense that you are not elected by the people, yet you do so much of the work that keeps Congress going?

Mr. Gribbin: The first thing that I think of when I begin working on something is how it will affect Wyoming and Wyoming's constituents. The congressman is here serving at their pleasure. The House was devised purposely to keep us in touch with what the folks back home think, and if the perception begins to emerge that you're losing touch with the folks back home, you may not be with us after the next election. In my opinion, the staff member who forgets that he isn't the one who took a chance to get elected, often at incredible financial risk, and begins to act as if he is the congressman—that guy is really off base. Members of staff are *not* the people's representative.

Ms. Boyle: I think it's very important to remind constituents that we are always thinking about them. In fact, we may be thinking about them, but if we don't let them know that, they might assume their views are forgotten. In that sense my job is very important. I aid my boss in representing the views of the people who elected him, and I do that by reaching constituents through the news media. But I would feel very uneasy about saying that I personally represent their views. I feel very strongly that I work to *aid* a member of Congress.

Mr. Hendricks: My position is a little different because I'm from the district the congressman represents, and I go back and work in the district office and then come back to Washington. That helps me to stay familiar with the concerns of constituents. However, my job is *not* to represent them. My job is to help them understand what pieces of legislation the congressman is working on and how his work can affect their quality of life.

I think each of us has our own personal sense of responsibility, but I think that in terms of accountability, I am and should be accountable to my boss.

Ms. Boyle: I think, by and large, most people come to work on Capitol Hill for the right reasons. We are advisors to our member of Congress, but you have to remember that the member has many other advisors as well. Most members had political careers before coming to the House. They served in city government or state government and have political advisors back home who helped them get started in their careers and who still influence the representative's decisionmaking. I also think that individual members of Congress have a great deal of influence on each other. Staff members are influential, but we are only one of many influential groups—and we certainly aren't always the most influential.

Mr. Gribbin: I'm familiar with the argument that congressional staff are behind the scenes manipulating Congress—affecting the way we live without being accountable to the general public. But I think you can also make the argument that if you're a staff person to a member of Congress, your behavior is circumscribed. Staff people have to ask themselves, "If this were on the front page of the Washington Post tomorrow, how would it affect my boss?" That puts a real brake on the abuse of power! And combine that with the fact that most staff people come to Washington out of a sense of public service— well, I just don't buy the idea that Machiavellian staff people are sitting in the background guiding the ship of state.

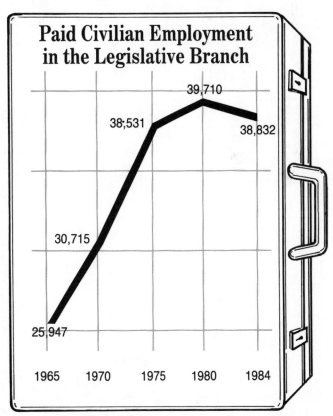

Paid Civilian Employment in the Legislative Branch

39,710
38,531
38,832
30,715
25,947

1965 1970 1975 1980 1984

Source: Office of Personnel Management

Employees in the legislative branch include members of Congress, their office staff, staff on committees, and workers at the Government Printing Office and the Library of Congress. Since 1965, more than 12,000 employees have been added to the legislative branch.

83

Ms. Boyle: I think it's important to remember that working as a staff member means working as a team. I find myself spending a great deal of my time talking to the legislative aides and to my AA, who's from Houston and has a better feel for what the people back home are saying. I find that almost all of our decisions are group decisions. Sometimes it's a challenge to reach a consensus, but one member of Congress can't make it alone on Capitol Hill, and one staff person can't do it either.

Trade Protectionism

No domestic issue is as important to the nation as the health of the economy—how many people are working, whether the price of goods is affordable, and whether businesses are growing. As the nation's legislators, members of Congress play an important role in keeping the economy on an even keel. They can use the federal budget to stimulate a sagging economy or to curb periods of high inflation. They can give tax breaks to help industries and pass job-training programs for the unemployed. When the nation's economy is in trouble, people often look to Congress to take action.

In deciding on a course of action, members of Congress take many considerations into account. They must satisfy voters in their local districts, respond to the president with his own legislative agenda, and balance the desire for short-term solutions against long-term needs.

Members often find themselves at odds with one another when weighing these considerations. For legislation to pass, procedures must be followed, compromises forged, and votes taken.

One piece of legislation that recently highlighted the deliberations of Congress was the Textile and Apparel Trade Enforcement Act of 1985. At the forefront of a growing movement to "protect" U.S. industries from foreign products, this bill sought to increase the amount of American-made textiles sold in the United States. Since 1980, many U.S. manufacturers had faced stiff competition from the rest of the world, and now they wanted Congress to take "protectionist" action.

Protectionism and Free Trade

Pressure for legislation to "protect" domestic industries from foreign competitors came in response to the economic problems of U.S. manufacturers in the early 1980s. Once the backbone of the largest economy in the world, U.S. manufacturers were now losing sales to foreign imports and being forced to lay off workers. Today, products of almost every sort can be manufactured abroad, shipped here, and sold for less than similar products made in this country.

"Protection," however, has been a dirty word in U.S. and world economics for decades. Most countries claim that they are for "free trade," the unrestricted sale of goods between nations. But few actually practice free trade. The temptation for nations to create barriers to protect their domestic industries from foreign competition is sometimes too great. Nevertheless, no country wants to admit that protection is a national policy for fear of retaliation from other countries.

As the world's leading trading nation, the United States has been in the forefront of the effort to remove barriers to the flow of goods such as *tariffs* (taxes on imports) and *quotas* (limits on the amount of imported goods). One of the main reasons the United States has opposed protectionism is because of the infamous Smoot-Hawley Tariff Act. In 1930, Congress enacted the Smoot-Hawley Act, named after its authors, Senator Reed Smoot (R-Utah) and Representative Willis Hawley (R-Ore.), to raise the tariffs on virtually all imported goods.

Passage of Smoot-Hawley came on the heels of the 1929 crash of the stock market and the beginning of the Great Depression. During the depression, jobs disappeared, the public stopped buying goods, and businesses went bankrupt. Pressure built on Congress to get the domestic economy rolling again by keeping low-priced foreign goods out of the country. Congress responded by passing Smoot-Hawley. Other nations immediately retaliated, raising their own barriers to the sale of American goods, which further cut sales of U.S. goods. Many economists blame the Smoot-Hawley Act for spreading the depression around the world.

After World War II, the United States took the lead in negotiating international agreements on free trade, such as the General Agreement on Tariffs and Trade. These agreements prohibited subsidies for exports and trade barriers, such as quotas and tariffs. In the decades following the war, world trade expanded and the American economy prospered.

But in the late 1970s and early 1980s, the United States began having serious trade problems. American consumers bought more and more foreign-made products, such as cars, stereo equipment, and clothes. And U.S. companies sold fewer goods overseas. The result was a *trade deficit*. By 1985, the trade deficit had grown to $150 billion. Economists estimated that the trade deficit was costing the United States tens of thousands of jobs a year, especially in "heavy" industries, such as steel and automobiles. The billions of dollars spent by American consumers on foreign goods were going to employ foreign workers.

To combat foreign imports, U.S. manufacturers began conducting "Buy American" advertising campaigns. They also lobbied Congress to pass protectionist legislation. Congress responded by approving laws that gave preference to American suppliers of products bought by the government; reduced the amount of steel and other products that could be imported into the United States; and limited imports of sugar, beef, and dairy products. According to a study at Georgetown University, 20 percent of all imports were covered by some sort of protectionism in 1985.

Despite these measures, American manufacturers continued to suffer. Especially hard hit was the textile industry. Between 1976 and 1984, imports of foreign clothes and fabrics doubled. By 1985, foreign imports accounted for more than 20 percent of the U.S. textile market and more than a third of the clothing market. Between 1980 and 1985, 300,000 textile workers in the United States lost their jobs. Industry spokesmen warned that the U.S. textile industry could disappear by 1990. They pointed out that since 1980, about 250 textile plants had shut down, many of which were the only employer in small southern towns.

The Move to Protect American Textiles

Alarmed by these figures, members of Congress were receptive to textile manufacturers' pleas for protectionist legislation. A textile bill was introduced in the House of Representatives on March 10, 1985. The original measure called for sharp limits on textile imports from twelve countries, including the People's Republic of China, South Korea, and Taiwan, where labor costs are only a fraction of what they are in this country. The textile industry said that the legislation would save domestic jobs by encouraging consumers to buy American-made products. The popularity of the textile bill in Congress was demonstrated by the fact that 291 House members—out of 435—signed on as original sponsors.

Because the bill dealt with tariffs (a tax on imported goods), it was referred to the House tax-writing committee—the Ways and Means Committee. The Ways and Means

subcommittee on trade held three days of public hearings on the textile bill in 1985—two in April and one in July. One other day, September 19, was needed for voting to send the textile bill to the full Ways and Means Committee. The full committee approved the bill a week later.

The committee's brief consideration of the textile measure reflected the committee members' strong support for the bill. Textiles are a $45-billion-a-year industry. Natural and synthetic fibers are used to manufacture clothes, home furnishings, automobiles, electronic circuit boards, and other products. One out of every eight manufacturing jobs in the United States is directly linked to textiles. The bill also benefitted because the Ways and Means Committee was spending most of its time considering an overhaul of the nation's tax code. The tax measure alone required several weeks of public hearings.

After passing the Ways and Means Committee, the textile bill was sent to the Rules Committee. The Rules Committee serves as a "traffic cop," deciding the rules under which legislation will be con-

sidered on the floor of the House of Representatives. Special rules for debate are necessary in the House because of its size. With 435 members, consideration of even noncontroversial legislation could drag on for days, thus limiting what the House could accomplish.

For the textile bill, the Rules Committee allowed two hours of general debate and, as is customary with Ways and Means revenue legislation, permitted no amendments to the bill. This is known as a "closed" rule and prevents House members from introducing endless amendments. House rules automatically permit one hour to debate the rules on the floor, but the time is almost always used to discuss the actual legislation.

Senators and representatives use debate on the House and Senate floors to persuade members one way or another on the merits of a particular piece of legislation. The debate is the first opportunity most members have to consider a bill. A complete transcript of the floor debate is published every day in the *Congressional Record.* This publication serves as a written record of

H. Edelman/Uniphoto

In recent years, Americans have bought more and more imported goods. As a result, sales of U.S.-made products have dropped and unemployment in industries such as steel and textiles has risen.

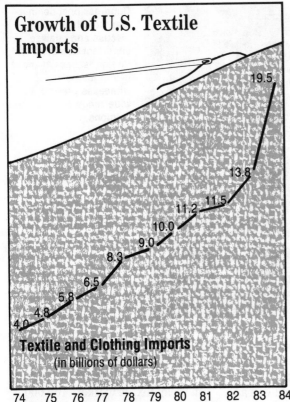

Growth of U.S. Textile Imports

Textile and Clothing Imports
(in billions of dollars)

4.0 — 4.8 — 5.8 — 6.5 — 8.3 — 9.0 — 10.0 — 11.2 — 11.5 — 13.8 — 19.5

Year: 74 75 76 77 78 79 80 81 82 83 84

Source: Congressional Quarterly and American Textile Manufacturers Institute

Textile manufacturers in countries such as Taiwan and Korea can make clothing cheaper because their labor costs are lower than those in the United States. Since 1974, American consumers have bought an increasing amount of inexpensive foreign-made goods. As a result, many American textile workers have lost their jobs.

the intent of Congress if and when a court questions what lawmakers meant when they passed a certain law.

A sponsor of the textile bill, Representative Butler Derrick (D-S.C.), opened the floor debate. He noted that forty textile plants had closed in South Carolina in the previous two years, resulting in the loss of 9,000 jobs. Nationwide, more than 300,000 jobs in the textile industry had been lost in five years. Derrick objected to calling the textile bill "protectionism." He argued that the bill would only reduce imports from major exporting nations to levels established by a 1981 international agreement. Because the agreement had not been enforced, Derrick charged, imports of textiles and textile products had jumped 19 percent in each of the last four years.

Representative Carroll A. Campbell, Jr. (R-S.C.), reported an incident from his district. The manager of a local department store wrote a letter to a textile plant superintendent, saying: "You have destroyed the town. You have shut

down your mill, and now I am going to have to shut down my department store." The superintendent of the mill visited the department store. Although most of the people who shopped there worked in the textile mill, he could not find anything made in America.

Representative James H. Quillen (R-Tenn.) and others focused their criticism on Japan, which accounted for much of the U.S. trade deficit. "After winning World War II," Quillen said, "we sent American dollars to build up Japan economically. Not only did we build up their industry, we also opened up our borders for them to ship their goods into the United States. We ended up winning the war, losing hundreds of thousands of brave Americans, and then in the end·losing [the war] economically. It simply does not make sense."

The bill's leading sponsor in the House, Representative Edgar L. Jenkins (D-Ga.), sought to broaden the measure's appeal, declaring that he was speaking for more than the textile industry. He argued that the bill might be the last opportunity in

1985 for Congress to vote on trade legislation because of time constraints. Jenkins said, "I have seen America's industrial base eroded," and pointed to producers of steel, automobiles, machine tools, televisions, pork, and cotton—all of them "on the way out, everything across the board."

But opposition to the textile bill was also strong. Representative Ed Zschau (R-Calif.) said that the textile bill was the "1985 equivalent of the Smoot-Hawley Tariff Act of 1930." Representative Robert S. Walker (R-Penn.) called the bill "a major budget-buster" because the bill would cause a drop in revenues from customs collected on the imported goods. The bipartisan Congressional Budget Office estimated that the loss in revenue over the first three years alone would be more than $1 billion. After five years, the loss could be as much as $2.5 billion. Other representatives charged that import limits would raise the average price of clothes and other textile products sold in the United States by 10 percent. Consumers would pay an additional $14 billion a year because of the higher prices.

Some representatives said that the textile bill would only benefit southern states and would lead to unemployment in U.S. port areas. Representative Thomas J. Downey (D-N.Y.) said that about 3,900 jobs would be lost in New York and New Jersey ports if the bill became law. Representative John R. Miller (R-Wash.) agreed, "Don't ask us to help your workers by taking away dock workers' jobs in New York, California, and Florida."

Some opponents were especially concerned that the textile bill could open the door for hundreds of other protectionist measures. These measures might lead to retaliation from other countries, which would hurt other U.S. industries. Representative Les AuCoin (D-Ore.) asked, "What right do the sponsors of this bill have to make my farmers pay the cost of retaliation?" Congressional opponents also said that

Congressional committees hold hearings to discuss and analyze important domestic and foreign issues. At the hearings, expert witnesses present a wide range of views and opinions.

the textile bill would hurt poor, Third World nations and damage our relations with our Asian allies, especially the People's Republic of China and Thailand.

Despite these objections, the House passed the textile bill by a vote of 262 to 159 and sent it to the Senate.

In the Senate

Across the Capitol in the Senate, South Carolina's senators, Republican Strom Thurmond and Democrat Ernest Hollings, had been pushing their own textile legislation for weeks. However, their job was more difficult because members of the Finance Committee, which considers tax and tariff bills in the Senate, opposed all protectionist measures. But the South Carolinians were lucky in that they were able to bypass the committee and bring the bill directly to the Senate floor. The senators were able to do this because Senate rules are more flexible than those of the House because of the Senate's smaller size).

Senators Thurmond and Hollings's main strategy was to attach the textile bill as an amendment (also called a rider) to other legislation related to tariffs. When Republican leaders in the Senate realized that Hollings and Thurmond intended to persist in this

effort, a deal was struck to permit consideration of the textile bill by itself.

Looming in the background was a Senate rule permitting unlimited debate (called a filibuster) on a bill, something not tolerated in the House. During a filibuster, one senator can hold up consideration of a bill by talking continuously day and night on any subject. (Thurmond himself once spoke on the floor for more than 24 hours in the 1950s to demonstrate his opposition to a bill.) Using a filibuster, a small group of senators can delay the Senate agenda almost indefinitely. Faced with the possibility of a filibuster blocking other pressing legislation—such as the federal budget—the Senate Majority Leader, who has a responsibility to keep the Senate agenda moving, compromised with Hollings and Thurmond. The textile bill was brought to the floor for consideration.

The two senators were not alone. They had the support of more than fifty other senators. Senator Howell T. Heflin (D-Ala.) argued for the bill: "For every 1 billion square yards of foreign-produced textiles, apparel, and fibers that we import, we can chalk up a loss of 100,000 American job opportunities. One billion square yards may sound like an extremely

high amount, but it isn't; that is less than the import level for September 1985—one month that cost American textile workers 100,000 job opportunities; 100,000 chances to support their families; 100,000 chances to build a better future for their children; 100,000 chances to dream the American dream. All this was lost in only one month!"

Senate opponents of the textile bill echoed arguments raised in the House of Representatives. They detailed the possibility of foreign retaliation and increased unemployment in other parts of the country. They also warned that approval of the bill could lead to more protectionist legislation. Senator John C. Danforth (R-Mo.) said, "If we don't say no to textiles, we can't say no to anybody [who wants protection]."

However, other senators were willing to support the bill if additional provisions were added. Six senators from the West wanted an amendment putting temporary limits on imports of copper, a major western industry. Some senators from New England (where most U.S. shoe manufacturers are located) sought a provision to limit shoe imports for a period of eight years.

Senate sponsors of the bill said that they were willing to consider these amendments. To gain further support, this time from the Reagan administration, the sponsors also met with officials from the White House.

Final Adjustments

Since President Ronald Reagan's election in 1980, he has been a strong and vocal supporter of free trade. He repeatedly vowed to veto any protectionist measure approved by Congress. The textile industry and its backers on Capitol Hill were aware of the president's opposition to protectionist legislation. Early on, they held private talks with White House officials about the textile bill to find a compromise that President Reagan would accept.

The officials explained that one of the administration's priorities was to maintain good relations with the People's Republic of China, an important ally in Asia. To preserve these relations, the White House believed that a relatively free flow of goods from mainland China, the fourth largest exporter of textiles to the United States, was necessary. In an effort to ease White House concerns, the Senate sponsors agreed to limit textile import quotas to only the top three textile exporters—South Korea, Taiwan, and Hong Kong—thus eliminating China and

eight other countries that would have been affected by the toughest provision of the House measure.

At the same time, opponents of the legislation were meeting with the president. They discussed strategies for defeating the bill. The legislators warned Reagan that his veto would be necessary to preserve the nation's free trade policies, since the bill was likely to pass in both houses.

Before bringing the bill to the Senate floor for a vote on November 13, 1985, Hollings and Thurmond made some other minor changes in the bill, such as dropping stuffed toys and dolls made of fabric and eliminating some silk products. The only substantive additions made during consideration of the bill were provisions protecting the copper and shoe industries. Amendments designed to soften the impact of the import restrictions were defeated by two-to-one margins or withdrawn. The Senate approved its version of the textile bill by a vote of 60 to 39.

Since only one version of a piece of legislation can become law, the House and Senate must meet to resolve any differences between their two bills. Normally, a few members from the two relevant committees get together in a "con-

ference committee" to work out a compromise. In this case, however, Senators Hollings and Thurmond had met with the principal House sponsors before the Senate had even voted and had won their approval for the changes. The agreement removed the need for a House-Senate conference. On December 3, the House voted 255 to 161 for the Senate version and sent the bill to the White House.

The final bill, named the Textile and Apparel Trade Enforcement Act of 1985, called for:

- cutting imports of textiles and clothing from South Korea, Taiwan and Hong Kong by as much as 30 percent;

- permanently limiting the growth of textile imports from eight other Asian nations and Brazil to 1 percent a year;

- limiting shoe imports to no more than 60 percent of U.S. sales for eight years; and

- directing the president to negotiate international agreements in 1986 to limit copper imports.

Members of Congress rely on the president to lend support to particular legislation. The president's influence and prestige can sway undecided representatives and senators.

The Pressures of Lobbying

Passage of the textile bill was a major victory for the textile industry. The industry had lobbied strongly for the bill, forming the Fiber, Fabric, and Apparel Coalition for Trade. The coalition deluged the lawmakers with dire warnings of what was happening to the textile industry. The coalition, along with the Man-Made Fiber Producers Association, Inc., spent a total of $1.8 million during the first nine months of 1985 in their efforts to sway Congress.

A grassroots effort was also directed at the White House. By the time the textile bill reached President Reagan's desk, nearly 3 million handwritten letters from apparel workers and their families had been sent to the president urging him to support the bill.

Opponents to the textile bill had revved up their lobbying machines as well. Retailers, who wanted to maintain their sources of less expensive supplies, and importers worked against the measure. While these forces were unable to defeat the bill in Congress, several House members who originally supported the measure were eventually persuaded to vote against it.

Sending the Bill to the White House

Despite earlier changes to ease limits of the bill on the People's Republic of China, President Reagan opposed the textile bill and vetoed the legislation when it reached his desk. In his statement explaining the veto on December 17, 1985, the president emphasized the benefits of a free-market economy, saying that protectionism would backfire and hurt consumers. Trade barriers would reduce the amount of inexpensive textiles available and force consumers to buy more expensive American-made textiles. As a result, consumers would have less money to spend on other goods, and the American economy would suffer even more. Protectionism would also prompt other nations to retaliate with barriers to American

Bob Daemmrich/Uniphoto

Many American workers have lost their jobs because of foreign imports. Protesters have called for quotas and tariffs to limit the sales of imported goods in the United States.

products, thus reducing the amount of American goods sold abroad and causing higher unemployment in the United States. The bottom line was that free trade, not protectionism, would best help American industries.

However, President Reagan did acknowledge Congress's concern over trade. He told Congress that he would not "stand by and watch American businesses fail because of unfair trading practices abroad." The president outlined a three-point program calling for: (1) additional retraining and relocation help for workers affected by imports, (2) renegotiation of pacts covering textile imports, and (3) investigation of whether imports had exceeded agreed-upon limits.

Although the president vetoed the bill, the measure did give U.S. trade negotiators more clout. The negotiators were trying to convince Japan and other major trade partners to lower their barriers to American goods. In effect, they could argue, "Look, we want to be reasonable, but you saw what Congress already has done, and that

could be only the beginning if we do not get some concessions."

Congress Responds to the Veto

Congress, of course, can enact legislation into law over the president's veto. Two-thirds of the members in both the House and Senate must vote again for the legislation. While the textile bill had broad support, it did not have enough to override a veto. Several legislators let it be known that while they had originally supported the measure, they would not vote to override the president. In fact, some supporters in Congress were actually relieved by President Reagan's veto.

The pressures on Congress to pass the textile bill had been immense. Not every member who voted "aye" wanted the measure to become law. Some members only wanted to send a message to other nations that they were concerned about the loss of American jobs. Other members had voted for the bill as a favor to a colleague whose home district was directly affected by the ailing textile industry. Still other members felt they could use the trade deficit to gain voter support. All were wary of the effects that protectionist legislation would have on the national economy.

A great deal of constituent pressure to vote for the bill was placed on several first-term Republican senators. Although they did not support the measure, the senators found it difficult to vote against it because their states were heavily involved in the textile industry. Their political position became even more tenuous by the fact that they were up for reelection in 1986 and wanted to get campaign help from the president. Voting to override the president's veto was not likely to keep them in the president's favor.

Because of the drop in support for the textile bill, the bill's sponsors decided not to try to override the veto for several months. By that time, they said, the administration would have had time to renegotiate bilateral trade agreements as promised by the president. Representative Carroll A. Campbell said that failure to get strict import limits in a new international agreement would "strengthen the chances of an override."

In the end, the congressional will seemed to have worked at least in prodding the administration into taking action on trade and sending a warning to other nations. Whether America's trading partners abroad heard the message as clearly as the president remains to be seen.

Activities

1. Reading Between the Lines

In her article, Representative Barbara Boxer states that "no matter what social or economic class people are in, they all want the same thing—a peaceful and secure world that is environmentally sound, where children can grow up with both opportunity and hope." Do you think it is possible for people to agree on what constitutes a "peaceful and secure" world? For example, some people believe that the United States needs a large nuclear arsenal in order to be secure, while others believe that the very existence of a nuclear arsenal makes our future very insecure. Some environmentalists argue that the use of pesticides poses a serious threat to our environment, while some farmers say our nation's food supply would suffer a tremendous loss if they were to stop using them.

Read the views on these and other issues of several different representatives from around the country, including your own. What do they think will make the world a peaceful and secure place to live? How are their views alike? How are they different? If you were a member of Congress, how would you go about resolving the differences?

2. Developing Your Own Perspective

Members of Congress can be divided into four types based on how they vote on legislative issues.

- *Trustees* see themselves as independents who judge each bill on its own merits. When voting, they usually do not take into account the views of their constituents or special interest groups.

- *Delegates* view themselves as representatives of their constituents and vote the way the people who elected them want them to.

- *Partisans* support their party's platform and vote according to the wishes of their party leaders.

- *Pragmatists* attempt to combine all of the above considerations when deciding how to vote on an issue. They try to decide what is best for their constituents, their party, and the country and then vote accordingly.

Imagine you are a member of Congress. Which type of representative would you be? Why?

3. Becoming an Active Citizen

Does your representative reflect your views? To find out, make a list of at least three issues that you feel strongly about. These could be national issues, such as the arms race, gun control, or school prayer, or local issues that pertain strictly to your area of the country. Jot down your views on these three issues. Now write to your member of Congress (see "Tips on Writing Your Member of Congress"), and ask for his or her views. You could also visit one of your representative's district offices and ask the staff aides if they can help you. You might also check your local newspaper to see if your representative has recently given a speech or made comments about one of your issues. How do your views compare with those of your senator or representative? Remember, a good voter is an informed voter!

★★★★★★★★★★

THE JUDICIARY

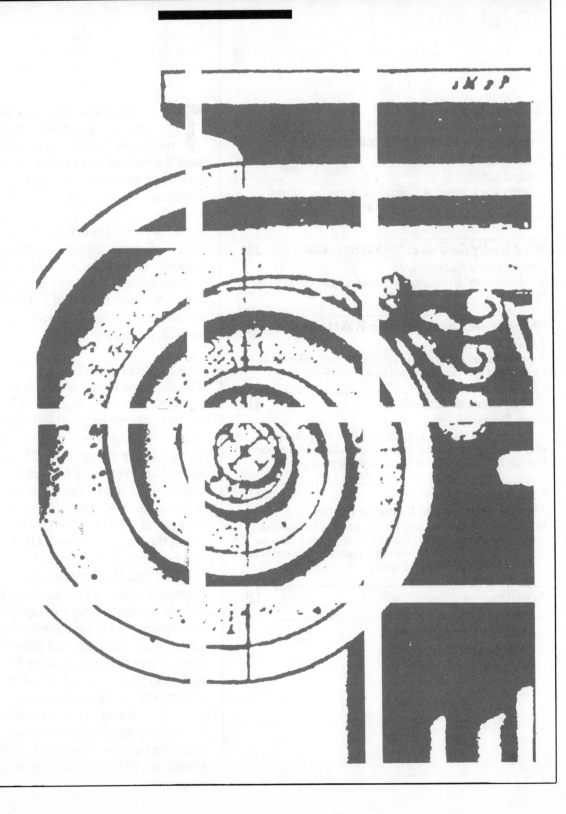

4. The Judiciary

In This Chapter

The Constitution gives few details on the structure of the judicial branch of government. Section I of Article III stipulates that the judicial power of the United States should be vested in one supreme and in as many lower courts as Congress decides to establish. Over the years, Congress has set up two major levels of federal courts below the Supreme Court—federal district courts and courts of appeals. In addition, each state has its own judicial system that tries cases involving state law. Together, state and federal courts have established the judicial branch as a powerful voice in our government.

The Supreme Court

The Supreme Court is composed of a chief justice and eight associate justices. While the Supreme Court has some original jurisdiction—such as in cases involving two or more states—most of the cases it hears are appeals of lower court decisions. However, very few cases ever reach the Supreme Court. Of the millions of federal and state cases tried every year in American courts, only about 4,000 to 5,000 petitions for review reach the Supreme Court. Of these, the Court will hear only 150 cases.

If you visit the Supreme Court, you will find an impressive marble building with the motto, "Equal Justice Under the Law," engraved over its imposing columns. Inside, the Supreme Court's surroundings and procedures suggest a bygone era: the justices wear long black robes and sit in front of a red velvet curtain. And many of their proceedings are conducted in private, away from the eyes and ears of the public. All of this is in keeping with the views of our nation's founders that the Supreme Court's decisions should not be subject to outside political pressures.

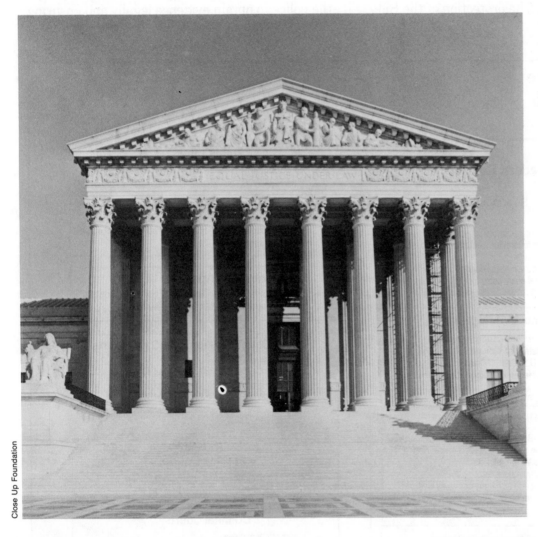

The Supreme Court and other federal courts comprise our judicial branch of government. Federal courts decide the constitutionality of actions, by Congress and the president, and resolve other legal disputes involving the government or private parties.

Judicial Review

The precedent for the Supreme Court deciding the constitutionality of laws was set in 1803. In the landmark decision, *Marbury* v. *Madison*, Chief Justice John Marshall established the concept of *judicial review*. Marshall declared that "it is the duty of the judicial department to say what the law is." He claimed that the federal judicial system—and especially the Supreme Court—

has the power to declare acts of Congress unconstitutional.

Since Marshall's time, the Supreme Court has expanded the concept of judicial review, giving it the power to declare unconstitutional the actions of public officials and even society as a whole. For example, in 1974, in *United States* v. *Nixon*, the Supreme Court ruled that President Richard Nixon's attempt to withhold tape recordings from a federal court was a violation of Article II of the Constitution and forced the president to release the tapes. And in 1954, the Supreme Court ruled in *Brown* v. *Board of Education* that separate schools for black and white students violated the equal protection of the laws guaranteed by the Fourteenth Amendment.

Individual Rights
In the past thirty years, the Supreme Court has shown a strong interest in protecting civil rights and liberties. First Amendment freedoms of speech, press, religion, and assembly have been defined and expanded. The protection of the Bill of Rights has been extended to people accused of crimes by federal and state authorities. The Supreme Court has insisted on a poor defendant's right to a lawyer; declared that illegally seized evidence cannot be used in state criminal trials; and held that a suspect must be advised of his or her constitutional right to silence and to have a lawyer before questioning.

Some complain that the Supreme Court has gone too far and is "coddling criminals" while "handcuffing the police." However, many argue that it is imperative to protect the legal rights of everyone, even suspected criminals. By forcing the police to obtain evidence legally and ensuring

Structure of the Judicial Branch

Federal Courts

U.S. Supreme Court
- Tries lawsuits between the states.
- Reviews decisions of federal appellate courts and specialized federal courts.
- Reviews decisions of the highest court of appeals in a state if a constitutional question or federal law is involved.

U.S. Courts of Appeals
Ten judicial circuits nationwide plus the District of Columbia
- Hears appeals from U.S. District Courts.
- Reviews decisions of federal administrative agencies.

U.S. District Courts
Approximately 90 district courts nationwide plus Puerto Rico and the Virgin Islands.
- Tries both civil and criminal cases.
- Serves as bankruptcy and admiralty courts as well.
- Reviews decisions of federal administrative agencies.

Tax Court of the United States
- Hears cases arising under federal tax laws.

U.S. Court of Claims
- Hears suits against the U.S. government. Evidence may be presented before court commissioners at various locations throughout the country.

State Courts
No two states have identical court systems, but all have similar outlines.

State Supreme Courts
- Hears appeals from all inferior courts. Court of last resort except for constitutional matters, which may be appealed to U.S. Supreme Court.

Intermediate Appellate Courts
- Hears appeals from the decisions of criminal courts and courts of general and special jurisdiction.

District, County or Municipal Trial Courts
- Hears civil suits and criminal cases.

Juvenile or Family Courts
- Hears domestic juvenile delinquency and youthful offender cases.

Probate Courts
- Reviews wills and hear claims against estates.

Criminal Courts
- Hears criminal cases.

Local Courts
- Hears minor criminal cases, traffic violations, and civil cases involving property. Cases cannot be appealed.
- Names vary according to locality but may include:
  Traffic Court
  Small Claims Court
  Police Court
  Justice of the Peace

that proper trial procedures are followed, the courts limit the power of the government to interfere in the private lives of citizens.

Poverty and the Law

The right of every defendant to have a lawyer present during a criminal trial might seem basic, but in fact it was not established by the Supreme Court until 1963. Clarence Earl Gideon petitioned the Supreme Court in 1962 from his Florida prison cell where he was serving time for allegedly stealing some beer, wine, and money from a pool hall. A drifter who had been in and out of prison on many occasions, Gideon could not afford to hire a lawyer. He claimed that he had not received a fair trial because he had not had a lawyer. The Supreme Court agreed, and Gideon was granted a new trial. This time, with the help of a lawyer, he was acquitted. The landmark Gideon decision entitled all poor defendants to a lawyer in felony cases. In 1972, the Supreme Court extended that right to people accused of misdemeanors.

It was left to each state to develop its own system for ensuring that all defendants receive legal counsel. Today, nearly 200,000 lawyers give legal advice to people who are caught up in the criminal justice system, but who cannot afford a private attorney.

The U.S Constitution only vaguely outlines the judicial branch of government. Though the system of checks and balances prevents any one branch of government from gaining too much power, the judiciary—and especially the Supreme Court—offers final voice in many legal matters.

Balancing the Rights of the Individual and the Needs of Society

Doug Bandow

Doug Bandow is a senior fellow for the Cato Institute, a public policy research institution. Prior to his present position, Mr. Bandow was a special assistant to President Reagan with responsibility for analyzing a wide variety of policy issues including energy, the environment, and federalism. In this article, Mr. Bandow examines how our judicial system protects the rights of all citizens by protecting the rights of the accused.

The basic building block of American society is the individual. For this reason, the express purpose of the nation's governing document, the Constitution, is to protect personal autonomy. In contrast to European countries like Great Britain, for instance, our political system is designed to diffuse power through different levels and branches of government. The Constitution expressly reserves important powers to the states and distributes the national government's limited authority among three separate branches.

More important, the federal government's power is restricted by the Bill of Rights, which guarantees freedom of religion, speech, gun ownership, and property; the first eight amendments also established strict limits on the government's power to arrest and prosecute its citizens. Finally, to reinforce the limitations on federal power, the Ninth Amendment proclaimed that "the enumeration in the Constitution, of certain rights, shall not be construed to deny or disparage others retained by the people," while the Tenth Amendment stated that "the powers not delegated to the United States by the Constitution, nor prohibited by it to the states, are reserved to the states respectively, or to the people."

Among the most important rights protected by the Constitution are those involving the criminal justice system. The Fourth Amendment prohibits "unreasonable searches and seizures"; the Fifth Amendment prescribes use of a grand jury, bars forced self-incrimination, and prevents multiple prosecutions for the same crime. The Sixth Amendment sets out the right of the accused to a "speedy and public trial," ensures the right of the defendant to confront the witnesses against him, and sets out additional procedural protections. Finally, the Eighth Amendment bars "cruel and unusual punishments."

The Supreme Court has applied most of these rights to the states through the so-called "due process clause" of the Fourteenth Amendment. Since most criminal prosecutions occur at the state level, imposing the bulk of the Bill of Rights on states has greatly expanded legal safeguards for individuals.

Over the years, there have been many conflicts between personal liberty and the desires of the majority in this area. During the 1960s, the Supreme Court, under the leadership of Chief Justice Earl Warren, greatly expanded the scope of the Constitution's guarantees, requiring that arrestees be read their rights and given access to an attorney, for instance. However, as the crime rate rose and the judicial system seemed increasingly unable to deliver justice—especially for victims of crime—a political backlash developed. Richard Nixon was elected president on a "law-and-order" campaign in 1968. Congress periodically sought to limit Supreme Court decisions by amending laws declared unconstitutional. The Reagan administration pressed the Supreme Court to back away from some of its more protective rulings, particularly in areas such as search and seizure.

The issues at stake are important ones, for victims, as well as defendants, are entitled to justice.

However, the criminal law is really less a question of *which rights* are more important (those of the individual or of the state) than of *which individual's rights* are more important. For the "right of society" is really the right of the people who make up society not to be assaulted or robbed, and, if they are, their right to collect restitution and punish their attackers.

The system that has evolved may seem weighted toward criminals, but most of the constitutional protections for defendants serve the innocent as well. Indeed, the purpose of the Fourth Amendment, which generally requires a warrant before the police can conduct a search, is to protect the privacy of people where there is no evidence that they have committed a crime. The right to a jury trial puts a barrier between all citizens and a potentially abusive government. The constitutional guarantees of bail, an attorney, and a public trial also protect the public generally by creating an independent, fair truth-determining process.

Nevertheless, do these protections sometimes result in a guilty person going free? Probably so, but how many critics of the current system would like to be the innocent person convicted if the Bill of Rights were swept away in an attempt to reduce crime? The fundamental difference between a free society like ours and totalitarian systems is that, in our society, the government respects the basic rights of its citizens. A country in which the police could arrest a person on the barest pretext or break into one's house at will would not be a pleasant—or safe—one, even if a few more criminals ended up in prison as a result.

There is a point, of course, where hard decisions must be made, even when the chance of an error persists. A search only requires reasonable evidence, not incontrovertible proof. Court appeals are necessary to review what may be life-and-death decisions, but the process cannot be endless. Indeed, it may be in the area of speed that the criminal justice system most fails to meet the theoretical ideal.

Yet widespread delay and inefficiency have not prevented America's prisons from being filled to overflowing. If we really want to put dangerous criminals in jail sooner, we should not eliminate rules that protect basic rights, but instead should reassess who deserves to be imprisoned. Might prostitutes, drug users, and stock manipulators, for instance, be better dealt with outside of the traditional criminal justice system? As much as 40 percent of local police resources are tied up dealing with essentially "victimless" crimes, so it is small wonder that the system moves slowly.

The perception that justice is never done is especially strong in death penalty cases. Inmates often spend years on death row; they receive stays of execution and make appeals ad infinitum. Though the Supreme Court has begun to remove some of the procedural impediments that have prevented executions in the past, it is probably inevitable that this form of punishment will only infrequently—and reluctantly—be carried out. For Americans have proved themselves to be immensely ambivalent about imposing the ultimate penalty. Short of abolishing capital punishment, no change in the law is likely to accelerate the disposition of murder cases. And we really shouldn't want it otherwise.

Is there a conflict between the rights of different individuals, particularly criminal defendants and victims? Yes, there is. But we must never allow dubious claims about the general good to override the very freedoms that make our society worth living in. Eliminating the fundamental legal rules that protect all of us, under the guise of cracking down on criminals, certainly will not promote the "public interest." For a system that does not protect individual liberty cannot preserve the common good.

Questions to Consider

1. How would you characterize the conflict between the rights of individuals and the desires of the majority in American society?

2. In this article, the author says that "criminal law is really less a question of *which rights* are more important than of *which individual's rights* are more important." What does the author mean by this statement?

3. The author states that people accused of "victimless" crimes—such as gambling and prostitution—should be prosecuted outside of our traditional judicial system. Do you agree with his argument? Why or why not?

Glossary of Legal Terms

adjudication—the process of determining what a law means in a specific case.

affirm—to uphold the decision of a lower court.

amicus curiae **brief**—"friend of the court" brief. A brief submitted to the Supreme Court by an interested person or group that is not directly involved in the case.

appeal—a petition, or formal request, to a higher court that it reexamine a verdict reached by a lower court.

brief—a document prepared by lawyers that presents legal arguments, facts, and other considerations that support their client's position.

certiorari—"to make certain." A petition to a higher court for a review of a lower court decision. The court can grant or refuse the petition.

de facto—a condition existing in fact. Example: *de facto* segregation means actual separation of the races whether or not that segregation is supported by the law.

de jure—a condition existing by law. Example: *de jure* segregation means the separation of the races sanctioned by the law.

defendant—a person charged with a crime.

due process of law—a clause in the Fifth and Fourteenth Amendments that guarantees that laws be reasonable and applied fairly and equally to all citizens.

habeas corpus—legal principle guaranteeing a speedy and public trial.

indictment—formal written accusation charging a person with a crime.

judicial activism—refers to judges who, in ruling on the cases before them, take an active role in directing public policy on social issues such as racial integration or school prayer.

judicial restraint—refers to judges who, in ruling on the cases before them, avoid broad policy implications.

judicial review—authority of the courts to examine legislative and executive acts to determine whether or not they are prohibited by the Constitution.

jurisdiction—the power of a court to hear a case. This power may be limited to specific geographic areas, subject matters, or persons.

litigation—legal proceedings.

original jurisdiction—the power of a court to hear and decide cases before they are considered by any other court.

plaintiff—person or group that brings a suit to court.

precedent—decision in a case that forms the basis for a future decision in a similar case.

stare decisis—"let the decision stand." The doctrine that principles of law established in judicial decisions should not be overruled.

subpoena—order for a person to appear before a court or to surrender evidence (tapes, documents, etc.) to a court or other official body.

writ—written document issued by a court requiring or prohibiting the performance of a specified act.

What Really Goes on at the Supreme Court

Justice Lewis F. Powell, Jr.

Justice Lewis F. Powell, Jr., was appointed to the U.S. Supreme Court in 1971 after a distinguished legal career. His article, adapted from an address given at the Southwestern Legal Foundation in Dallas, Texas, explains the inner workings of the Supreme Court.

Asked to name the problems of greatest concern to Americans, most people probably would include unemployment, drugs, Soviet aggression, increasing terrorism in the world, and whether we have the will and the capability to defend vital interests.

Yet, with all of these perplexing and even disquieting problems, public interest in what goes on at the Supreme Court continues to be high. Rumors—often perceived to be facts—have circulated for years. Those of us who work quietly in our marble palace find it difficult to understand this apparent fascination with how we go about our business.

The Court is a place where justices and their small staffs work extremely long hours; where the work is sometimes tedious, although always intellectually demanding; where we take our responsibility with the utmost seriousness; and where there is little or no time for socializing.

The constitutional duty of the Court, as John Marshall said in *Marbury* v. *Madison*, is to "say what the law is." In discharging this function, the Court is the final arbiter, and therefore its role in our system of government is powerful and unique. But the Court is remote from the mainstream of day-to-day government.

However, it is natural to be curious about secrets. For years—perhaps throughout the history of the Supreme Court—there have been stories and gossip about secret goings-on behind the Court's closed doors. I remember an article in which the Supreme Court was described as the most "secret society in America."

The fact is that the extent of our secrecy is greatly exaggerated. The doors of the Court are open to the public. Both the press and the public are welcome at all of our argument sessions. Our decisions in the argued cases are printed and widely disseminated.

The charge of secrecy relates only to the discussions, exchanges of views by memoranda, and the drafting that precede our judgments and published opinions. As lawyers know, we get together almost every Friday to discuss petitions by litigants who wish us to hear their cases and to debate and vote tentatively on the argued cases. Only justices attend these conferences. There are no law clerks, no secretaries, and no tape recorders—at least none we know about.

The chief justice and the most junior justice have the responsibility of recording our votes.

These votes always are tentative until the cases are finally decided and brought down. Justices may—and usually do—keep their own notes at conference.

We rarely discuss cases with one another before going to conference, where our discussions are thorough. After a tentative vote has been taken, the drafting of opinions is assigned to the individual justices. When a justice is satisfied with his or her draft, he or she circulates it to the other chambers. Comments usually are made by exchanges of memoranda, although we feel free to visit justices and discuss differences. There is less of this than one would like, primarily because of our heavy caseload and the logistical difficulties of talking individually to eight other justices.

The process that I have described actually may take months after a case is argued. The preparation of an opinion often requires painstaking research, drafting, and revising, and additional efforts to resolve differences among justices to the extent that is feasible. It is this unstructured and informal process—the making of the decision itself, from the first conference until it is handed down in open Court—that simply cannot take place in public.

Nevertheless, there are recurring demands that the public and the media have front-row seats on the decisionmaking process. Some urge that reporters be admitted to our conferences, be afforded access to the preliminary drafts of opinions, and even see informal memoranda that we exchange with each other.

The integrity of judicial decisionmaking would be impaired seriously if we had to reach our judgments in the atmosphere of an ongoing town meeting. There must be candid discussion, a willingness to consider arguments advanced by other justices, and a continuing examination and reexamination of one's own views. The confidentiality of this process assures that we will review carefully the soundness of our judgments. It also improves the quality of our written opinions.

Both litigants and the public could be harmed if total openness were to prevail. For example, the decision in an antitrust case may affect the market prices of securities. Unless our initial conference votes were final, the weeks or months of the opinion-writing process would be a continuous sideshow, with investors uncertain as to what to do. Or in a capital case that involved the death penalty, the condemned defendant would agonize over each memorandum circulated among the justices.

Our decisions concern the liberty, property, and even the lives of litigants. There can be no posturing among us and no thought of tomorrow's headlines.

Over the years, security at the Supreme Court has been exceptionally good. It also is only fair to say that the reporters who regularly cover the Court respect the institutional need to preserve confidentiality until an opinion is handed down.

Smithsonian Institution

The Supreme Court, from left to right: Sandra Day O'Connor, Lewis F. Powell, Jr., Thurgood Marshall, William J. Brennan, Jr., William H. Rehnquist, Byron R. White, Harry A. Blackmun, John Paul Stevens, and Antonin Scalia.

Two Myths

Two of the myths about the Supreme Court have been repeated so often that they have attained a life of their own. One is simply untrue; the other reflects a fundamental misconception of the Court's role.

The nine justices often are portrayed as fighting and feuding with one another. In the past, news stories have described the Supreme Court as torn by personal discord and lack of mutual respect.

This is a wholly inaccurate picture of the relationships at the Court. At the personal level, there is genuine cordiality. No justice will deny this. We lunch together frequently, visit in one another's homes, celebrate birthdays, and enjoying kidding one another to lighten our long and demanding conferences.

It is true that over the years there have been some fascinating examples of personal animosity on the Supreme Court. There are three justices on the present Court who were law clerks when some notable rivalries existed. Justice John Paul Stevens, one of these former clerks, recently told the Richmond bar that he had been pleasantly surprised to find no such animosity on the present Court. "Reports to the contrary," he stated, "are simply not true."

The erroneous perception of discord on the Court perhaps is based on a failure to distinguish between personal and professional disagreement, although misconception as to differences among the justices is not confined to the media. Law clerks, who are at the Court only for a year and usually have not practiced law, may take personally the professional disagreements among us. A clerk's loyalty to his or her justice tends to be high. This sometimes may cause a clerk— disappointed by the outcome of a particular case—to think harshly of justices who have disagreed with his or her "boss."

Many cases present extremely close and difficult questions of law. Often these questions are intertwined with sensitive collateral judgments of morality and social policy. Examples include those cases involving capital punishment, abortion, obscenity, and the vast ramifications of equal protection and civil rights.

We do indeed have strong professional differences about many of our cases. These are exposed for the public to see. Unlike the executive branch, for example, we record fully our disagreements in dissenting opinions. Frequently, the language of a dissent is not a model of temperate discourse. We fight hard for our professional views. But, contrary to what one may reason, these differences reflect no lack of respect for the members of the Court with whom we disagree. In the course of a given term, I find myself more than once in sharp disagreement with every other justice.

It is fortunate that our system, unlike that in many other countries, accepts and respects the function of dissenting opinions. The very process of dissent assures a rigorous testing of the majority view within the Supreme Court itself and reduces the chance of arbitrary decisionmaking. Moreover, as "courtwatchers" know, the forceful dissent of today may attract a majority vote in some future year.

A more substantive misconception concerns the role of the Supreme Court and the way it functions. One writer has described the Court as "rudderless, its nine justices still searching for a theme." Other commentators have said that the Court lacks strong leadership and has no consistent judicial or ideological philosophy. Those who write this nonsense simply do not understand the responsibilities either of the Supreme Court or of the chief justice.

The "Rudderless" Burger Court

In the early years of what was called the Warren Burger Court, one often read that the more recently appointed justices would vote consistently as a conservative bloc (the "Nixon bloc") to dismantle the great decisions of the Warren Court.

There was never justification for the alarm about a monolithic "Nixon bloc." The long history of the Supreme Court happily makes clear that justices recognize no obligation to reflect the views of the president who appointed them. Tenure during good behavior and the strong tradition of an independent federal judiciary have assured this.

I have wondered whether those who decried the "rudderless Court" would like to be judged by a different kind of court. For example, if one's liberty were at stake, would he or she like to be judged by a Court whose members were dominated by a willful chief justice? And what confidence could a litigant have in a Court that decided cases according to some consistently applied philosophy or "theme," rather than on the facts of his or her case and the applicable law?

To be sure, sweeping constitutional phrases such as "due process" and "equal protection of the law" cannot be applied with the exactitude of the rule against perpetuities. And in cases involving these and like phrases, justices may tend to adhere to what often are called their own "liberal" or "conservative" interpretations. But in the application of these views, judgments are made on a case-by-case basis in light of one's perception of the law and relevant precedents.

Each of us has an equal vote, and although we endeavor to harmonize our views to reach a Court judgment, the members of this Court vote independently.

There is a long tradition at the Supreme Court of independent decisionmaking. Indeed, this is the sworn duty of each justice. In discussing some of the perceptions of the Burger Court, Professor Gerald Gunther of Stanford Law School commented on the shallowness of the criticism that the Court "lacked strong, overarching [ideological] value commitments. . . ."He characterized the independent quality of the judging process as "admirable."

I recognize the difficulty that the media may have in covering the Supreme Court. Our work is important to the country, and the public needs to be informed about it promptly. But few of our opinions will ever make a "best-seller" list. Assuring that news stories about the Court will be readable may well require some romancing about justices' disagreements.

But most of the media coverage of our decisions is professional, and we certainly do not expect or want it to be uncritical. In an address, Justice Brennan, who often has written eloquently about the First Amendment, spoke of the "fundamental. . . interdependence of the Court and the press." He noted that "the press needs the Court" because we are the "ultimate guardian of the constitutional rights" enjoyed by it. The Supreme Court also needs the press to report our judgments accurately to the public.

If I seem partisan on behalf of the Court, it is because I am. As a traditionalist, I profoundly respect the Court as an institution.

Courts Make Dream of "Ordered" Liberty a Reality

Our most precious ideal is that of ordered personal liberty. Its principles are stated in the Bill of Rights, but no mere exposition of these principles, however eloquent, would have assured their survival. The ideal of ordered liberty is rooted in many centuries of English history. It dates back to the great charters of the rights of the English: Magna Carta (1215), the Petition of Right (1628), the Habeas Corpus Act (1679), and the English Bill of Rights (1689).

I emphasize the word "ordered" in speaking of personal liberty. The rights now guaranteed by our Constitution have been interpreted and preserved in our country by a judicial system, both state and federal, that inherited many of the doctrines, traditions, and practices of the English courts. For liberty to be ordered, there must be institutionalized courts that function within a system of government. To state an extreme contemporary contrast, the revolutionary courts that operated in Iran during 1980 were hardly institutionalized. Nor did they protect liberty.

All three branches of our government have supported the great ideal of ordered liberty. Yet it is the courts—led by the Supreme Court—that have assured it. The American people have respected the courts, and they have placed special trust and confidence in the Supreme Court.

In my view, this trust has been merited. I speak not of the membership of the Supreme Court today or at any particular time. Justices, with varying degrees of wisdom and legal scholarship, come and go. The institution, nourished by its inherited traditions, is what merits respect and confidence. Those who denigrate the courts do a disservice to liberty itself.

Questions to Consider

1. Do you agree with Justice Powell that the integrity of judicial decisionmaking would be seriously impaired if the media had access to judicial conferences and draft memoranda? Why or why not?

2. Why are dissenting opinions important?

3. What does Justice Powell mean when he writes about "ordered personal liberty"?

The Supreme Court: Deciding What to Decide

Phillip L. Spector

Phillip L. Spector, currently a partner in the law firm of Goldberg & Spector in Washington, D.C., served as a law clerk to U.S. Supreme Court Justice Thurgood Marshall from 1977 to 1978. In this article, Mr. Spector explains the criteria used by Supreme Court justices in deciding whether to hear a case.

When most of us think of the Supreme Court, our first thought is of the major cases that grab the headlines in our nation's newspapers. Whether the subject is affirmative action or abortion, the rights of the press or the rights of criminals, government budget-cutting or school prayer, the Supreme Court often plays a crucial role in deciding the critical issues that we face as a government and a people. Thus, when a news announcer says, "The Supreme Court decided today...," we all stop and listen.

As we listen, most of us do not think about the many, many cases that the Supreme Court chose not to decide. For example, if you were a litigant and had asked the Supreme Court to review your case in 1984–85, you would have had about one chance in seventeen of succeeding with your request. And, of course, succeeding in having the Supreme Court hear your case does not mean that you will necessarily win in the Supreme Court; it only means that the justices have decided to decide.

To understand the Supreme Court's discretion to decide which cases it will hear, one must first understand how cases reach the Supreme Court. Whether coming from a state court or from a federal court, a case typically will not end up in the Supreme Court until it has been considered by a trial judge, sometimes working with a jury. Once the trial judge or jury has ruled, the facts of a case are generally assumed to be as the judge or jury found them, but the losing side almost always has a right to appeal the trial-level decision to a higher court. The appeal is based primarily on how the law was applied to the facts of the case. In our judicial system, every litigant is entitled to at least one—and sometimes two or three—appeals before a case may reach the Supreme Court.

Once lower court appeals have been exhausted, the losing party may file a request for review with the Supreme Court. The most common form of request is a petition for "certiorari" (or review). Once a certiorari petition or appeal is filed, the opposing side may reply, and then the petition and reply are reviewed by the justices and their law clerks. Despite the fact that more than 4,000 requests for review may be filed with the Supreme Court in a year, every petition is read by a justice or clerk before a decision to deny is made.

On most Fridays from September through June, the nine justices sit together in "con-

Peter ©1986

Speech bubbles (part of image):
HOORAY!

BOY, HE'S EXCITED. WHAT DID HE DO... WIN THE LOTTERY?

NO... THE SUPREME COURT DECIDED TO HEAR HIS CASE.

typically by granting certiorari—if four of the nine justices vote to hear it. Any justice who wants to hear a case, but cannot persuade his or her colleagues, may ask that the announcement of the certiorari petition's denial be delayed while that justice writes memoranda or talks to colleagues in an effort to persuade them to join him or her.

What factors do the justices consider in deciding which cases to hear? Although each justice has his or her own reasons for voting to grant or deny, certainly the overriding criterion for all justices is one of importance. If a case has something important about it, something unique and significant for the country or the legal system, it is likely to be heard. If there is nothing important or unique about a case, the certiorari petition will almost always be denied.

Beyond this general criterion of importance are a few more specific criteria:

- If two appellate courts in the federal system are in conflict on a legal principle—that is, the two courts have reached different conclusions as to what the law requires in a particular situation—the Supreme Court is likely to grant certiorari to resolve the conflict.

- If a lower court has declared that a federal or state statute violates the U.S. Constitution and accordingly cannot be enforced, the justices are also likely to grant certiorari, unless the lower court has followed clear Supreme Court precedent in reaching its conclusion.

- In criminal cases (which constitute a large percentage of the Supreme Court's docket), the justices will take a hard look at any decision that might lead to a convicted criminal's going free because of a lower court's perception of what the law requires.

- If the federal government asks the Supreme Court for review, the request will carry more weight than if an ordinary citizen is seeking review.

- If the case deals with large issues of concern to us all (such as school prayer), review is more likely than when the Court's decision would affect only the litigants in the case.

- When the Supreme Court is struggling to establish useful guidelines in particularly controversial areas, such as abortion or libel, review is more likely than when the case is in

ference.'' No other persons—secretaries, law clerks, or assistants—are with them as they discuss not only the decisions in the cases that they have accepted for review, but also which of the thousands of cases they should agree to hear. Any justice who thinks that a particular case might be worth reviewing may put it on the list for the conference; and in the conference, an informal "rule of four" is followed.

This rule, which is not written anywhere, means that a case is reviewed on its merits—

an area in which the body of law has been relatively stable for a long period.

One frequent question is whether a rich person's chances of being heard in the Supreme Court are better than a poor person's. At first glance, the statistics would seem to indicate that this is the case. In 1984–85, the Supreme Court granted review in just 1 percent of the cases filed "in forma pauperis"—cases for which the Supreme Court waived the normal filing fee. By contrast, review was granted in 11 percent of the paid cases.

However, these statistics are misleading. A large proportion of the in forma pauperis cases are filed by prisoners seeking relief from the Supreme Court after they have exhausted all other avenues of appeal, sometimes in both the state and federal judicial systems. These prisoners are understandably desperate for relief, but their desperation does not necessarily mean that they have a case worthy of Supreme Court review.

Moreover, many in forma pauperis cases are filed directly by litigants without the assistance of lawyers. While this fact does not mean that their petitions are treated more lightly by the Supreme Court, it does mean that no lawyer has

given the petitioner a realistic assessment of his or her Supreme Court chances. Because a lawyer has a professional responsibility to advise a client that the Supreme Court is not likely to hear the case—and because a lawyer will expect to be paid for filing a certiorari petition—the cases that are filed after a lawyer's screening are more likely to be worthy of review and thus more likely (about ten times more likely, according to the 1984–85 statistics) to be heard by the Supreme Court.

From my own experience, I believe that those filing in forma pauperis, including those without lawyers, are given a fair shake, and that the justices and their clerks may even bend over backwards to make sure that they understand a particular poor person's claim. If that claim has any merit in terms of the Supreme Court's criteria for hearing cases—i.e., if the case is important enough or if there appears to have been a serious miscarriage of justice—counsel will be appointed for a poor person, and the case will be heard.

In fact, the Supreme Court's history over the past fifty years has been one of protecting the weak and defenseless, the minority citizens and the accused criminals, and the unpopular causes. The popular causes and the rights of the majority have always been protected by the legislative and

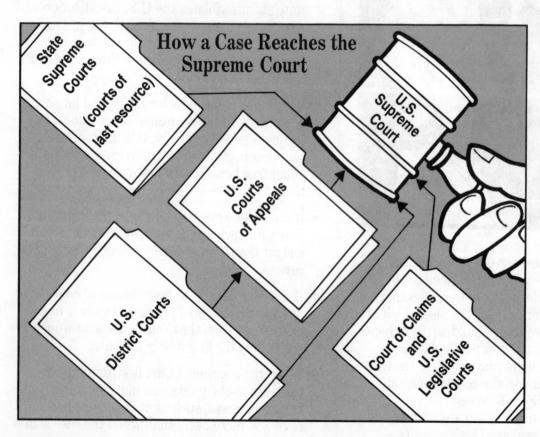

How a Case Reaches the Supreme Court

State Supreme Courts (courts of last resource)

U.S. Courts of Appeals

U.S. District Courts

U.S. Supreme Court

Court of Claims and U.S. Legislative Courts

The Supreme Court hears cases that involve basic constitutional principles, important questions of federal law, or conflicts between state and federal laws. Petitions and appeals reach the Supreme Court from the highest courts in each state or from a lower federal court. The Supreme Court considers only a small percentage of the cases brought before it. During its 1985-86 term, the Court received petitions and appeals for 4,287 cases, but agreed to hear only 186.

executive branches of the government, whose officials are elected by virtue of their popularity with the majority. Because the Supreme Court does not have to face election, it has played a key institutional role as the defender of the Bill of Rights.

The Supreme Court's ability to decide what it will decide has had a strong impact on its history and institutional role. By concentrating its attention on those cases where major issues need to be resolved, the Supreme Court has gained a certain legitimacy that it could not have had if it were required to decide every case that came before it. Moreover, nine justices, no matter how intelligent or hardworking, could not possibly reach individualized determinations on the merits in more than 4,000 cases per year. Just attempting to write full opinions in 150 or so cases per year, while reading and denying thousands of certiorari petitions, taxes the resources of the justices and their staffs. For these reasons, the Supreme Court's discretion to review only the most significant cases is absolutely essential to its continued effectiveness and to the respect accorded the Supreme Court by the American people.

Questions to Consider

1. How does the Supreme Court decide which cases it will hear each year?

2. Do you think the Supreme Court should hear *every* case that is brought before it? Why or why not?

3. What does the author mean by the following statement: "Because the Supreme Court does not have to face election, it has played a key institutional role as the defender of the Bill of Rights."

Two Systems of Justice?

Mary Broderick

Mary Broderick is the director of the defender division of the National Legal Aid and Defender Association, which represents more than 2,000 public defender offices throughout the country. She also spent eight years as a trial and appellate attorney with the Defender Association of Philadelphia. In this article, Ms. Broderick examines the public defense system in the United States.

As visitors to the Supreme Court mount the steps in front of that impressive building, they can see the words "Equal Justice Under Law" emblazoned across the top of the entrance. That ideal is one of the corner-stones of our Constitution. But all too often in America, the kind of justice you get depends on how much money you have.

Our Constitution is 200 years old, but up until a little more than twenty years ago, many people charged with felonies—and most people charged with misdemeanors—did not have a lawyer to defend them unless they could afford to hire one. And defendants without lawyers were no match for the prosecuting attorneys who had gone to law school and were used to arguing cases in court. As a result, many innocent people wound up in jail, all because they were too poor to hire a lawyer.

Then in 1963, the Supreme Court changed everything with its decision in *Gideon* v. *Wainwright*, reversing the conviction of a man who was convicted and sent to jail after the court refused to appoint a lawyer in his trial on the charge of breaking into a poolroom. The Supreme Court said that the states must appoint a free lawyer for felony defendants who could not afford to hire their own. That decision was extended to misdemeanor and juvenile cases a few years later. However, it was left up to the states to decide how they would fulfill this obligation, and the different systems now in place across the country mean that defendants get widely different kinds and quality of representation.

In many states and counties, there is a public defender office, usually staffed by a combination of young lawyers a few years out of law school and more experienced lawyers with many trials behind them. Many people believe that this system works best for the client, because the defense lawyer is part of a law firm that does nothing but represent poor defendants. These people believe that public defenders are dedicated to the concept of equal justice for their clients, have the benefit of working in an office that does nothing but criminal defense work, and have the benefit of the support and training provided by other lawyers in the office.

So while clients are frequently heard to complain, "I don't want a public defender, I want a real lawyer," in most cases they are not only getting a real lawyer, but a good one as well.

In other jurisdictions, private lawyers are appointed by the court to represent poor defendants and are paid a fee, either by the hour, the day, or the case. And in some counties, the county government contracts with private law firms to handle blocks of cases, either for a lump sum or for a set fee per case.

These systems can work well if they are properly administered and if the lawyers who participate in them are monitored to make sure they are providing clients with high-quality representation.

The biggest problem facing all these systems is lack of funding. Most Americans agree with the Constitution that a person accused of a crime is innocent until his guilt has been proved. But the fact is that state and local governments spend almost four times as much money to prosecute people as they do to provide defense services, despite the fact that most of the people accused of crimes are too poor to hire their own lawyers.

There are many dedicated public defenders and assigned counsel who do a conscientious job, often at great personal sacrifice. However, the imbalance in funding between the prosecution and the defense means all too often that poor defendants are shortchanged:

■ In Massachusetts, 36 percent of the court-appointed lawyers who responded to a recent survey admitted that they did not perform some essential defense duty because they were being paid such a low fee.

■ In San Diego, the county gave contracts for indigent defense services to low bidders in a money-saving attempt, but eventually had to drop two contractors after repeated complaints from judges and other lawyers about the contract lawyers' negligence and incompetence.

■ In Georgia, defendants can spend months in jail without ever talking to a lawyer and or having any kind of hearing—much less a trial——to determine whether they are guilty as charged.

In addition, I could name dozens of other jurisdictions across the country where court-appointed lawyers are not screened before they take appointments to see if they know anything about criminal law and where they are not disciplined if they mishandle a case.

Perhaps the most critical area is in death penalty defense. The death penalty is a highly emotional issue, with strong feelings on both sides. But there should be no disagreement about the fact that someone charged with a crime that could result in a death sentence is entitled to the best possible representation before, during, and after his trial. Unfortunately, in many jurisdictions that representation is severely hampered by lack of funding. For example, in some jurisdictions, there is a cap on the amount of money attorneys can recover for their work in death penalty cases, despite the fact that these cases can take months or even years to litigate. Consequently, the defense attorney is forced to make a choice between continuing to represent the client without fee or withdrawing from the case. Yet the judge and the prosecutor get paid no matter how long the case takes.

In the final analysis, these issues all relate back to the second-class status that state and local governments impose on defense services for the poor.

What is the solution?

State and local governments must first be willing to acknowledge that the provision of high-quality representation to poor people in criminal cases is an important function of the government, equal in importance to the provision of a court system and a prosecutor.

State and local governments must also be willing to fund the defense system adequately, so public defender offices can be properly staffed

111

and appointed defense lawyers will be paid a fair amount for their services. In addition, support services, such as investigators and expert witnesses, should be provided without the lawyer having to foot the bill.

Finally, state and local governments must make a commitment to screening lawyers who want to be appointed in criminal cases to make sure those lawyers have the training and skill to give their clients the best possible representation. Governments should also monitor the lawyers' performance to make sure they do a competent job for their clients and remove those lawyers who don't measure up.

When state and local governments begin to live up to these obligations, poor people who are accused of crimes will begin to get the same quality of justice as those who can afford to hire their own lawyers.

Questions to Consider

1. Why do you think there was no public defender system in the United States until the 1960s?

2. Do you think there are two systems of justice in the United States—one for those who can afford to hire private lawyers and one for those who must rely on public defenders?

3. Do you think our judicial system lives up to the creed of "equal justice under the law"? Why or why not?

Judicial Activism and Busing in Boston

On the first day of school in September 1974, Boston's public schools were integrated—most without incident—in response to an order for prompt desegregation by U.S. District Court Judge W. Arthur Garrity. At South Boston High School, however, buses bringing black students from Roxbury were stoned. In the days that followed, white students boycotted classes, and incidents of racial violence—including arson, vandalism, and rock throwing—increased.

Most people thought that Boston, with its small black population, would be able to integrate its schools without problems. Yet in some areas—like South Boston—the sentiment against integration was strong. Many of the reasons are historical. Starting in the mid-1800s, many immigrants came to Boston to seek a new life, to work in the city's expanding economy. They settled in ethnic neighborhoods, some of which remain: South Boston and Charlestown residents are predominantly Irish, and East Boston is populated by Italians. Those who prospered moved out to the suburbs; those who stayed in the city cherished their sense of community. This "pride of neighborhood" was especially prevalent in South Boston, where the worst racial violence occurred.

South Boston High School sits on a hill overlooking the entire South Boston community. The high school was a symbol of neighborhood pride, a place that reinforced what the community valued: home and family, neighborhood and church. The old building that housed the school was a link to the past—and the beginning of the future for most of its graduates.

But South Boston was also a neighborhood that felt threatened by the expansion of the Roxbury ghetto. Many of the black people who came to Boston after World War II settled in Roxbury, seeking the same "good life" that the Italians and the Irish searched for in the 1800s. As the Roxbury community grew, tension and resentment between the two neighborhoods increased. Nearly thirty years of fear and hatred was brought to the surface by Judge Garrity's ruling in a case brought before him in 1974.

Garrity's decision in *Morgan* v. *Hennigan* was based on evidence that Boston city schools had been deliberately segregated for years by school officials. Garrity did not expect his ruling to arouse the resentment and violence that occurred at South Boston High School. He believed firmly in the rule of law. Garrity knew that his decision was constitutional and that desegregation was as important for white students as it was for black students. His order and the plans he put in place to implement desegregation are a clear example of *judicial activism*, that is, when a judge establishes or changes public policy through his or her judicial decisions.

Where Does the Power for Judicial Activism Come From?

The U.S. Constitution set up three branches of government—executive, legislative, and judicial. In order to make sure no one branch got too much power, the Constitution also established a system of checks and balances. One of the powers of the judicial branch is called *judicial review*—the power of a court to rule on the constitutionality of the laws passed by a government or on acts of a government official. Judicial review is a power not written into the Constitution. Rather, it was first expressed by Chief Justice John Marshall in the 1803 case of *Marbury* v. *Madison*. Marshall's decision in this case held that the Constitution was the paramount law of the land, and that, based on this paramount law, the Supreme Court could declare a law of Congress unconstitutional and therefore void. Marshall also extended the practice of judicial review to state statutes, thus giving federal courts the authority to ensure the rights of all citizens and the federal government.

Judicial review has two aspects: *judicial restraint* and *judicial activism*. Judicial restraint generally refers to decisions that only apply to the case at hand and that do not initiate broad changes in public policy. Judicial activism refers to court decisions that cause significant change in public policy. For the most part, the courts defer to the elected branches of government to decide and legislate policy. However, there are some cases in which a judge feels that circumstances do not allow any other course but for the court to order changes in policy. The desegregation decisions of the early 1950s was one such time.

Although segregation in the public schools had been declared unconstitutional by the Supreme Court in the 1954 case of *Brown* v. *Board of Education*, Boston school officials continued segregation policies. Garrity handed down a decision in which he changed the segregation policy of Boston's public schools to one of desegregation. When judges find they cannot rely on administrative officials to enforce laws to cure social ills, they—like Garrity—often become judicial activists.

Judicial review, by which the judiciary can invalidate laws or

In 1974, Judge W. Arthur Garrity ruled that the Boston Public School system was racially segregated. He then ordered the schools to be desegregated. His ruling is an example of judicial activism.

actions judged contrary to the Constitution, has become an important part of our policymaking process. While it may be controversial at times, it remains the most effective process in the U.S. court system to effect change. It is also a process in which the Supreme Court has the last word.

Desegregation Efforts Before Judge Garrity's Decision

Efforts to end school segregation in Massachusetts began in earnest in the 1960s during the height of the civil rights movement. As a result·of a boycott of schools by black parents to protest the inferior education they believed their children were receiving in rundown, segregated schools, a commission was established to study the situation. The commission— made up of educators, clergy, and community leaders— found that segregated schools seriously damaged the confidence, self-esteem, and motivation of black children. The commission called for speedy integration.

In response, black and white leaders joined together to force the issue and secure passage by the Massachusetts state legislature of the Racial Imbalance Act in August

1965. Considered a model for integrating northern schools, the act prohibited minority student enrollments of more than 50 percent in any Massachusetts school. It also required school boards to conduct a yearly census of students to determine the racial composition in their schools and to take prompt action to correct any racial imbalance uncovered. The act also provided funds to state authorities to ensure enforcement.

The Boston School Committee (Boston's school board) had evaded all efforts by state authorities to enforce the Racial Imbalance Act. As a result, schools in Boston became more and more segregated. In 1967, 56 percent of Boston's black students attended predominantly black schools; by 1971, the number had risen to 68 percent.

When members of Congress— especially from those states with schools that were ordered to follow federally mandated desegregation plans—heard these figures, they demanded an immediate investigation of this "monstrous hypocrisy." They claimed that if segregation was unconstitutional, it was illegal in *all* areas of the country—not just the South. The U.S. Department of

Health, Education, and Welfare (HEW) responded, and in December 1971 reported that Boston's schools were not only segregated, but also violated the 1964 Civil Rights Act, which prohibited segregation in federally funded programs. Boston became the first major northern city to be accused of operating a segregated school system by the deliberate action of school officials.

One of HEW's findings was that the Boston School Committee was operating two sets of schools at the intermediate level. One set was made of middle schools (grades 6 through 8) that fed into 4-year high schools. Students in the middle schools were predominantly black. The other set was made up of junior high schools (grades 7 through 9) that fed into 3-year high schools. Students in the junior high schools were predominantly white. The Boston School Committee explained that the original plan had been to use middle schools throughout the school system, but that only four schools were changed and these just happened to be predominantly black. However, the committee could not explain, at least to HEW's satisfaction, why the original plan had not been continued beyond these four schools in the system.

Other findings included in the HEW report were that 1,100 school-age children in Boston with Spanish last names were not on school enrollment lists, that in some cases predominantly white schools were located in black neighborhoods, and that in other cases black students were bused past underutilized but predominantly white schools to more distant, predominantly black schools.

HEW did not press the school committee on separate items, but instead insisted that, unless a satisfactory desegregation plan was forthcoming, the Boston school system would lose its federal funding under the provisions of the 1964 Civil Rights Act. Boston school officials denied the HEW charges, although they agreed to work on a plan that would ensure keeping federal funds and that would correct the problems HEW listed. However, Boston school officials maintained that the problems were caused by *de facto* (in fact) segregation; that is, by changes in neighborhoods (white families moving out, black families moving in) that have nothing to do with the law but that might change school enrollments.

In March 1972, believing that the state would not enforce the Racial Imbalance Act in Boston, a group of black parents and the National Association for the Advancement of Colored People (NAACP) filed suit in U.S. District Court for the District of Massachusetts, charging Boston school officials with segregation and discrimination in the city's school system. Defendants included the chairperson of the Boston School Committee, the Boston superintendent of schools, and the state education commissioner.

The suit called for equalized spending (the same expenditure per pupil in every school). It challenged the traditional autonomy of local school boards by urging that city and suburban schools be linked through educational methods, transportation, and rezoning in order to achieve the greatest degree of integration.

Judge Garrity's Decision

In June 1974, after nearly two years of testimony and deliberation, Judge Garrity handed down 148 pages of legal and factual analysis of the *de jure* (in law—or by official action—as opposed to de facto—in fact) nature of Boston's segregation. Among Garrity's findings of unconstitutional and illegal actions were that: (1) the Boston schools had been segregated deliberately and systematically for years; (2) the Boston School Committee had built facilities, drawn attendance zone lines, and channeled students through middle schools and junior high schools to promote segregation; (3) new teachers and black teachers were assigned to black schools, while experienced teachers and white teachers went to white schools; and (4) white students were allowed to transfer out of predominantly black schools on a hardship basis, thus dissipating any natural integration that grew out of residential desegregation. Garrity also suggested that the school committee was guilty of evading and procrastinating on agreed-to compliance with desegregation requirements.

Based on these findings, Garrity ordered prompt desegregation—to "secure the rights of the plaintiffs"—to start in September 1974. He ordered the Boston School Committee to develop and implement a plan to reduce racial imbalance through busing and redistricting so that desegregation could be achieved within city limits. (The order to use busing and redistricting within city limits was based on the fact that the Supreme Court had not yet ruled on the constitutionality of busing over city lines—although the NAACP as well as many officials, including Boston's mayor, argued that desegregation in Boston could not be accomplished unless the suburbs were tied into an area-wide busing plan.) Garrity's decision superseded the Massachusetts Racial Imbalance Act and put the Boston school system under federal control, with the judge himself in charge.

The chairperson of the Boston School Committee called Garrity's decision "ludicrous" and announced that the committee would not

More than 17,000 students were bused as part of Phase One of the plan to desegregate Boston's public schools. As a result, the city of Boston was struck by a wave of violence.

In Boston, protesters sometimes used violence to disrupt court-ordered busing. As a result, police were assigned to protect students on their way to and from school.

develop a desegregation plan for Boston's schools. Instead, the committee planned to appeal the judge's decision in the courts.

However, Garrity's decision was in line with a series of Supreme Court decisions that changed public school policy. These cases include:

- *Brown* v. *Board of Education* (1954): In this unanimous, landmark decision, the Supreme Court found that schools segregated by state law are "inherently unequal" and violate the Fourteenth Amendment's guarantee of equal protection under the law.

- *Brown* v. *Board of Education* (1955): This second *Brown* decision stated that desegregation should take place "with all deliberate speed."

- *Swann* v. *Charlotte-Mecklenburg Board of Education* (1971): The Court's decision in this case stated that all feasible means, including extensive busing if necessary, must be used to create a nonracial school system, no matter how much inconvenience was caused.

- *Keyes* v. *School District No. 1, Denver, Colorado* (1973): The

Court found that the board of education had located schools and drawn attendance zones so as to encourage segregation, that this was de jure (by law) segregation, and that by presumption the entire school system was segregated.

Between 1974 and 1976, the Boston School Committee appealed Judge Garrity's decision three times—once to the U.S. Court of Appeals and twice to the U.S. Supreme Court. In all three cases, Garrity's decision to desegregate Boston's public schools was upheld.

Integrating Boston's Schools: Phase One

When the Boston School Committee refused to develop a desegregation plan to implement the court's integration order, Garrity turned to the state department of education. There, staff members designed a plan (called phase one) that tried to apply the Racial Imbalance Act by bringing together black and white children living near each other and integrating as few white schools as possible. The phase one plan affected only 40 percent of Boston's

schools (most white schools remained unaffected). There were sixty-eight predominantly black schools: the phase one plan reduced that number to forty-four by reassigning 45,000 students to different schools and by busing 17,000 students. The shortest bus routes were between South Boston and Roxbury, so the plan called for large numbers of black students from Roxbury to be bused into predominantly white South Boston. The plan worked for the elementary schools, despite the tension and resentment that had long existed between the two neighborhoods, but not for South Boston High School. In essence, the state created a crisis for the entire city by establishing a desegregation plan based solely on geography, not community.

A month after school opened, after four weeks of court-ordered busing, school attendance was down. Incidents of violence and arrests were up—although principally limited to only four of the eighty schools affected by phase one. State police were brought in to aid the metropolitan police in maintaining order. In South Boston, the watchword was "resist." In Roxbury, parents were fearful and students were angry. City officials were exhausted from trying to cope.

As the school year progressed, the resistance to busing increased. The city of Boston, and its problems with school desegregation, attracted national attention. News stories depicted Boston as a city torn apart by racial hatred:

- Massachusetts Senator Edward Kennedy was spattered with garbage and driven off the stage by shouting members of ROAR (Restore Our Alienated Rights), a militant antibusing group, when he spoke in favor of complying with Judge Garrity's decision.

- Five thousand people expressed their anger at the court that had forced integration on them at a rally held in South Boston during the third week of school. The crowd recited a parody of the pledge of allegiance: "I will not pledge allegiance to the court order of the United States District Court or to the dictatorship for which it stands, one law, incontestable, with liberty and justice for none."

- The national director of the Ku Klux Klan came to Boston and addressed an enthusiastic group, arguing against the mixing of the races.

- The American Nazi Party came to march in Boston in full uniform. However, the police escorted their bus to the state line.

- Graffiti on a restaurant wall near South Boston High School reportedly proclaimed, "This is Klan country," amidst other racist slogans.

- Frankie Freeman, a member of the U.S. Commission on Civil Rights, said that the racism she saw at South Boston High School was worse than anything she had ever witnessed in the South.

But despite the turmoil in some areas of the city, integrated programs were successfully developed in most of the affected schools and learning was accomplished. Most school officials honored Judge Garrity's orders, illustrating their belief that the Constitution must be obeyed, and tolerated the need for police to protect the black students. The archbishop of Boston, Cardinal Humberto Medeiros, announced that the Catholic church would not allow students to transfer into parochial schools for the purpose of avoiding integration. And beginning in July 1974, the local news media made an enormous effort to promote the positive aspects of integration and to downplay the violence.

As it turned out, the money saved by shorter bus routes did not make up for the state aid lost because students withdrew from public schools or the costs to the city of providing extra police protection to prevent racial clashes. In the year before court-ordered busing (1973–74), enrollment had been 93,647 (53,593 white students; 31,963 black students); for 1974–75, when phase one was implemented, enrollment dropped by 8 percent to 85,826, with most of the decrease occurring in the number of white students (44,957 white students, 31,737 black students). Desegregation costs were estimated at $18 million.

Integrating Boston's Schools: Phase Two

In late October 1974, a little more than a month after the phase one desegregation plan had begun, Judge Garrity once again ordered

Busing in Boston polarized the city. Groups both for and against busing organized rallies to demonstrate their concern.

117

the Boston School Committee to develop a desegregation plan of its own to be implemented during the next school year (1975-76). This plan (called phase two) would provide the greatest amount of desegregation possible for all grades, for all schools, and for all parts of the city. Garrity hoped that the new plan—designed by local school officials who were more familiar with Boston's neighborhoods—would be based on educational goals and not simply geography. To help the committee begin its work, Garrity provided the following guidelines:

- The existence of schools that can be identified by race must be eliminated because racial or ethnic isolation can generate a feeling of inferiority that may never be undone, and because minority students, if cut off from the majority, may be deprived of the opportunity to learn the cultural standards of that majority society.

- Some schools can end up with one race predominant if the reason is nondiscriminatory (as in the case of East Boston, which is separated from the rest of the city by Boston Harbor).

- Practical matters essential to consider are minimizing forced busing, drawing districts to limit busing distances, and drawing districts to include proper school facilities.

- The possibility of "white flight" (the movement of families out of one school system into another to avoid racial turmoil or desegregation) cannot be a consideration in planning. The constitutional rights of children to receive a desegregated education cannot be traded to appease some parents.

- To provide equal educational opportunities, a responsible administration must be in place in each school. Further, the instruction given must be nondiscriminatory, must avoid racial stereotypes, and will be monitored by citizen groups.

- City-wide magnet schools, open to all students and with distinctive educational programs, must be developed, using the assistance of Boston's colleges, universities, businesses, and the cultural community.

- Each school must have a racial distribution that is the same as every other district so that families will not move to resegregate any district.

In late January 1975, the school committee submitted a plan for desegregating all of Boston's schools. Unlike phase one's court-ordered busing, the committee plan provided for voluntary student enrollment in biracial classes. The committee plan relied heavily on *magnet schools*—schools with special programs that would attract students city-wide—to be located in the different zones throughout the city. Children already attending integrated schools would be given first chance to enroll in these varied learning programs.

Judge Garrity appointed a biracial panel of experts to study the committee's plan and to determine if it was suited to local conditions and met his guidelines. The four members of the review panel were: Francis Keppel, a former commissioner of education and dean of the Harvard Graduate School of Education; Charles V. Willie, a professor of education at the Harvard Graduate School of Education; Edward McCormack, Jr., a former Massachusetts attorney general who had been born in South Boston; and Jacob Spiegel, a retired justice of the Massachusetts State Supreme Court. On their recommendation, two Boston University education experts—Robert Dentler and Marvin Scott—amended the committee plan, emphasizing districts in which schools would reflect the ethnic composition of the district rather than the city. Students were to be assigned to schools within their districts on a nearest available seat basis (as long as the assignment contributed to racial balance) and Boston's

seventeen colleges and universities would be paired with magnet schools for consultation on programs and for instructional support, assistance, and development.

After reviewing the panel's report, Judge Garrity issued his final desegregation order on May 10, 1975. In it he adopted most of the review panel's recommendations. The city was divided into eight districts. Nearly 21,000 students in the Boston school system were to be bused, with a maximum travel time of twenty-five minutes and an average commute of ten to fifteen minutes. Garrity could not order the colleges to cooperate. Instead, he made them an offer they could not refuse—the opportunity to be involved in the most extensive collaboration of colleges and public schools in the country.

To finance the new desegregation plan, the state provided $900,000 to help with formulating and implementing the distinctive educational programs for the city-wide magnet schools. More state and federal money was to be available later to facilitate the extensive collaboration of public schools, universities, colleges, and businesses working to reshape curricula, improve teaching practices, and motivate students to realize their college or vocational ambitions.

However, the problems in the Boston school system did not change overnight. Reaction to the phase two plan included a comment by Boston's mayor Kevin White that the plan has "virtually guaranteed a continuation of the present tension and hostility throughout the city." Antibusing leader Louise Day Hicks called the order "outrageous" and the "death knell of the city."

In September 1975, as phase two implementation began, enrollment in Boston's city schools dropped to 76,461 (from 85,826), almost 11 percent from the phase one year and nearly 19 percent from the year before Garrity's court-ordered busing began. Again, most of the decrease was in white enrollment:

Boston Public School Enrollment

Year	Black Students	White Students
1972	31,634	56,893
1974	31,737	44,957
1976	31,631	34,561
1978	31,789	28,716
1980	31,080	24,060
1982	29,039	18,592
1984	28,477	16,946
1986	28,551	15,842

Source: Boston School Committee

While Boston's public schools have experienced a decline in enrollment generally since 1972, the number of white students decreased much more rapidly than the number of black students. Some experts attribute declining white enrollment to parents enrolling their children in private schools or moving from the city altogether.

the number of white students dropped to 36,243 from 44,957 the year before; the number of black students increased slightly from 31,092 to 31,737. Where did these students go? Some dropped out of school entirely, others moved out of the city with their parents, and still others transferred to parochial schools (despite the cardinal's order) or to private, unaccredited academies.

At South Boston High School, black students complained that they were being harassed and beaten by white students, ignored by teachers and administrators, and discouraged from playing football. Judge Garrity conducted an investigation and as a result put South Boston High School into federal receivership. That is, he transferred the headmaster, his staff, and the football coach to another school and put a federal officer in charge. Trouble followed the judge's action, but the situation was soon controlled by placing police officers in the school's halls.

After this incident, the crisis at South Boston High School eased. Although violence and hostility continued to flare occasionally, the phase two plan, based on educa-

tional concepts and offering some attractive programs at the end of bus rides, provided benefits to students and helped reduce the tension. By 1977, Boston's voters elected their first black member in seventy-six years to the school committee.

The Boston School System Today: The Results of Judicial Activism

The Boston School Committee has expanded from five to thirteen members, all of whom are now elected by district rather than at large. As a result, there are now four minority members.

The percentage of black teachers and administrators employed by the system is roughly equal to the percentage of black citizens in Boston.

On tests administered in August 1985, most Boston students scored at or above the fiftieth percentile in grades 1 through 8, but below the fiftieth percentile in grades 9 through 11—yet most grade levels showed improvement over the preceding tests in 1983.

Enrollment in the Boston school system in 1985–86 was approximately 56,000 (down from the 93,647 students in 1973–74). Of

these 56,000 students, 48 percent were black (approximately 26,900—down from 31,963 in 1973–74). The remaining 24 percent—almost 13,500 students—were Hispanic, Asian, and native American. The city continues to be predominantly white.

In the fall of 1985, after eleven years of court supervision, Boston public schools were returned to the control of the Boston School Committee, and Dr. Laval Wilson took over as the new superintendent of schools. Wilson, a black man, faced a school system with an illiteracy rate of 20 percent and a dropout rate of 48 percent, but one in which Scholastic Aptitude Test (SAT) scores had gone up, violence had subsided, and attendance had improved overall. He also faced the city's parents, who challenged him to continue to improve scores (particularly for black and Hispanic students), to reduce racial tension, and to restore confidence in their schools.

Judge Garrity retired in the summer of 1985. He was characterized by today's headmaster of the completely integrated South Boston High School as "the bravest guy in Boston in the past fifteen years."

Activities

1. Reading Between the Lines

The Supreme Court is considered by most people to be the most invisible of the three branches of government. In order to break down some of the mystery that surrounds the Court, examine the backgrounds of the nine men and women who make up the current Court. Find out their age, religion, educational and career experience, and their opinions on key decisions. Do you think a justice's background plays an important role in deciding how he or she will vote in the Court's decisions? See if you can determine how each justice will vote on some of the key cases that the court will be facing this year. Compare your guess with the actual voting when the Supreme Court's decision is made public.

2. Developing Your Own Perspective

In 1803, Chief Justice John Marshall, in his decision in the case of *Marbury* v. *Madison*, established *judicial review* as one of the basic functions of the Supreme Court. To understand this important decision better, study the facts in *Marbury* v. *Madison* and Marshall's decision. Do you think the chief justice was correct in ruling that the Supreme Court has the right to review and determine the constitutionality of laws? What has been the impact of Marshall's ruling in the case?

3. Becoming an Active Citizen

You may think that the only time you will ever have any contact with the American judicial system is when you have broken a law or are accused of a crime. However, the courts—and especially the Supreme Court—have a tremendous impact on all of us, even if we never enter a courtroom.

To become aware of the impact of the Supreme Court on our daily lives, talk to some local officials about how particular Court decisions have affected their jobs. You might want to talk to a police officer, your mayor, your principal, and your teacher. Have certain Court rulings made their jobs easier or more difficult? Why do they think the Supreme Court decided the case the way it did? How would things be different if the Court had not made this ruling?

★ ★ ★ ★ ★ ★ ★ ★ ★ ★

THE BUREAUCRACY

5. The Bureaucracy

In This Chapter

he growth of our national government over the past fifty years and the variety of tasks it has confronted have produced a large and complex administrative system. Today, more than 2.5 million people work as *bureaucrats*, or ad-ministrators, in the government, carrying out the policies of our elected officials. Most of the bureaucracy is part of the executive branch and includes thirteen Cabinet-level departments and more than fifty regulatory commissions with some 2,000 bureaus, divisions, and local offices.

The Cabinet

The Cabinet departments are the major admin-istrative organizations of the federal government. Originally, there were only three Cabinet departments—State, War, and Treasury. Today there are thirteen. The expansion of the Cabinet is due largely to the fact that people wanted the government to deal with more and more problems. For example, the creation of the Department of Energy in 1977 reflects the concern of government officials and citizens over the energy crisis of the 1970s and the demand that government do something about it.

Cabinet members are appointed by the presi-dent and serve a variety of functions. As secretaries of a department, they ensure that their departments run smoothly and that the policies of the administration are carried out. As members of the Cabinet, they advise the presi-dent on matters of public policy. They also repre-sent the president before Congress where they testify on behalf of administration positions.

Although Cabinet secretaries report to the president, they must also respond to political demands outside the White House. For example, farmers may ask the secretary of agriculture to support higher farm prices, which the president

As the role of government has grown over the years, the job of the bureaucracy has grown increasingly complex. The bureaucracy is now the largest component of the federal government and employs almost three million people.

may oppose. Car manufacturers may try to pressure the secretary of transportation to relax automobile fuel consumption standards even though the president may be against such action. While Cabinet secretaries are generally in agreement with the president's policy agenda, no president can completely control the Cabinet.

Regulatory Commissions

Another large group of federal agencies, the independent regulatory commissions, are responsible for regulating industry. Regulatory commissions work to ensure that private industry acts in the public interest. These commissions establish standards for industry in areas such as product safety, pollution control, and health risks to consumers. All industries must conform to government-issued standards or face fines and possible criminal indictment. Examples of regulatory commissions include the Interstate Commerce Commission, which regulates the railroad, bus, and trucking industries; and the Federal Communications Commission, which oversees telephone, radio, and television transmissions. In addition, various bureaus within Cabinet departments, such as the Food and Drug Administration (which is part of the Department of Health and Human Services), play prominent regulatory roles.

The independence of regulatory commissions from the rest of the government has raised the question of whether the public has too little control over their activities. Critics charge that the commissions are often pressured by the groups they are supposed to be regulating and end up giving in to industry demands. Industries, on the other hand, often argue that government regulations are an unnecessary and costly burden.

The Bureaucrats

Someone has to perform the jobs that the federal bureaucracy creates. In the past, politicians who won an election usually gave their friends and supporters a job in the government as a reward for helping in the campaign. But in 1881, President James Garfield was assassinated by a man who had failed to get a government job. Public outrage over Garfield's assassination forced Congress to pass the Pendelton Act, which established the civil service system. Under this system, government employees are hired after passing an examination and promoted only on the basis of job performance. Today, the civil service system covers practically the entire bureaucracy and ensures that government hiring practices are fair.

For many people, the word "bureaucracy" means incompetence and red tape. A bureaucrat is seen as a faceless, nameless person who unthinkingly follows rules despite their impact on people's lives. The size and complexity of a large bureaucracy make it hard to tell who is responsible for a particular action, and the bureaucracy is largely outside public scrutiny and control. However, most bureaucrats see themselves as dedicated public servants working for the public good. They work as scientists, inspectors, social workers, budget analysts, and clerical workers. Many are aware of the negative image of the bureaucracy and work to improve the efficiency of their departments.

Congressional Oversight

Although housed in the executive branch, nearly all bureaucratic agencies have been established by Congress to implement legislation. Therefore, Congress sees itself as ultimately responsible for supervising the bureaucracy. In the past, the bureaucracy was small, and keeping an eye on the administrative agencies was fairly easy. As the government grew, however, congressional oversight of the bureaucracy became more difficult. In the 1970s, some members of Congress accused several agencies, including the Central Intelligence Agency (CIA) and the Federal Bureau of Investigation (FBI), of acting outside of the law.

Recently, Congress placed more emphasis on its oversight responsibilities to ensure that the bureaucracy carries out the intent of its laws. The number of committees and subcommittees charged with oversight has increased. In addition, Congress now requires bureaucratic agencies to report their activities to appropriate committees. For example, all covert action by the CIA and the FBI now must be reported to the House and Senate committees on intelligence.

Today, the government is involved in a wide range of activities. Some agencies set safety standards for new baby toys, others determine the amount of lead permitted in gasoline, while still others establish guidelines for the construction of nuclear power plants. These and other responsibilities make oversight of the federal bureaucracy vital to the health of our political system.

The Role of the Federal Government in Education

William Bennett

William Bennett is secretary of the Department of Education. Prior to his appointment, Mr. Bennett chaired the National Endowment for the Humanities. He holds a Ph.D. in philosophy from the University of Texas and a law degree from Harvard Law School. In his article, Mr. Bennett describes the importance of education to a democracy and his role as a Cabinet secretary.

Some 2,000 years ago, Plato observed that the education of children is the most important issue with which a republic must concern itself. So it is not surprising that education is one of the foremost topics of debate in our democracy today.

A central characteristic of education in America has always been that it is a local enterprise. Before the Civil War, our nation's educators directed their energies toward gaining support for the very idea of a public school system. Obviously, much has changed since then. The public schools not only have become accepted, but are now a basic assumption in our idea of American society. We now take for granted the right of every American to a free education.

But the existence of a public school system should not be equated with the centralization of local schools. Early public schools were still very much creatures of their locality. They were usually built, furnished, financed, and run by people within walking distance of the schoolhouse.

Today, of course, schools must serve larger areas and more diverse groups of students. But the fact remains that schools work best when under local control. America is a large and diverse nation, and no single curriculum—no single method of instruction—would be proper for all students.

But this does not mean that we expect American children to end up educated differently from one another—that children will be learning one thing in Portland, Maine, and another in Portland, Oregon. In fact, people with a common cultural and intellectual heritage can usually agree on what the basics in education are. They do not need the federal government to tell them that their children need a firm knowledge of English, math, history, and science. State governments should make sure that the basics are being taught. Whether a local school district stresses short stories over poetry or solid geometry over trigonometry will, of course, vary. But this variety is not to be condemned. Americans have always prided themselves on their diversity. As long as the basics are being taught, localities ought to be left to determine for themselves how their children will be educated.

An example of the how the federal government can become too restrictive toward local education initiatives can be found, I think, in the area of bilingual education. As it stands now, only 4 per-

Structure of the Executive Branch

Executive Office of the President

President
Vice-President
White House Staff
Central Intelligence Agency
Council of Economic Advisors
Council of Environmental Quality

Domestic Policy Staff
National Security Council
Office of Management and Budget
Office of Science and Technology Policy
Office of Special Representative for
  Trade Negotiations

Cabinet Departments

Agriculture | Commerce | Defense | Education | Energy | Health and Human Services | Housing and Urban Development | Interior | Justice | Labor | State | Transportation | Treasury

Components of the Bureaucracy
Independent Agencies, Regulatory Commissions, and Other Offices (partial listing)

ACTION
Administrative Conference of the United
  States
Advisory Commission on
  Intergovernmental Relations
American Battle Monuments Commission
Appalachian Regional Commission
Commission on Civil Rights
Commission of Fine Arts
Commodity Futures Trading Commission
Consumer Product Safety Commission
Environmental Protection Agency
Equal Employment Opportunity
  Commission
Export-Import Bank of the United States
Farm Credit Administration
Federal Communications Commission
Federal Deposit Insurance Corporation
Federal Election Commission
Federal Home Loan Bank Board
Federal Maritime Commission
Federal Mediation and Conciliation
  Service

Federal Reserve System
Federal Trade Commission
Foreign Claims Settlement Commission
General Services Administration
Inter-American Foundation
Interstate Commerce Commission
National Aeronautics and Space
  Administration
National Credit Union Administration
National Foundation on Arts and the
  Humanities
National Labor Relations Board
National Mediation Board
National Railroad Passenger Corporation
  (Amtrak)
National Science Foundation
National Transportation Safety Board
Nuclear Regulatory Commission
Occupational Safety and Health Review
  Commission
Office of Personnel Management
Overseas Private Investment Corporation

Pennsylvania Avenue Development
  Corporation
Pension Benefit Guaranty Corporation
Postal Rate Commission
Railroad Retirement Board
Securities and Exchange Commission
Selective Service System
Small Business Administration
Smithsonian Institution
Tennessee Valley Authority
U.S. Arms Control and Disarmament
  Agency
U.S. International Trade Commission
U.S. Postal Service
Veterans Administration

cent of federal funds going to bilingual education programs around the country can be used to teach bilingual education in a manner that local authorities deem best. All other funds must be employed in a method known as "transitional bilingual education," in which students are instructed in both English and their native language. This method may be fine in some districts and for some students, but other methods may work better in other places. We at the Department of Education believe that all American children should learn English, because it is the language of our society. As long as students learn the language, local school districts are in a much better position to determine what works best than is a federal bureaucracy or congressional committee in Washington, D.C.

Despite the traditional—and appropriate—limits to the federal government's role in education, there is certainly a place for federal involve-

Department of Education. For armed with the right information, the American people can fix their own schools.

The Department of Education can also serve as what Theodore Roosevelt called a "bully pulpit." As secretary of the department, I have the responsibility of making the best case I can for the best ideas we have about education and of doing so publicly. I have the job of stimulating the national discussion on education among the American people.

Education is the steward of democracy. And we—all of us—must be, in turn, the stewards of education. It is for this reason that we are doing all we can to help the educational pursuits of the American people.

Questions to Consider

1. In Mr. Bennett's view, what is the proper role of the federal government in the nation's public schools?

2. How does Mr. Bennett see his role as secretary of education?

3. Why is education the "most important issue with which a republic must concern itself"?

ment. For instance, the federal government must protect the civil rights of students. It should ensure that every child, regardless of religion, sex, race, or financial circumstances, is given the opportunity for a good education.

The federal government also has a special obligation to disadvantaged children—children from poor families and handicapped children. The largest program at the Department of Education is one that provides school districts with funds to offer remedial courses to poor children with low academic performance. These programs are the kind of undertaking that goes to the very heart of the American belief that everyone should have a fair shot at the American dream.

There are still other duties that are proper for the federal government to fulfill. The Department of Education acts as a clearinghouse for information on education in the various states, student performance, education expenditures, and analysis of recent research on what has been proven to work in the field of education. These activities supply the American people with accurate and reliable information about education. They are a crucial responsibility of the federal

Increasing the Responsiveness of the Federal Bureaucracy

John M. Palguta

John M. Palguta is director of external service and studies for the U.S. Merit Systems Protection Board (MSPB), a federal agency that protects the rights of government workers. In this article, he discusses the image of the federal bureaucracy and why individual bureaucrats try (or do not try) to increase its responsiveness by "blowing the whistle" on fraud, waste, or inefficiency.

A recent study conducted by the University of Michigan asked a cross-section of American citizens to rate government bureaucrats and the services they provide. Many of the people questioned said they had problems the government could or should be able to solve, but that they were never able to find the right agency—or had no idea an agency existed—which could help them. The study asked the same people what they thought of those bureaucrats they had personally met. In this case, the results were almost the exact opposite of what might have been expected. Individual government employees were generally seen as helpful and responsive. Having dealt with an individual bureaucrat, two-thirds of the people questioned said they were completely satisfied with the way their problems were handled. Why the difference?

The authors of the university study concluded that "Americans have tackled the great bureaucratic beast and found it not such a dragon after all. But stereotypes live long and die hard, and the image of the insolent bureaucrat and his inefficient organization survives in spite of people's experiences, not because of them."

The Image of the Federal Bureaucrat

For the most part, the general public does not have a positive image of federal bureaucrats or the federal bureaucracy. Some critics maintain that the bureaucracy is simply too large and that this damages its image. In some parts of the bureaucracy, of course, this may be true. However, bureaucracies, by their nature, are characterized by job specialization and formal rules. Government (and large private corporations, for that matter) has not yet found a better way to organize.

One individual cannot become an expert in all the different activities carried out by most agencies. For example, just imagine the problems that would arise if each of the several thousand social security claims examiners or Internal Revenue Service tax examiners applied individual judgment, without rules or guidelines, to determine how large a benefit one person receives or how much tax an individual pays.

Another problem for bureaucrats stems from the fact that a number of politicians have campaigned over the past ten years, in part, by complaining about the weaknesses and inefficiencies of the federal bureaucracy and promising to do something about it. In most cases, the rhetoric was directed at specific programs that the politician disliked rather than at the employees hired to administer those programs. This distinction was seldom made clear, however, and the employees often ended up being portrayed as ineffective or wasteful.

Finally, in any institution as large as the federal government, there are bound to be some inefficient or ineffective programs and employees. However, even most critics would agree that the inefficient or ineffective programs and employees are greatly outnumbered by the good ones. Unfortunately, upon hearing of any problems within the government, many people assume the worst about government as a whole.

The Reality of the Bureaucracy

Is the size of government a problem? If so, then an easy solution would be to make it smaller. A smaller government would have to be more efficient and responsive. Or would it? While government as a whole has grown substantially over the last twenty-five years, most of the growth has come at the state and local level. At the federal level, however, the size of the bureaucracy, as measured by the number of full-time civilian employees, has not increased very much over the last twenty-five years. And if measured as a proportion of the total U.S. population, it has actually gotten smaller (see chart).

In 1960, there were an average of 12.4 civilian federal employees for every 1,000 U.S. residents. Twenty-five years later—in 1985—there were only 11 employees for every 1,000 U.S. residents. This decrease may be offset somewhat by individuals who work for private companies or businesses that have contracts with the federal government. Even so, the federal bureaucracy has been remarkably stable over a long period of time.

Calls to reduce the size of the federal government raise another issue—reaching agreement on what precisely is to be cut or reduced. In 1984, almost half (49 percent) of all executive branch civilian employees worked for the Department of Defense, and roughly one-fourth of the federal budget was for defense spending. While disagreements exist over how much to spend, there is no disagreement that government programs serve a need, whether in defense, health, or agricultural research. For example, the Department of Health and Human Services

Full Time Civilian Employees in Executive Branch		Total U.S. Population	Number for every 1,000
2,231,081	**1960**	179,323,175	12.4
2,495,641	**1965**	194,303,000	12.8
2,775,620	**1970**	203,302,031	13.6
2,840,140	**1975**	215,973,000	13.1
2,658,224	**1980**	226,545,805	11.7
2,612,870	**1985**	237,318,000	11.0

Federal Civilian Employment

Source: U.S. Office of Personnel Management/Bureau of the Census, U.S. Department of Commerce

administers social security, the Food and Drug Administration, the Centers for Disease Control, and the National Institutes of Health, among other activities. The Department of Agriculture administers the food stamp program; conducts meat and poultry inspections; and maintains the Agricultural Research Service, the Soil Conservation Service, and a myriad of other functions. The list goes on and on.

While some agencies do outlive their usefulness and some programs are cut (and more perhaps should be cut), by and large the big budget items and the larger agencies are there because Americans either want or need the services provided. Entitlement programs (so called because everyone who qualifies is entitled to receive benefits) account for close to half of the federal budget. These programs include social security, Medicare, and Medicaid. Reaching agreement on which programs are no longer necessary or are too generous is understandably a difficult task since someone usually stands to lose.

A common mistake made by many people is to assume that all federal government agencies and employees are basically the same. Of course, federal agencies vary widely in size ranging from those with less than a dozen employees to the Department of Army with more than 385,000 civilian employees. (The U.S. Postal Service has the largest number of civilian employees with close to 700,000, but it is also an independent part of the federal government with separate personnel policies and procedures.)

In addition to size, each federal agency has a unique mission and a unique work force to carry out that mission. For example, the National Aeronautics and Space Administration (NASA) has a high concentration of engineers and scientists among its employees, while the Forest Service in the Department of Agriculture relies heavily on foresters and rangers who work in an environment totally different from NASA.

In sum, the bureaucracy is best understood when it is seen in terms of its component parts.

The Role of the Bureaucrat in Improving the Bureaucracy

There is always room for improvement in the operation of most agencies, and individual bureaucrats can become key players in those efforts. In 1980, the U.S. Merit Systems Protection Board sent a questionnaire to 13,000 randomly selected employees in 15 major federal departments and agencies. In 1983, a related questionnaire was sent to approximately 7,500 randomly selected employees government-wide. The results from both surveys provide some interesting insights into the motivations of federal bureaucrats who "blow the whistle" on fraud, waste, or mismanagement.

In both surveys, a significant percentage (45 percent in 1980 and 25 percent in 1983) admitted that they had direct knowledge of some type of illegal or wasteful activity. When we asked those employees who had observed the wrongdoing if they reported it, 70 percent of them said they did *not* report it. Among those who did report it and were identified as the source of the report, about one in five claimed they suffered some type of reprisal by management as a result.

These findings are disturbing because federal employees themselves may be in the best position to help make improvements in government. When we asked employees why they did not report an observed violation of the law, more than half of the employees in both surveys (53 percent) gave as a primary reason their belief that nothing would be done about the activity even if they were to report it.

What we conclude from these and other studies is that federal workers want to do a good job and want to improve the effectiveness and responsiveness of their agencies. And given the

opportunity, most will do so. The 1983 survey found that most federal senior executives stayed in government because they enjoyed their work (85 percent), and more than three-fourths (76 percent) wanted the opportunity to make an impact on public affairs.

Our studies also show that whistle-blowing is usually not the most effective means of improving the bureaucracy. One exception may be when whistle-blowing calls attention to deliberate violations of law, such as major theft or fraud. In most cases, however, federal employees "blow the whistle" on less clear-cut issues such as poor management practices or a difference of opinion on agency policies. When such issues become public, agency managers may feel a need to defend their record and become even more resistant to change—even constructive change.

I believe that federal managers can take steps within their agencies to move the bureaucratic "climate" toward one of open communication and cooperation between managers and employees so that "blowing the whistle" becomes less necessary. Some of the steps that can be taken include: (1) actively and sincerely soliciting the

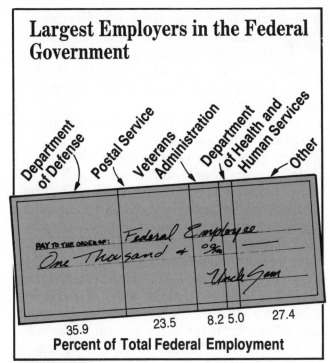

Largest Employers in the Federal Government

Department of Defense
Postal Service
Veterans Administration
Department of Health and Human Services
Other

PAY TO THE ORDER OF: *Federal Employee*
One Thousand + 0%
Uncle Sam

35.9   23.5   8.2 5.0   27.4

Percent of Total Federal Employment

Source: Statistical Abstract of the United States, 1986

In 1984, the federal government employed more than 2.5 million people, yet 72 percent worked in only four government departments. Despite efforts by Congress and the Reagan administration to decrease the size of the bureaucracy, civilian employment in the federal government rose by 2.7 percent to more than 3 million people in 1985.

views of employees; (2) providing prompt feedback to employees on their ideas or opinions; and (3) recognizing employees who become involved in improving agency effectiveness and responsiveness. In the long run, of course, it is all of us who gain from these efforts.

Questions to Consider

1. Why do you think most people have a negative view of the federal bureaucracy?

2. How do you explain the difference in attitude toward the bureaucracy and individual government workers?

3. In a survey cited by the author, almost half of the federal employees questioned admitted that they knew of wrongdoing in their agency but did not report it. Would you "blow the whistle" if you worked for a government agency and felt that it was violating the law? What problems might you encounter because of your decision?

The Role of Congressional Oversight

Senator Albert Gore, Jr.

Senator Albert Gore, Jr. (D-Tenn.), was elected to the Senate in 1984 after serving in the U.S. House of Representatives for eight years. While a member of the House, he served on several committees with oversight responsibility in the areas of health, environmental quality, and consumer issues. In his article, Senator Gore explains why congressional oversight is essential to our system of checks and balances.

While Congress spends much of its time making laws, passing bills is only half the battle. Legislators also have a duty to oversee the executive branch. It is not enough to make laws; Congress must also make sure that they work.

Congressional oversight is vital to our system of checks and balances. When the nation's founders gave the three branches of government distinct powers, they wisely designed each branch to keep an eye on the other two. The Constitution enumerates several of these checks and balances, from the presidential veto and the congressional override to Senate approval of Supreme Court nominees.

Oversight is not spelled out in the Constitution, but courts have held that the power of oversight is inherent. The Constitution gives Congress the power "to provide for...the general welfare of the United States." In recent years, Congress has relied heavily on oversight to carry out that charge.

The History of Congressional Oversight

Since as early as 1792, Congress has asserted itself as a watchdog over the executive branch, uncovering scandals ranging from Civil War profiteering to the notorious Teapot Dome affair in 1923.* Modern congressional oversight came of age in 1950, when Senator Estes Kefauver, a Democrat from Tennessee, held televised hearings on organized crime. The Kefauver Committee was the first of many widely publicized congressional investigations into law enforcement, fraud, and abuse.

In the early 1970s, the Watergate scandal galvanized Congress into policing the executive branch more actively and sparked public interest in government ethics. A new generation of senators and representatives came into office eager to ask questions and challenge tradition. Congress passed strong conflict-of-interest laws and expanded its investigative powers through oversight subcommittees.

*Editor's Note: Teapot Dome was a federally owned oilfield, which was supposed to be used for emergency fuel for the U.S. Navy. When the Harding administration leased the fields to private developers who made a great profit, the scandal was uncovered by a congressional oversight committee.

Congress uses oversight committees to ensure that the bureaucracy faithfully administers the nation's laws. The power of legislative oversight was spelled out in the Legislative Reorganization Act of 1946, which called for "continuous watchfulness" by Congress.

Congressional Oversight at Work

Over the past decade, I have had an opportunity to join in several important congressional probes. As a member of the Subcommittee on Oversight and Investigations, I took part in a 2-year probe into the Environmental Protection Agency's (EPA) enforcement of the Superfund program for toxic waste cleanup. We found evidence not only of EPA's failure to carry out the law, but of criminal mismanagement by EPA officials. The agency had deliberately manipulated the Superfund to delay cleanup and gave certain companies favorable treatment.

Our subcommittee also exposed price-fixing by an international uranium cartel, widespread overcharges by major oil companies, and illegal dumping of toxic waste by organized crime. Another investigation revealed that officials of the Federal Emergency Management Agency had diverted public funds for their own use.

Congress uses its oversight powers not only to uncover scandals in government, but to reexamine laws it has passed. Often an oversight hearing will reveal the need for new or revised legislation. During committee hearings in 1983, for example, I became convinced that Congress should establish a computerized national network for organ donors. A year later, we passed the National Organ Transplant Act. Committee hearings on infant formula, bioethics, and health insurance for the elderly led to progressive legislation and regulation in these areas as well.

A thorough investigation—or the prospect of one—helps to keep federal agencies on their toes.

Congressional committees have the power to subpoena witnesses, who can be held in contempt of Congress for lying under oath or refusing to testify. In 1974, the Supreme Court ruled in the case of the Richard Nixon tapes that the president could not invoke executive privilege to shield officials or evidence from congressional investigations or the courts.

The Limits of Oversight

Congressional oversight can not solve all of the government's problems. Oversight does not always produce dramatic results. Keeping watch over the federal bureaucracy takes a great deal of effort, and a lengthy investigation can sometimes fail to produce anything substantial. Unless Congress catches the offenders red-handed, it may not be able to stop some offenses or questionable practices.

In addition, some members of Congress are more interested in legislation than oversight. A few may hesitate to launch investigations or hold hearings that could jeopardize industries or government workers in their home states or districts. In some cases, committee members have grown too close to agencies under their jurisdiction.

More often, Congress simply fails to ask the right questions. It is easier to pass laws and never look back than to admit that past statutes or programs may not be working. Until the explosion of the space shuttle Challenger in 1986, for example, Congress did little to oversee the space program. Even now, there are doubts as to

LOOKS LIKE THE ROBOTICS INDUSTRY HAS FINALLY GOT THEMSELVES A HEAD OF THE FEDERAL ROBOT CONTROL AGENCY THEY CAN LIVE WITH...

CONGRESSIONAL OVERSEERS

UNITED STATES OF AMERICA
FEDERAL ROBOTIC CONTROL AGENCY

Peter © 1986

Questions to Consider

1. Do you think congressional oversight of the bureaucracy is necessary? Why or why not?

2. What are some of the limits of congressional oversight?

3. Do you think congressional oversight helps or hinders the workings of the federal bureaucracy?

how well we are reviewing our responsibility in this area.

The Tools of Democracy

I believe that congressional oversight is getting better all the time. While a few areas of the government still escape notice, an active Congress has made the executive branch more accountable. As the philosopher Samuel Johnson once observed, "Nothing is so conducive to a good conscience as the suspicion that someone is watching."

Our democracy depends on the right to know. By watching over the executive branch, Congress helps to keep the public—and itself—informed. A strong and curious legislative branch will become still more important as the federal government strives to make the most of limited resources. Congressional oversight is one way to make democracy work.

Government Regulation: Two Views

The government regulates industry in a variety of ways. For example, government regulations determine the minimum miles per gallon of gas required for domestically produced cars, the amount of pollutants a factory can release into the air and water, and the types and amounts of insecticides that can be sprayed on the foods we eat. CLOSE UP asked two Washington lobbyists—one representing business, the other consumers—to comment on the advantages and disadvantages of government regulation.

James Carty

James Carty is vice-president for the Government Regulation, Competition, and Small Manufacturing Department of the National Association of Manufacturers (NAM). He is responsible for NAM's dealings with Congress and federal regulatory agencies in the areas of economic regulation, antitrust legislation, and corporate governance. Mr. Carty discusses what government regulation should and should not be.

Government regulation is an integral part of our everyday lives. The clothes we wear, the food we eat, and the water we drink are all subject to some sort of government action. As an indication of how pervasive regulation is, the Code of Federal Regulations now comprises more than 20 feet of bookshelf space. And the cost is enormous—the Office of Management and Budget (OMB) estimates that regulatory compliance last year cost the economy $200 billion.

Government regulation of products is a legitimate function. Citizens should be assured that the medicine they take is safe and effective and that the airplanes they fly in and the trucks they share the road with are safe. However, many regulations are unnecessary or go far beyond what is needed. These regulations are an excessive burden to industry and drive up the prices we pay for goods and services.

Part of the problem lies with the fact that Congress often enacts legislation, but does not define how the new law is to be implemented. This job is left to government agencies. The problem with this is that agencies often have little knowledge of the impact their decisions will have on a business. Also, a regulation imposed by one agency may conflict with a regulation of another agency, leaving those affected in a quandary.

Take the example of children's sleepwear. In 1971, the government ordered the makers of children's sleepwear to put the flame-retardant Tris into all of their products. In 1977, however, the Consumer Products Safety Commission ordered the removal of all such garments from store shelves because Tris was shown to be a potential cause of cancer.

The most important aspect of regulation to most business owners, large and small, is the cost of compliance through paperwork. These costs, while hidden, are ultimately paid for by the consumer. However, some recent developments have reduced the amount of paperwork entailed with government regulation.

The first ray of hope was the enactment of the Paperwork Reduction Act of 1980, which granted OMB the power to oversee the issuance of rules and regulations by the various government agencies. OMB's mandate was to reduce the amount of paperwork involved in complying with federal regulations. In addition, the president directed government agencies to perform cost-benefit analyses of proposed regulations and to submit new regulations to OMB for review to ensure compliance with the Paperwork Reduction Act.

For example, in 1985, the General Services Administration, the National Aeronautics and Space Administration, and the Department of Defense attempted to issue regulations governing the Defense Procurement Reform Act of 1984 and the Small Business and Federal Procurement Competition Enhancement Act of 1984. These laws were intended to prevent the federal government from paying more for an item than it would for the same item on the open market. Initially, the three agencies proposed a regulation that would require all companies doing business with the federal government to submit a "Certificate of Commercial Pricing." This certificate would have required suppliers to track every single price of every item that may someday be sold to the government. To the surprise of the agencies, few companies maintain such detailed records. And because the agencies wanted this information stored and filed for three years, implementation would have been a strain for computer storage capacity, physical files, or both.

The cost of tracking, analyzing, maintaining, and submitting such records would have been astronomical. Of course, such costs would have been considered legitimate overhead and would have been passed on to taxpayers, so the agencies' attempt to lower the government's purchase price would have been counterproductive, anyway. OMB rejected the proposal because the costs far outweighed the benefits.

The recent deregulation of several industries shows how costly regulation can be. Deregulation demonstrates just how much more efficient and responsive industry becomes when it is allowed to respond to consumer demands rather than being run by a government agency charged with "protecting the public interest." Two good examples are the trucking and airline industries.

Prior to 1980, when the Motor Carrier Act of 1980 was passed, it was extremely difficult for new trucking companies to enter the market because they had to demonstrate conclusively to the Interstate Commerce Commission (ICC) that their services were needed for "the public convenience." Carriers were authorized to operate only between certain cities and were forced to return with their trailers empty. In addition, requests for rate increases were nearly always granted by the ICC while requests for rate reductions were contested strongly by competing companies and at least delayed if not denied.

After 1980, when the new law went into effect, 17,000 new carriers entered the market. Today, carriers and shippers negotiate truck routes and delivery times that are mutually beneficial. Shippers generally report that truck charges are down, efficiency in operations is up, and the quality of service is at least as good as (if not better than) when the ICC exercised complete regulation. One estimate of the savings resulting from the Motor Carrier Act has been cited as $56 billion.

However, the trucking industry is not yet completely free of government regulation. Carriers still must file every rate with the ICC. Each year, over one million rates are reported, and over three trillion are on file.

The airline industry, which has been totally deregulated, is perhaps an even better example of the benefits of deregulation. The Civil Aeronautics Board (CAB) regulated the industry from 1938 until 1978. It is easy to understand why the regulated companies were the most vocal opponents of deregulation when one realizes that not one new interstate air carrier was able to demonstrate the "public convenience" necessary to begin operations during the forty years of the CAB's existence. Since such regulatory barriers to entrance were removed, however, the number of interstate air carriers has increased enormously. Consumers have benefitted from reduced fares, increased route competition, and an increased choice about the type of service they wish to purchase.

No one who supported the removal of federal regulatory oversight of either the motor carrier or airline industry believes that safety standards, requirements, or inspections should be decreased. Where problems exist in the safety of deregulated industries, efforts should be made to correct the problems. Economic regulation of an industry is a separate issue from safety regulation. Protection of the public safety is a legitimate function of government, along the same line as police and fire protection.

Another legitimate function of government regulation is to increase and preserve competition. Antitrust regulation, in particular, has served both the public and the business community well. All entrepreneurs should be able to rely on rules and laws to protect them from unfair competition. The key, of course, is that the rules have to be clear, unambiguous, and reasonable.

In August 1985, the Federal Communications Commission wrote what should become a maxim for other agencies. "Regulation was never intended to impede the development of competition. Rather, it is a surrogate for effective competition." These words strike at the heart of what government regulation should and should not be. It was not intended to interfere with the efficient operation of the economy, and it was not conceived to increase the costs of products to consumers just to justify the existence of an agency. Instead, a good system of regulation protects the health and safety of citizens while guarding against the imposition of rules and requirements that would result in the inefficient and unproductive use of economic resources.

Bruce Silverglade

Bruce Silverglade is legal affairs director of the Center for Science in the Public Interest, a nonprofit consumer advocacy organization in Washington, D.C. He oversees the litigation of federal court cases involving a variety of consumer health issues and coordinates the center's legislative activities on environmental health. Mr. Silverglade claims that government regulation, though a burden at times, might be necessary to protect the rights of consumers.

It has been more than five years since the business community's cries of "get government off our back" have been sympathetically received by both the White House and a majority of Congress. Those who echoed this cry told us that regulation was a waste of taxpayers' money, a burden on American industry, and even idiotic at times. Now that the deregulators have had their way for a while, it is fair to say that many Americans are thinking twice about whether regulation is as bad as we have been led to believe.

The difficulty of trying to get a telephone installed has made many people nostalgic for the old system. A recent epidemic of airline crashes has caused second thoughts about airline deregulation. All in all, public opinion polls show that while most Americans are against regulation in the abstract, they now support specific consumer, health and safety, and environmental protection measures.

Surely, some aspects of deregulation have been a success. For example, the elimination of so-called "economic regulation" of airline fares and long-distance telephone rates has produced lower prices that are a boon to consumers. More deregulation of this type is called for.

However, increases in airplane crashes illustrate the need for continued government regulation of a different sort. Advocates of deregulation rely on the theory that informed citizens should be able to decide for themselves whether to pay an extra $5 or $10 to fly in a plane with some added safety feature. In practice, however, an individual consumer does not have the technical expertise needed to make that decision. That's why government regulation is actually the most efficient way of making these decisions for everyone.

Similarly, while deregulation of the telephone industry has produced lower prices, it has also produced a variety of substandard, low-quality products and long-distance services. Such situations ring out for increased regulation by consumer protection agencies because individual consumers cannot be expected to know whether one telephone company's communications satellite is as good as the next guy's.

However, this simple fact often eludes the business community and Washington policymakers alike. For example, after airline fares were deregulated, both Congress and the White House failed to beef up the staff of the Federal

Aviation Administration (FAA), which is in charge of ensuring airline safety. Although more people than ever took to the skies, the FAA was unable to increase the number and frequency of its inspections in order to keep up with the growing number of flights and carriers. Similarly, while the Federal Communications Commission placed its stamp of approval on telephone deregulation, it failed to issue adequate regulations that would protect consumers from being cheated in a newly competitive marketplace. The public will increasingly question the benefits of deregulation unless the business community and government officials recognize that deregulation in one area often calls for re-regulation in another.

Americans are also having second thoughts about deregulation because of the way deregulators use cost-benefit analysis to justify the rollback of health and safety regulations.

While no one would quibble with the notion that government regulators should consider the costs and benefits of proposed regulatory actions, few people understand how such estimates are arrived at. Program administrators often place a dollar value on a human life (sometimes as low as $100,000) and then compare that figure to the cost of the regulation. According to the cost-benefit experts, a human life should be sacrificed if, for example, the cost of forcing factory owners to filter out cancer-causing chemicals from their smokestacks is more than the dollar value of the lives that will be saved from taking such steps.

The problem with this approach to regulation—apart from its callous attitude toward human life—is that it is unfair to weigh the cost of a regulation against its benefits. Even if the cost that factory owners must bear to reduce cancer-causing chemicals in the air is more than the dollar value of the lives saved from such action, the factory owners should still be required to take steps to protect the public.

Consumers are not the only ones thinking twice about whether regulation may be worth it after all. Even the business community has recently come around to the position that some government regulation is good. For example, the National Association of Manufacturers itself has led the fight *against* the elimination of affirmative action regulations for government contractors. Affirmative action regulations require that any company doing business with the federal government must employ appropriate numbers of minorities and women. In an attempt to "get the government off the back of industry," the Reagan administration proposed to rescind such requirements. However, it now appears that, far from creating any "burdens," such regulations help corporations maintain employee morale, increase worker productivity, and take advantage of a changing labor market that includes an increasing number of women and minorities.

Similarly, the Federal Trade Commission (FTC) proposed eliminating a requirement that all advertisers maintain records that prove that claims in television commercials and magazine ads are truthful. In other words, if an advertising company claimed that its skin cream worked better than a competitor's, it would have to have scientific data on hand if asked by government authorities to prove the claim. However, the FTC decided that the requirement placed undue burdens on advertisers and proposed to eliminate the measure to save the industry money. The advertising industry itself—not consumer organizations—persuaded the FTC to back down. Advertisers understand that without government requirements insuring that advertising claims are true, unscrupulous claims would fill the airwaves and consumers would eventually come to disbelieve all ads.

In sum, important segments of the business community have come to realize that the hoopla about "getting government off our backs" may not be so great after all. While the business community as a whole still argues that regulations cause a significant burden on our economy, the fact is that economic problems such as declining innovation, trade imbalances, budget deficits, inflation, and unemployment have much deeper causes than federal regulation. For example, government regulators never forced American car manufacturers to continue building big cars

when the handwriting was on the wall that consumers wanted smaller automobiles. The flood of Japanese imports that followed was the result of poor corporate planning, not government regulation.

Consumer organizations hope that, in the future, the business community will work with government officials to address the root causes of our economic problems and not simply blame such ills on scapegoats such as consumer and environmental protection regulations.

Evolution of the Cabinet

The original Cabinet of President George Washington had only three departments—State, Treasury, and War. Over time, new departments were added or established ones changed names and responsibilities. Today, the Cabinet officially consists of the secretaries of thirteen executive departments, but may include other government officials (such as the U.S. Ambassador to the United Nations) if the president wishes.

Department	Year Established
Department of State	1789
Department of the Treasury	1789
Department of War	1789
Department of the Interior	1849
Department of Justice	1870
Department of Agriculture	1889
Department of Commerce	1913
Department of Labor	1913
Department of Defense (formerly the Department of War)	1947
Department of Health, Education, and Welfare	1953
Department of Housing and Urban Development	1965
Department of Transportation	1966
Department of Energy	1977
Department of Health and Human Services (formerly the Department of Health, Education, and Welfare)	1979
Department of Education (formerly the Department of Health, Education, and Welfare)	1979

Questions to Consider

1. Do you think government regulation helps to promote product safety and fair competition, or does it place an undue burden on industry? Why?

2. In what areas do the authors think that government regulation is necessary? Do you agree with them? Why or why not?

3. Do you think the government's method of cost-benefit analysis—putting a price tag on human life—is a fair way of assessing the cost of government regulations? Why or why not? Can you think of a better way to evaluate whether a regulation should be put into effect?

The Federal Aviation Agency: Preventing Chaos in the Skies

Regulation of economic activity by governments has historical roots going back to ancient Babylonia, the Roman Empire, medieval towns, and the American colonies. The U.S. Constitution gives the federal government the power to regulate commerce with foreign nations and among states, and, according to a 1945 Supreme Court ruling, the power is as broad as the economic needs of the nation.

The government's power to regulate commerce was exercised primarily through the courts until the late 1800s, when this traditional machinery proved insufficient to deal with the complexities of a modern industrial economy. The first regulatory agency was the Interstate Commerce Commission (ICC). The ICC was set up in 1877 by the Interstate Commerce Act in response to citizen outrage over the monopolistic practices of the railroad companies. (In fact, the large railroad companies also supported the ICC because they saw that the establishment of a government-sponsored cartel would ensure them a steady rate of return.)

The ICC's broad mandate was to keep a continuous eye on railroads throughout the country. It was given the traditional authority to punish wrongful acts after they were committed and a new authority to prevent wrongful acts from occurring at all. This large discretionary power was shared among five commission members, no more than three of whom could be from the same political party, with their tenure and decisions independent of presidential authority.

This first independent, expert, nonpartisan agency brought together the worlds of politics and industrial economics. It set the form for all the regulatory agencies to come. All were created by Congress in response to particular needs, pressures, crises, and technologies. As pointed out in a 1949 report, the purpose of government regulatory agencies was "to correct or prevent abuses without impeding the effective operation of the industry or imposing unnecessary expense and waste."

The Federal Reserve System was established in 1913, the Federal Trade Commission in 1914, and the Federal Power Commission in 1920. Other major regulatory agencies—including the Food and Drug Administration, the National Labor Relations Board, the Securities and Exchange Commission, and the Federal Communications Commission—were created during

In December 1903, the Wright brothers made their first successful flight. Within twenty years, civil air transport became a major business.

National Air and Space Museum Smithsonian Institution Photo No. A45528 the 1930s as part of President Franklin D. Roosevelt's New Deal. Also during the 1930s, some agencies, such as the ICC, in reaction to Depression-caused setbacks, began to promote the industries they regulated. Regulation surged in the 1970s with the creation of new agencies such as the Consumer Product Safety Commission, the Environmental Protection Agency, and the Occupational Safety and Health Administration.

Today, in the widest sense, there are probably close to 100,000 people employed as federal regulators. According to the General Accounting Office, the number of agencies engaged in regulation is well over 100. These agencies were defined in a 1977 Senate study on federal regulation. A federal regulatory office, the report said, was "one which (1) has decisionmaking authority, (2) establishes standards or guidelines conferring benefits and imposing restrictions on business conduct, (3) operates principally in the sphere of domestic business activity, (4) has its head and/or members appointed by the president...[generally subject to Senate confirmation], and (5) has its legal procedures generally governed by the Administrative Procedure Act."

The new agencies established in the 1970s were not focused on particular industries and illustrate the fact that there are two kinds of regulations. The first kind of regulation is aimed at a specific industry and pursues essentially economic objectives. It is used to correct for market failures, that is, for those instances of "natural monopolies" where no competition exists—as in the case of public utilities. It is also used to prevent economic failure in a given industry (e.g., banking) in which the public perceives that a failure may be so costly as to be intolerable. This kind of regulation has also been used to allocate limited space or resources, as in the case of the airlines and the broadcast spectrum.

The other kind of regulation is aimed at protecting the health and safety of workers and consumers. It deals with public welfare. In some areas (e.g., drugs, insurance, and medical services), this type of regulation helps consumers make more informed decisions. It is used to give workers information about the possible risks they may face in various jobs. It is also used to set certain requirements for public safety. For example, seatbelts are required to be made of a specific type of material, at a certain length, and installed in all cars; aircraft must undergo certain prescribed maintenance procedures.

In the 1970s, a movement for deregulation—especially *economic deregulation*—began. An increasing number of Americans were unhappy with what they considered unnecessary and costly government regulation. (Some people also saw the second kind of regulation—public welfare regulation—as both excessive and too expensive. (The air-transport industry in particular became a target for deregulation, in part because the two kinds of regulation were already separated and because public interest groups and others saw the Civil Aeronautics Board as cooperating with the industry to keep profits high.

Regulation of the Aviation Industry

In December 1903, the Wright brothers made their first successful flights in motor-powered airplanes. In the next few years, other aviators demonstrated how airplanes could be flown all over the world. During World War I, more advances were made. After the war, civil air transport became a major business.

Soon it became clear that regulation—both national and international—was necessary. In 1919, representatives from various nations met at the Paris Convention. The rules adopted pertained to such areas as airworthiness and certification and licensing of pilots. The

United States signed but did not ratify the convention.

In the United States, the availability of cheap aircraft encouraged barnstorming and stunt flying as well as transport. By 1925, private airplane companies had contracted to carry airmail. But some states set standards for the certification of pilots and planes; others did not. In many cases, there were fewer restrictions on flying a plane than on driving a car.

A group of businessmen and engineers known as the Aero Club believed that the federal government should get involved. The club wanted the government to impose order on the industry by regulating pilot licenses, plane licenses, ground operations, routes, and rates charged. Only with such regulation could the aviation industry become a truly dependable means of transportation for people and merchandise. Club members called upon Congress to end the "chaos of *laissez-faire* in the skies."

In 1926, Congress passed the Air Commerce Act, which was based on the same regulation developed at the 1919 Paris Convention. The act created the Bureau of Air Commerce within the Department of Commerce and gave the bureau the authority to license pilots, certify aircraft, develop air-navigation systems, advance flight safety, issue flight information, investigate air crashes, and promote the aviation industry in general.

In the next year, 1927, Charles Lindbergh made the first nonstop crossing of the North Atlantic, in his plane named the Spirit of St. Louis, in 33½ hours. Lindbergh's flight captured the public's imagination and made people begin to consider seriously the possibilities of travel by air. Lindbergh's achievement was also helpful in securing sufficient funds from Congress for the Bureau of Air Commerce to keep pace with the fast-growing aviation industry.

In its first years, the bureau spent most of its efforts on pilot training

In 1927, Charles Lindbergh made the first nonstop crossing of the North Atlantic in his plane, the Spirit of St. Louis. Lindbergh's achievement was helpful in securing sufficient funds from Congress for the newly created Bureau of Air Commerce.

and certification. Its first set of regulations consisted of approximately 225 lines of type—as compared with today's hundreds of pages and daily bulletins. Those regulations made a difference. The accident rate fell as more and more pilots were certified. By 1931, the number of accidents had dropped 20 percent, and by 1932, another 20 percent. The bureau also worked to promote both public safety and the aviation industry by setting up air highways and travel routes, a system of beacons on landing fields that made night travel possible, and radio control to help pilots fly in bad weather. A system of air-traffic control developed by private controllers in Chicago also contributed to improved safety. (All such systems were managed privately until 1986.) Technological improvements in testing, the design of engines and airframes, and maintenance equipment soon combined to provide larger, faster, and stronger

National Air and Space Museum Smithsonian Institution Photo No. 78-3983

UNITED AIR LINES

UNITED AIR LINES

A 1935 air crash, in which well-known humorist Will Rogers was killed, prompted Congress to pass the Civil Aeronautics Act. This act created a separate panel to investigate air disasters.

airplanes. Transportation of passengers became profitable both nationally and internationally.

However, shortcomings in the system of controls were brought to light by two air tragedies. In the first, in 1931, the Notre Dame football coach, Knute Rockne, was killed. The bureau, empowered by the 1926 act to investigate all accidents, was reporting all crashes as simple statistics. Members of Congress, who had been trying to get more detailed information on air crashes, now used public opinion about the accident to force the bureau to release additional information. It turned out that the plane in which Rockne was killed was a new type of Fokker—with a defective design. The planes were taken

out of service, and the bureau (and its successor organizations) henceforth provided more detailed information to Congress on all crashes. The question was raised as to whether it was good for public safety to have one agency regulating and controlling an industry while at the same time promoting it.

The question became more acute after a second air tragedy in 1935 in which aviator Wiley Post and humorist Will Rogers were killed near Point Barrow, Alaska. The crash was attributed to weather, as a great many other crashes had been. Some members of Congress began to suspect that the bureau was actually covering up some of its own errors.

In 1938, Congress passed the Civil Aeronautics Act. The Bureau of Air Commerce became the independent Civil Aeronautics Authority. To separate the function of crash investigation from the function of setting and enforcing industry standrds, the act created a 3-person investigative board that reported only to the head of the Authority. The new organization had grown from a small bureau to a full-fledged agency with seven divisions and forty specialized offices, each one focusing on a particular aspect of aviation safety such as pilot education, aircraft inspection, plane maintenance, radio controls, international flights, and enforcement of regulations. To help the new Authority respond more quickly to local needs and to make onsite investigations, a field staff was put in place.

Further reorganization in 1940 assigned the functions of the Civil Aeronautics Authority to the Civil Aeronautics Administration, within the Department of Commerce; the Civil Aeronautics board (CAB), located administratively within the Department of Commerce, reported directly to Congress. The Civil Aeronautics Administration enforced safety regulations, operated traffic-control services and navigational aids, encouraged development of a national system of airports, and allocated air space. The new 5-member CAB was given authority to determine the routes and fares of every airline company operating in the United States. The CAB was also responsible for investigating accidents.

With the introduction of commercial jet aircraft in the 1950s, air travel increased and the problems of the air industry became more complex. However, a series of accidents in the late 1950s—as in the 1930s—instigated new regulatory legislation. "Recent mid-air collisions of aircraft," said President Dwight D. Eisenhower, "occasioning tragic losses of human life, have emphasized the need for a system of air-traffic management which will prevent within the limits of human ingenuity a recurrence of such accidents."

The 1958 Federal Aviation Act established the Federal Aviation Agency. The agency assumed authority over the nation's air space, combining the functions of the Civil Aeronautics Administration with the safety functions of the CAB. The CAB retained jurisdiction over plane fares, routes, and investigation of accidents. Responding to criticism that the CAB allowed a few big carriers to split among themselves the most profitable traffic, the act charged the CAB to foster "adequate, economical, and efficient services by air carriers at reasonable charges."

History of Airline Regulation at a Glance

1926 The Air Commerce Act establishes a Bureau of Air Commerce within the Department of Commerce to regulate "the chaos of *laissez-faire*" in the skies.

1938 The Civil Aeronautics Act expands the Bureau of Air Commerce into the independent Civil Aeronautics Authority. Within the authority is a separate board to investigate crashes.

1940 In a further reorganization, the functions of the Civil Aeronautics Authority are assigned to the Civil Aeronautics Administration (within the Department of Commerce) and the Civil Aeronautics Board (CAB) (administratively within the Department of Commerce but reporting directly to Congress).

1958 The Federal Aviation Act establishes the Federal Aviation Agency to replace and expand the Civil Aeronautics Administration.

1967 Congress creates the Department of Transportation. The Federal Aviation Agency becomes the Federal Aviation Administration (FAA) and is placed within the new department. Congress also creates the National Transportation Safety Board, which takes over the investigation functions of the CAB.

1975 The National Transportation Safety Board becomes an independent regulatory agency.

1978 The Airline Deregulation Act ends government regulation over air fares and routes. The act provides for the CAB to be phased out by January 1, 1985. The FAA's authority to promote and issue safety regulations remains unchanged.

1981 The FAA takes over limited regulation of domestic routes and fares from the CAB.

1985 The CAB is phased out on January 1.

How Regulations Are Made in the Federal Aviation Administration

Regulations are generated by:

— new laws

— internal recommendations made by FAA program offices

— petitions from outside groups

FAA Program Office produces an "issue paper" detailing a new regulation

FAA management reviews new regulation

FAA Office of General Counsel provides advice*

Economist's Office conducts informal review*

Originating office compiles comments and writes a formal proposal

Formal proposal is sent to all involved FAA offices for review*

Originating office compiles comments from FAA offices and writes new proposal

FAA administrator reviews new proposal*

Secretary of Transportation reviews new proposal*

Office of Management and Budget reviews new proposal*

New proposal returns to FAA originating office via Department of Transportation and FAA Office of Chief Counsel

Originating office compiles all comments and makes changes

FAA Office of Chief Counsel reviews changes

Federal Register publishes proposed regulation

Public comments are received on proposed regulation

Originating office reviews public comments and proposal is put into final form

Final proposal is reviewed by FAA Office of Chief Counsel, FAA Administrator, Department of Transportation, and Office of Management and Budget

FAA Office of Chief Counsel compiles final reviews, makes changes, and sends new regulation to Federal Register for final publication

New regulation becomes effective from date stated

*A "no" from management or a negative review can kill the new regulation here.

Eight years later, under the Department of Transportation Act, the Federal Aviation Agency became the Federal Aviation Administration (FAA) within the newly created department. The act also set up the National Transportation Safety Board (NTSB) and transferred the responsibility for investigating air accidents from the CAB to the NSTB. The function of crash investigation remains solely with the NTSB, thus ensuring that that function is kept separate from the function of setting and enforcing economic and safety standards for the air industry. Through this reorganization, Congress hoped to prevent problems of possible conflicts of interests.

The Push for Deregulation

In the late 1960s, at the same time that Congress began creating a spate of new regulatory agencies (such as the Occupational Safety and Health Administration and the Environmental Protection Agency), an equal push was under way for government deregulation. But the emphasis was not on deregulation of the health and safety protections; rather it was on deregulation of the economic protections of the various industries. Public interest groups, such as the Center for the Study of Responsive Law, declared that the regulatory agencies made monopolies. The agencies were accused of serving industries rather than consumers. The CAB, now concerned with only economic regulations, was a good target. Without CAB regulation, said one study, interstate airline prices "would be from 9 to 50 percent lower." Furthermore, if air fares were less, empty seats would be full, and airlines would end up making more money.

In 1975, President Gerald R. Ford proposed an Aviation Act based on the idea that, because of excessive economic regulation, air travel had "become a luxury too expensive to afford." He said, "The rigidly controlled regulatory structure now serves to stifle competition, increase costs to travelers, makes the industry less efficient than it could be, and denies large segments of the American public access to lower cost air transportation." In the extensive hearings that followed, proponents of airline deregulation described how fares were artificially high because no competition was allowed. Some airlines saw opportunities to increase their routes, but most industry officials predicted chaos. The enactment of such a law, industry representatives said, could cause serious trouble for every segment of the system and result not in greater access and lower costs but in reduced convenience and increased fares.

Typical were the comments of Arthur A. Kelly, president of Western Airlines. Lower fares, he said, would mean lower costs on popular routes, but cutbacks in service of less profitable routes. He predicted fare wars, the addition of new firms that would hurry pilots through training, less attention to airplane maintenance, and, in the end, fewer airlines to serve the public. Kelly also emphasized his belief that although economic and safety regulations were handled by separate organizations (the CAB and FAA), in fact they were closely linked.

Other opponents of deregulation agreed: they feared that open skies would overload the FAA's ability to oversee the industry. In addition, safety might be sacrificed to fill

Since economic deregulation of the airline industry in 1979, more than two dozen new airline carriers entered the market. Many of the new companies offered cheaper fares. As a result, more Americans are travelling by air today than ever before.

Close Up Foundation

147

seats. To keep company profit levels high, pilots might be forced to fly more often in bad weather or with "short" fuel.

However, proponents (including United Airlines and Continental Airlines) predicted that competition would benefit consumers and increase opportunities for airline companies. William Coleman, secretary of the Department of Transportation under President Ford, emphasized that safety would not be affected because the legislation would only affect economic regulation. "Safety is not handled by CAB, it is handled by FAA . . . There is nothing in this legislation which in any way will affect safety . . . ."

When Jimmy Carter became president in 1977, he joined in the support for deregulation. In 1978, after numerous hearings and more than 4,000 pages of written testimony, the Airline Deregulation Act was signed into law. The guiding policy for the CAB was now to increase competition with the airline industry by helping new carriers enter the market and preventing monopolistic practices. The policy was also to maintain service to small, isolated communities. The CAB was to use its remaining authority over economic, routing, and pricing practices to advance innovative, more efficient, and cheaper service "consistent with public convenience and necessity." The CAB was also to be phased out by January 1, 1985.

After Deregulation

What changes—if any—in the Federal Aviation Administration and its regulation of safety have resulted from deregulation? Were the proponents of economic deregulation right in their belief that consumers would benefit from lower fares, increased competition, and new opportunities for airlines? Or has airline safety suffered, as opponents feared, and air service decreased?

As before, the FAA today continues to be responsible for establishing and enforcing safety standards covering all aspects of civil aviation. As in the original Bureau of Air Commerce, the training and certification of air personnel is a primary concern—although now, in addition to pilots, these workers include navigators, mechanics, flight engineers, air-traffic controllers, parachute riggers, and aircraft dispatchers. Other concerns continue to be the manufacture, maintenance, and operation of aircraft; the development of air-traffic rules and regulations; and the allocation of the use of U.S. air space. More recent areas of concern include security measures at airports, expansion and modernization of airport facilities, and exhaust emissions from aircraft (the latter in conjunction with the Environmental Protection Agency). Operation of the air-traffic control network continues to be one of FAA's most important safety functions. The FAA also continues the tradition of promoting the industry it regulates. For example, one of its offices is devoted to educating the public, particularly schoolchildren, about aviation. As already noted, the National Transportation Safety Board continues to be responsible for investigating civil aviation accidents, with FAA cooperation. The NTSB also makes independent recommendations to improve safety.

One change in FAA's operations is that the FAA took over the reduced regulation of domestic routes and fares from the CAB in 1982, with maximum reliance on competition. Another change concerns new airline companies. Since 1979, more than two dozen new air carriers have entered the market—and existing airlines have added new routes—to take advantage of new opportunities in such highly trafficked (and profitable) areas as the shuttles between New York and Washington, D.C. The FAA has not only had to provide certification, but

it has had to inspect operations, aircraft, and maintenance for the new companies.

One result of the increased competition has been lower fares, as predicted. More and more people are flying. *Time* magazine (September 1, 1986) described the change this way: "What was long an elitist and expensive but comfortable means of transportation has been transformed into a democratic, cut-rate, mass-transit system that is straining to serve the new hoard of passengers." And business travelers, long the mainstay of the airline trade, are complaining.

Another result is that the FAA's push for expansion and modernization of airport facilities has been made more urgent by the crowds of people arriving and departing—and waiting. Sometimes mechanical problems are the reason for waiting; most often it is that planes cannot depart because there is no space to land at their destination. The FAA reported that in the first seven months of 1986, delays for flights were up 30 percent over the same time period for 1985. At a few of the busiest airports, delays were up 40 percent. The FAA claims that cities say that the FAA needs to hire more air-traffic controllers.

The cities have a good point. In 1981, air-traffic controllers went on strike, citing increased job stress. President Ronald Reagan fired the 12,000 controllers because they were federal workers who had violated their union's no-strike clause. The FAA had to scramble for new recruits and use supervisory personnel to control traffic at the same time that airlines were offering more flights and were working to attract new business by offering low-cost, no-frills flights.

As the proponents of deregulation were correct in predicting that consumers would benefit from increased competition, so were opponents correct in predicting that airline safety would be jeopardized. An example was the accident in

The task of investigating air crashes lies with the National Transportation Safety Board (NTSB). After determining the cause of a crash, the NTSB makes specific recommendations to prevent similar tragedies in the future.

which an Air Florida jet crashed into a bridge across the Potomac River shortly after takeoff from National Airport in Washington, D.C. The accident occurred on a snowy day in January 1982. A major reason for the crash was found to be that the regulations governing deicing were inadequate, particularly for pilots with little experience flying in snowy, icy weather. If the industry had not been deregulated, points out former pilot John Nance in his book *Blind Trust,* Air Florida would not have been flying jets to Washington. Instead, the pilot would have stayed in Florida, shuttling people between warm Florida cities in propellor planes. The FAA has since issued comprehensive regulations on deicing procedures.

Nance points out that the shortage of inspectors is another safety hazard resulting from deregulation. The FAA is allowing some small airlines to be "on their honor." The October 1983 crash of an Air Illinois flight in Pinckneyville, Illinois, which killed 48 people, bears out his

contention. In its investigation, the NTSB found that the airline had been falsifying its maintenance records and reports to the FAA. As a result, the NTSB strongly recommended that FAA inspectors make more onsite inspections to confirm the accuracy of airline records.

In March 1986, FAA officials admitted that they had not anticipated that so many new airline companies (more than two dozen since 1979) would be set up after deregulation. The FAA had also not anticipated that the airlines would contract out their maintenance work. Both of these effects strained the FAA's ability to ensure that safety standards were met. Nevertheless, it is important to note that—despite an increase in air traffic, a shortage of air-traffic controllers, and abnormal weather patterns—accident rates and fatalities have declined fairly steadily since the Airline Deregulation Act was passed.

The Federal Aviation Administration is required to report to Con-

gress each year on the effects of airline deregulation on the level of air safety. The executive summary of the report made in January 1986 emphasizes the decline in aviation-related accidents. The major points of the summary are as follows.

- Activity in all segments of commercial aviation, including air carriers, commuter carriers, and air taxis increased in 1984 over previous years.

- The increase in activity, together with changes in commercial operating practices, created delays at major airports. To avoid excess airborne holding and to maintain a high level of safety, the FAA took steps to reduce "peaking" at selected airports.

- The rates for total accidents and fatal accidents declined for air carriers in 1984 and represented the best annual record since deregulation.

- In 1984, the FAA increased the number of safety inspectors by 25

149

Economic deregulation, the air-traffic controllers' strike, and abnormal weather patterns have all strained the ability of the FAA to supervise the airline industry and ensure passenger safety. To compensate for these problems, the FAA has recently hired more than 500 new safety inspectors and has prohibited planes from taking off until they are cleared to land at their destination.

percent; introduced the Safety Activity Functional Evaluation Program to assess new staffing requirements, inspector qualifications, and training requirements; and began the National Air Transportation Inspection Program (NATI) to study the efficiency and effectiveness of FAA inspection and surveillance programs.

- As a result of these safety reviews, along with the increased numbers of air carriers and passengers, the Department of Transportation expects to hire more FAA inspectors over the next three years.

- As a result of the NATI program, the FAA found that most operators complied with federal aviation regulations. The FAA also identified problems that will require regulatory changes.

- In cases of noncompliance with federal aviation regulations, the FAA took immediate corrective actions. Other short-term initiatives, such as enhanced inspector training, were also implemented.

The FAA is acting on its recommendations. The agency has hired more than 500 new inspectors. Fines for violations of FAA regulations have risen from $1.4 million in 1984 to $3 million in 1985. In 1986 one airline alone was fined $2 million for violations of FAA regulations for airplane maintenance.

Problems related to deregulation remain. Now that airlines are free to set their own fares, consumers are often confused with so many to choose from. Do flights that cost more offer better safety features? Travel agents are also confused. In some cases, they receive so little commission that, for the first time

in history, they are starting to charge customers for their services. Many small cities no longer have scheduled air service. Delays continue to mount, with the FAA blaming weather, increasing air traffic, and overscheduling of flights at some airports. One former senator is suing for false imprisonment because the airline would not let him off the plane after a lengthy delay made the reason for his flight unnecessary. Some of the new and some of the older airlines have failed. Others have merged. Some critics have suggested that the air-transport system has returned to the chaos of *laissez-faire* that produced the push for regulation in the 1920s. Others feel that as poorly managed companies go out of business, competition will help order return. Still others point out that the true results of the Airline Deregulation Act are not yet known.

The 12,000 air-traffic controllers fired in 1981 have not yet been replaced; and not until they are back at least to their former numbers will it be clear if the exasperating delays will persist.

What is noteworthy is that questions of aviation safety are being addressed, even in the "chaos" of *laissez-faire* in the 1980s. For example, new regulations are being developed on deicing procedures in reaction to specific accidents, just as new regulations were made in the 1930s in reaction to accidents involving Knute Rockne and Will Rogers. Airlines agree that current ground delays are being handled more safely than before: instead of letting airplanes "stack up" in the air—circling and waiting to land—they now are required to wait on the ground at their departure point until there is room to land at their destination. The figures are undeniable. The accident rate per 100,000 miles flown has steadily declined since economic deregulation. Although problems still exist in aviation, federal regulation continues to perform its most important function—safety.

Activities

1. Reading Between the Lines

In his article, John M. Palguta explains that people sometimes "blow the whistle" on a government agency or business to expose waste, fraud, or mismanagement to the public. Look through your local newspaper to see if you can find a recent incident of whistle blowing. Find out what motivated the person to "blow the whistle" on their coworkers and bosses. What price have they had to pay for their efforts? Has safety or efficiency improved? In the long run, do you think whistle blowing is an effective way to improve the performance of a business or government agency?

2. Developing Your Own Perspective

The bureaucracy affects virtually every aspect of your daily life. Literally hundreds of regulatory commissions and agencies determine such things as the amount of chlorine permitted in the water you drink, the number of television stations to which your town can have access, and the amount of impact a car bumper can withstand.

Make a list of the ways that the federal government affects your life. Do you think there is too much or too little government regulation? How might your life be different if there weren't any government regulation?

3. Becoming an Active Citizen

Without the thousands of people who make up the bureaucracy, the programs and services provided by the government could not be carried out. Try to find out as much as you can about this vital part of our government.

■ Contact a representative of a local business or industry, and ask how the bureaucracy regulates their operation. Does this person think that government regulations are a burden or that they are necessary to ensure safety and competition?

■ Locate any extension offices of a federal agency in your area. Call the office, and find out what the office is responsible for and who or what they regulate. See if you can arrange a meeting to discuss their jobs, their feelings about whistle blowers, and what they think of government regulations.

Most important, become aware of the hundreds of ways that government regulations affect your community.

★ ★ ★ ★ ★ ★ ★ ★ ★ ★

INTEREST GROUPS

6. Interest Groups

In This Chapter

In this century, America has witnessed a continuous growth in the number of interest groups. During the Progressive era many citizens banded together to fight exploitation of workers, unfair business practices, and corruption in government. In more recent times, citizens have organized around a wide variety of issues such as equal rights, the environment, and nuclear arms.

The Growth of Interest Groups

It is hard to determine the exact number of interest groups that exist today, since groups form and disband as the issues change. Some experts estimate that there are more than 10,000 interest groups in America. Several factors account for the large number of such groups. One is the sheer size of our country and the variety of people, occupations, levels of wealth and education, and ethnic origins that are found in the United States. Also important is the decentralized nature of our political system. The principles of federalism and separation of powers allow interest groups many opportunities to exercise political influence. They seek to persuade opinion on local, state, and national issues.

Economic concerns account for a large number of interest groups. Business groups are concerned with government regulation of industry, tax laws, government subsidies, and international trade policies. Interest groups are also formed to represent a certain occupation or profession. For example, teachers, doctors, lawyers, and farmers all have organizations that present their views to elected officials. In addition, ideological or single-issue groups are created to educate elected officials and the public on issues of national importance. These groups represent a wide variety of conservative and liberal viewpoints.

To build support for their cause, lobbyists talk to members of Congress, meet with congressional aides, and testify before congressional committees. Although critics claim that lobbyists exert undue influence on Congress, others say that lobbyists publicize important issues and provide legislators with vital information.

Lobbying

When interest groups try to influence the government to act in their favor, it is called lobbying. Some interest groups maintain professional staffs in Washington, D.C., to protect their interests. These staffs often include former members of Congress or former government employees.

Lobbyists use different methods to express their views to members of Congress. *Direct* lobbying involves face-to-face meetings between lobbyists and members of Congress, congressional aides, or bureaucrats. Sometimes a group of lobbyists with similar views will join together to present their case to a member of Congress; this method is called the *coalition* approach. Lobbyists also organize *indirect* lobbying campaigns that involve grassroot activities. These can include massive letter-writing campaigns in which constituents from a legislator's home district send letters to Capitol Hill expressing support or opposition to a particular piece of legislation.

Regardless of the methods lobbyists use, they all offer members of Congress the same thing—information. Lobbyists provide busy senators, representatives, and other government officials with information about the concerns they represent and their position on pending legislation. The main purpose of lobbying is to educate public officials about a specific point of view.

Political Action Committees

Interest groups are not political parties. They do not nominate candidates for political office. But they can try to influence the outcome of elections. Many interest groups form political action committees (PACs), through which they solicit funds from their members. This money can then be contributed to individual candidates or

political parties who support the PAC's interests. In addition, interest groups can work to defeat the candidates they oppose by sponsoring negative ad campaigns. There has been a tremendous growth in the number of PACs over the past decade and an enormous increase in the sum total of their campaign contributions.

The large expansion of PACs occurred after Congress passed campaign finance reform laws in 1974. These laws stated that an individual could donate only $1,000 to a candidate running for public office, making it impossible for wealthy individuals to contribute vast sums of money to political campaigns. But the campaign contribution limit for interest groups was set at $5,000. Many interests groups formed PACs and began fundraising efforts to collect money for the candidates they supported. Today, there are more

than 4,000 PACs in the United States.

Many people, both in and out of Congress, fear that candidates who accept large sums of money from PACs owe those PACs favors. The concern is that legislators who owe their elections to PAC money will feel obligated to pass legislation favorable to the group's interests. PACs claim that campaign contributions do not influence members of Congress. On the contrary, PACs claim that they serve as a link between the voters and the candidates and make it possible for more people to be involved in the electoral process.

PACs—and interest groups in general—are a permanent fixture in American politics. While the extent of their influence on the decisionmaking process may be debated, PACs provide many people with the opportunity to participate in government.

Lobbying: The Good, the Bad, and the Pinstriped

Nancy M. Neuman

Nancy M. Neuman is president of the League of Women Voters, an organization that promotes voter participation and public education on a variety of political issues. She has been a member of the League since 1966, serving as a local League president, president of the Pennsylvania League, and a member of the national board of directors. In her article, Ms. Neuman discusses lobbying and the public interest.

If ever a profession needed a public relations makeover, it's lobbying. The very mention of the word conjures up distasteful images of pinstriped, cigar-chomping power brokers sneaking about the halls of power with money-stuffed briefcases and evil intentions.

The reason for public mistrust of lobbyists is that most people believe that lobbyists exert undue influence on the legislative process. Lobbyists—or at least the ones we imagine—are concerned not with producing legislation that serves the public good, but that serves the more narrow interests of the people who sign lobbyists' paychecks: the special interests.

However, it's not always that way. Lobbyists come in all shapes, sizes, and genders. They don't all operate in the shadows. And most importantly, they don't lobby just on "special interest" issues.

For example, the League of Women Voters has a full complement of professional lobbyists and an army of volunteer lobbyists—all working in the public interest on issues ranging from civil rights to taxes to the environment. That's hardly the stuff of which the popular image is made.

Whether a lobbyist works for a *special interest* or the *public interest* generally depends on whether you agree with his or her position. While most lobbyists couch their arguments in terms of the public good, it's their real motivations that don't always bear up well under closer scrutiny.

Why Allow Lobbying Anyway?

If lobbyists have the capacity to distort the processes of government, why do we permit it? For one thing, lobbying is an exercise of the constitutional right to free speech. James Madison addressed the issue in his discussion of factions in *The Federalist Papers.* While recognizing the threat such narrow interests pose, Madison argued that in a large pluralistic society, creating a balance in the marketplace of ideas is preferable to suppressing the right to free speech.

But does that balance really exist? Frankly, no. The reality is that there's a very real imbalance in the marketplace of ideas. The reason? Money.

Lobbying and Money

If you have money in Washington, you can afford a number of valuable weapons for your arsenal. You can afford the most expensive lobbyists, lawyers, and public relations experts. You can

pay for the computers, mailing lists, and fancy offices to help them do their jobs. You can buy television, radio, and newspaper ads to get public and congressional attention. You can publish books and leaflets to amplify your message. Money is a big advantage.

Also, the marked increase in the cost of running a campaign makes legislators much more susceptible to the persuasions of lobbyists who come equipped with money from political action committees (PACs). PACs are the fund-raising arms of lobbying organizations. They distribute campaign funds to candidates and parties. One need not look far to find testimony to the influence of special interests with ideas to sell and lots of money to sweeten the deal.

That's why the government keeps track of who's lobbying Congress by requiring them to register and report on their activities. At least we now know who is spending what to lobby whom.

If the money were spread out across the political spectrum, then we'd have the balance that Madison sought. But it's not. Money has a way of clustering on one side of an issue, and over a range of issues. It tends to cluster on one side of the political spectrum.

What About the Rest of Us?

It's not just big business and special interests that have lobbyists. There are public interest organizations like the League of Women Voters, civic associations, trade groups, student groups, church organizations, environmental groups, and many more making their cases in Washington—all competing for Congress's attention.

And those lobbyists do more than just whisper in an elected official's ear. In many cases, they function as a resource for senators and representatives—gathering data, counting votes, cajoling the press, and sometimes even drafting legislation. I know my organization frequently works closely with members of Congress to draft bills and develop legislative strategies.

The fact is that Congress depends on the Washington lobbying community for its expertise on the issues. No member of Congress can learn the intricate details of every issue. Even congressional staffers are hard-pressed to master all aspects of an issue. Between the number of issues and the weight of the congressional mail, the workload is just too great. So Congress often turns to lobbyists for help. In this way, knowledge is power. And indeed, lobbyists do better when they have knowledge to sell. That's what citizen organizations like the League of Women Voters depend on. We can't afford to wrap our message in high-priced wrapping paper; it has to sell on its own merits.

You're a Lobbyist, Too

Madison's balance may be tipped, but it's not broken altogether. It's important to remember, too, that members of Congress pay a great deal of attention to what their constituents say. As Speaker of the House Jim Wright says in his book *You and Your Congressman*:

> With exceptions so rare that they are hardly worth mentioning, members of Congress positively do read their mail. Moreover, they are interested in its contents. The mood and tenor of the daily mail from home is a recurring topic of conversation in the rear of the House and Senate chambers or around the coffee cups in the dining rooms of the Capitol.

So the power of the people cannot be ignored. But it can be overstated. While members of Congress remember who elected them, they also remember who paid for their campaign. To be sure, the balance that Madison hoped for is missing. The narrow special interests are over-represented in Washington, and the result has been a number of pieces of legislation that serve the interests of a very few at the expense of very many.

But the cynical cry that the people's voice is never heard is just plain wrong. The people can make their case—by letting public officials know where they stand and by supporting public interest organizations that can help hold Congress accountable to the people who elected them.

Questions to Consider

1. According to the author, what is the difference between a special interest lobby and a public interest lobby?

2. How would you respond to the question: "If lobbyists have the capacity to distort the processes of government, why do we permit it?"

3. Do you agree with the author that money buys power and influence in Washington? Why or why not?

THE LOBBYISTS ARE LOOKING FOR A FEW FORMER LAWMAKERS TO JOIN THEM

Lobbyists and Lobbying

Michael Ware

Michael Ware is director of legislative affairs for Conoco, Inc. Prior to his present position, he was director of regulatory reform and consumer affairs for the National Association of Manufacturers and an aide to former Representative David Treen (R-La.). In his article, Mr. Ware explains why he views lobbyists as an indispensable part of our political system.

Senator James Reed of Missouri once said, "A lobbyist is anyone who opposes legislation I want." Probably most people feel that way. Traditionally, lobbyists have been envisioned as unshaven, cigar-smoking political "fixers" carrying money-filled bags so they can bribe legislators. This image—besides being negative—implies that all lobbyists are men. In the past, that may have been true, but today, women comprise a large percentage of the working lobbyists in Washington.

Although the term "lobbyist" is held in low esteem, everyone is, to some degree, a lobbyist. Any person who attempts to persuade someone with political power, whether it is in regard to community activities, the PTA, or social welfare programs, is actually lobbying.

What Is a Lobbyist?
Legally, a lobbyist is a petitioner of the government, exercising a right granted in the First Amendment of the U.S. Constitution:

> Congress shall make no laws...prohibiting...the right of the people peaceably to assemble, and to petition the government for a redress of grievances.

The assumption that all individuals and groups are entitled to representation in the making of public decisions forms the basis for all lobbying activities. It is the essence of participatory government.

Political analyst Lester W. Milbrath describes lobbying this way:

- Lobbying relates only to governmental decisionmaking. Decisions made by private organizations or by corporations may be influenced by special interests within those organizations or from without, but they do not affect the entire body politic.

- All lobbying is motivated by a desire to influence governmental decisions.

- Lobbying implies the presence of an intermediary or representative who provides a link between citizens and governmental decisionmakers. A citizen who, of his own volition and by his own means, sends a message to a governmental decisionmaker is not considered

THAT'S THE SENATOR WHO THE LOBBYISTS THINK IS THE **SWING VOTE** ON THE NEW TRADE BILL. LAST WEEK ALONE HE ATE **27 LOBSTER DINNERS,** WENT ON 5 **VACATIONS,** SAW 12 **SPORTING EVENTS,** AND RECEIVED 3 TONS OF INFORMATIONAL PAMPHLETS AND BROCHURES

NO MORE, PLEASE... NO MORE.

a lobbyist—though he is attempting to influence governmental decisions.

■ All lobbying involves communication. Without communication, it is impossible to influence a decision.

Broadly defined, then, lobbying is the stimulation and transmission of communication by someone other than a citizen acting on his own behalf directed to a governmental decisionmaker with the hope of influencing decisions.

"If It Walks Like a Duck..."
If this definition is correct, why then is lobbying often viewed as corrupt? The reasons are simple. The general assumption is that the "public interest" is somehow subverted by the lobbying process. The defeated party in a political battle often charges that the opponent won because of the evil activities of lobbyists. Citizens readily accept these charges because they confirm their preconceptions. The public generally receives only negative information about lobbyists.

Given this kind of public image, it's no wonder lobbyists call themselves by different titles, such as "Washington representative," "legislative liaison," or "coordinator of government affairs."

Borrowing an analogy from the late Senator Sam Ervin (D-N.C.), however, "If it walks like a duck, sounds like a duck, and when I see it, it is always in the company of other ducks, I just naturally assume it is a duck."

For the same reason, some groups attempt to disassociate themselves from the negative image of lobbying by proclaiming that they are "public interest" lobbyists in contrast to "special interest" lobbyists. They refer to their own activities as educational and those of their opponents as lobbying. In other words, sometimes a duck prefers to be seen as a peacock.

Lobbyists: Sources of Information
Whatever titles are used, the principal function of a lobbyist is education and the principal commodity is information.

In every session of Congress, more than 20,000 pieces of legislation are introduced. The subjects of these bills cover every aspect of American society: energy, environment, health care, job safety, the economy, and many other complex issues. No representative or senator can be an expert in all of these fields, yet expertise is often required in making decisions on the issues. Although members of Congress rely on their staff to assist them, most staff members spend their time doing constituent services, such as responding to letters from people in their districts or helping constituents solve problems with government agencies. Congressional staff is also constrained by the enormous complexity of issues and the amount of work that is required of them. They too need outside expertise. This expertise is provided by the lobbyist.

On many occasions, the lobbyist is the only individual to whom legislators and staff can look to for the specialized information they need. Without the information provided by the lobbyist, the legislative process would be severely hampered.

Lobbyist: Spokesperson for Organized Interests
In a complex society, everyone cannot come to a town meeting or go to Washington, D.C., to present their views. People need someone to act for them when they cannot. Members of Congress thus "hear" from their constituents by listening to a business lobbyist, a labor lobbyist, or a consumer lobbyist. Combined with the letters

Types of Lobbyists

Political Interest Groups

Organizations whose members hold similar viewpoints on issues. Examples include:

- American Conservative Union—lobbies on all issues in which conservatives are interested
- Americans for Democratic Action—lobbies on all issues in which liberals are interested
- American Security Council—funds research on national security and supports a strong national defense
- Common Cause—lobbies on issues such as open government, public financing of political campaigns, defense spending, and energy
- Council for a Livable World—lobbies for arms control and reduced military spending
- Sierra Club—lobbies on environmental issues including energy, water resources, and land use

Foreign Governments

Foreign nations are permitted to hire lobbyists to represent their views. Examples include:

- Canada—lobbies on issues such as acid rain, fishing rights, and U.S. trade policy.
- Israel—lobbies on issues such as military aid, U.S. policy in the Middle East, and U.S. intervention on behalf of Soviet Jews.
- Japan—lobbies on trade issues such as quotas on automobiles, agricultural products, and electronic equipment; and restrictions on foreign investment in the United States.
- Mexico—lobbies on issues such as immigration and border control, oil imports, and foreign aid.

Professional Lobbyists

Washington lawyers with extensive personal connections often offer their services as lobbyists. Examples of such law firms and their clients include:

- Arnold & Porter—Canadian Meat Council, Embassy of Switzerland, Philip Morris Inc., Recording Industry Association of America
- Covington & Burling—American Watch Association, American Telephone and Telegraph (AT&T), General Electric Company, National Football League, Procter and Gamble Company
- Shaw, Pittman, Potts, & Trowbridge—Federal Express Corporation, Knights of Columbus, People Express Airlines, Wisconsin Power and Light Company
- Walker Associates—Anheuser-Busch Companies, Inc., Ford Motor Company, Goodyear Tire Company, International Business Machines Corporation (IBM), Union Carbide Corporation

Corporations, Unions, and Trade Associations

Some organizations have their own lobbyists who are part of the companies' "government relations" divisions. Examples of these organizations and the issues on which they have lobbied include:

- Dr. Pepper Company—nutrition, health, food safety, franchise matters, and bottle laws
- Gulf Oil Company—legislation affecting the oil and gas industry
- Major League Baseball—legislation affecting professional sports
- American Federation of Labor and Congress of Industrial Organizations (AFL-CIO)—legislation affecting workers
- American Gas Association—legislation affecting the natural gas industry
- American Hospital Association—legislation affecting the health care industry

---

legislators receive from the people back home, this assists members of Congress in representing the people who elected them.

The presentation of the people's views is a service for which there is no substitute. Officials might find other sources for the information that lobbyists provide, but they could never find a substitute for the representational function of lobbyists. This function is also the one most clearly protected by the constitutional right to petition.

Former Representative Emanuel Celler of New York sums up his view:

It is true that the pressures generated by a well-organized group can become irritating. But despite this, I believe that too much lobbying is not as dangerous as too little. The congressman may know or suspect that there are serious opposing considerations to legislation, but they are simply not presented. He is faced with a dilemma as to how far he should go to supply the omission.

In addition, the lobbyist has a responsibility to protect the legitimate interests of his or her employer and to keep the employer informed on specific and general trends that affect the lobbyist's business or special interest.

To those not familiar with the workings of Congress, this may seem to be a rather insignificant assignment. However, most lobbyists work for someone who is located in another part of the country and who, in many instances, lacks a detailed understanding of the legislative process. The employer or the constituent who is made

Origin of the Term "Lobbyist"

The term "lobbyist" can be traced back to the early nineteenth century when citizens waited in the lobbies and hallways outside legislative chambers to talk to—and influence—their elected representatives. The phrase "lobby-agents" was first used in 1829 to describe special favor-seekers who congregated in the New York state capitol lobby in Albany, New York. The term was shortened to "lobbyist" and quickly spread around the country. By the mid-1830s, the word "lobbyist" was being used at the U.S. Capitol to describe persons attempting to influence a legislator's decision on a particular bill.

aware of the present political situation and of possible future governmental actions is a much more knowledgeable individual than the one who operates in a political vacuum.

There are many methods by which lobbyists get their views presented to legislators. There is the *direct* approach—meeting with members of Congress and their staffs. There is the *coalition* approach—where a group of people all working toward the same goal join together to present a collective viewpoint. And there is the *indirect* approach—where special interests attempt to influence the constituents of a legislator by conducting local or grassroots campaigns. Every lobbyist will probably utilize all of these methods or a combination of them at one time or another. Whatever the method, by whomever conducted, the purpose remains the same—to educate the legislator to a specific point of view.

Indispensable Parts of Our Political System

The fundamental questions remain: What contributions do lobbyists make to the political system as a whole? Do these contributions tend to make the political system more or less workable?

Many congressional officials claim they could function adequately without lobbyists. However, I think lobbyists are indispensable to our political process. Cutting off lobbying communications would eliminate a valuable source of creativity. There is no assurance that government on its own could discover all the possible alternatives to our problems. As a matter of fact, there is a great deal of evidence that points to the opposite.

A decisionmaker whose mind is made up may well have to have new points of view forcefully presented before he or she can perceive and accept them. The clash of viewpoints between contesting groups is not only informative, it is also creative. According to philosopher John Stuart Mill, the best way to teach the realities of life is to hear the opposition. Let the position be challenged, and let the challenge fail. This method was considered by Mill to be so important that he recommended inventing a challenging position if a real one was not forthcoming. Thus, formerly unperceived alternatives may arise from the newly created challenge.

Through lobbyists and lobby groups, officials know what the effects of a given policy will be and how citizens will react to that policy. The lobbyist defines opinions regarding government issues in real and specific terms to a degree that cannot be achieved through political parties, the mass media, opinion polls, and staff assistants.

There is good reason to conclude that the political system without lobbyists would not produce wiser or more intelligent decisions. Instead, the assumption could be made that if we had no lobbyists, they would probably have to be invented to improve the functioning of our political system.

Questions to Consider

1. Why do you think the public receives only negative information about lobbying and lobbyists?

2. Do you think lobbyists represent the people or the interests of the organizations who hire them?

3. Do you agree with the author that lobbyists are an indispensable part of our political system? Why or why not?

A Member of Congress Looks at Lobbying

Senator Malcolm Wallop

Malcolm Wallop (R-Wyo.) was elected to the U.S. Senate in 1976. He previously served in the Wyoming State Senate and the Wyoming House of Representatives. In his article, Senator Wallop examines lobbying and lobbyists from a legislator's point of view.

Lobbying is an integral part of our system of government. It's been around as long as legislators have, and at one time in the history of our country, lobbyists were referred to collectively as the "third house of Congress."

Registered professional lobbyists help to inform Congress and the general public about problems and issues. Lobbyists stimulate public debate, open a path to Congress for the wronged and needy, and inform Congress of the practical aspects of proposed legislation—whom it would help, whom it would hurt, who is for it, and who is against it.

Although the term *lobbyist* often carries negative connotations, in the eyes of a legislator a lobbyist is someone who voices support or opposition on a particular issue. Paid or unpaid, a Washington attorney or your hometown neighbor, a lobbyist is *anyone* with an interest in legislation. A lobbyist is not always the paid and powerful, but is often the needy or the threatened. Any citizen with a concern about a particular issue can function as a lobbyist merely by contacting an elected official. Any person who writes a member of Congress expressing an opinion on an issue is, in effect, lobbying for a special interest. And, in my opinion, the "lobbyists" I listen to the most, and whose advice I seek most often, are the constituents from my home state of Wyoming.

In fact, a recent survey of legislators and their staffs found that lawmakers are influenced more by letters from individual constituents, press clippings from hometown papers, constituent surveys, and meetings with constituents than by lobbyists.

Be that as it may, Washington is filled with people who, as a paid profession, visit the offices of members of Congress with the intention of influencing lawmakers in some way. The how, when, and who depends upon the issue, the lobbyist, and the legislator. But as organizations seek to enact laws that suit their purpose, they must realize they are not alone in seeking the attention of Congress. There are nearly 20,000 lobbyists in Washington, an average of about thirty-five for each member of Congress. Lobbyists can be economists, association executives, lawyers, or publicists. Yet they all have something in common—in their eyes, their issue is the most important and the most pressing.

Congressional committee assignments play a big part in determining a lobbyist's involvement with a particular member of Congress. Not only is it advantageous for a lobbyist to have a sympathetic ear, it is also advantageous to find someone who can do something about a particular issue. As a member of the Finance Committee—the Senate's tax-writing pencil and eraser—I am lobbied extensively by financial institutions, realtors, insurance executives, small businesses, and a wide array of other groups, all of which try to preserve their special interests.

As a member of the Energy and Natural Resources Committee, I often hear from the oil and gas industry, the coal industry, independent drillers and refiners, and other energy interests. The list goes on. Lobbyists' contact with a legislator occurs throughout the legislative process—when a bill is first introduced, being considered in committee, or debated on the Senate floor.

But it is when the committee is in the heat of a markup session (where they put certain things in the bill and take certain things out) that lobbyists

are drawn to Congress much like moths to a light.

The most important point to be made is that, ultimately, legislators are responsible to their constituency. It generally does little good to lobby a member of Congress on an issue that would be detrimental to the lawmaker's home state. Instead, a lobbyist may ask members of his organization from the legislator's district to contact the member of Congress personally. That way, a lobbyist can "lobby" through the voice of a constituent—which, after all, is the most effective way to draw attention to an issue.

Although still sometimes portrayed as an evil influence, lobbying is a much "cleaner" profession than it was in the past. In prior decades, dollars were said to be passed under the table and votes bought and sold without a second thought. Today's lobbyists are much more accountable for their actions.

Professional associations and lobbying groups now use communication, education, and public

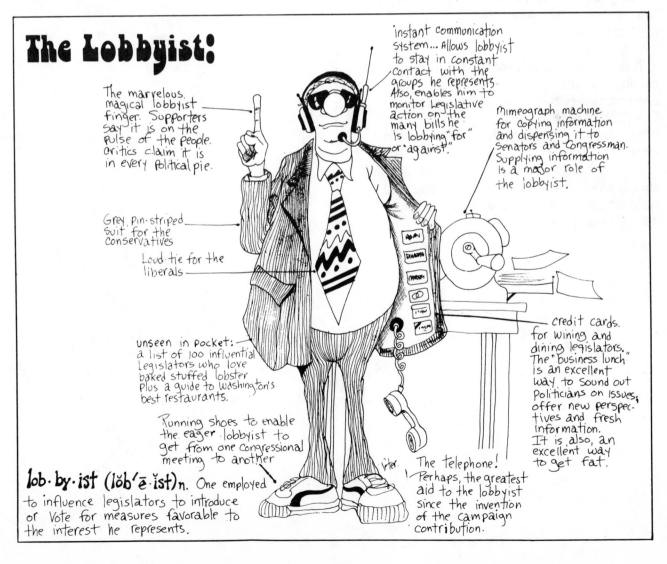

The Lobbyist:

The marvelous magical lobbyist finger. Supporters say it is on the pulse of the people. Critics claim it is in every political pie.

instant communication system... Allows lobbyist to stay in constant contact with the groups he represents. Also, enables him to monitor legislative action on the many bills he is lobbying "for" or "against."

Mimeograph machine for copying information and dispensing it to Senators and Congressman. Supplying information is a major role of the lobbyist.

Grey, pin-striped suit for the conservatives

Loud tie for the liberals

credit cards. for wining and dining legislators. The "business lunch" is an excellent way to sound out politicians on issues, offer new perspectives and fresh information. It is also, an excellent way to get fat.

unseen in pocket: a list of 100 influential legislators who love baked stuffed lobster plus a guide to Washington's best restaurants.

Running shoes to enable the eager lobbyist to get from one congressional meeting to another

lob·by·ist (lŏb′ē·ĭst) n. One employed to influence legislators to introduce or vote for measures favorable to the interest he represents.

The telephone! Perhaps, the greatest aid to the lobbyist since the invention of the campaign contribution.

Questions to Consider

1. How does the author view lobbyists? Do you think most members of Congress share his views? Why or why not?

2. Do you think lobbying is good for our system of government? Why or why not?

3. If you were a member of Congress, would you be more influenced by the views of your constituents or by lobbyists? Why?

relations techniques to support political and legislative objectives. For example, to tailor their services to new realities, the U.S. Chamber of Commerce now spends more of its manpower and budget on spreading the word than on twisting the arm. It has built a multimillion-dollar satellite communication network that beams news shows and issues forums to subscribers all over the country.

Today, a lobby's influence is directly tied to its candor, its honesty, and the quality of the arguments it is able to present to policymakers. The content and quality of a lobby's arguments are even more important these days, given the ever-increasing depth and complexity of the issues confronting our democracy—a democracy specifically designed to give every citizen the right and opportunity to participate in the process of making laws.

Political Action Committees and the Government: Two Views

Political action committees (PACs) are formed by interest groups to raise money for campaign contributions to particular candidates. After Congress passed campaign finance laws in 1974, which limited the amount of money an individual could directly contribute to a candidate, PACs became a major source of campaign funding. Their influence on elections has grown steadily—and some would claim dangerously—over the past decade. CLOSE UP asked two Washington insiders to comment on the impact PACs have on the electoral process.

Senator David L. Boren

David L. Boren (D-Okla.) was elected to the Senate in 1978 after serving as governor of Oklahoma. He sees PACs as a growing threat to our democratic system and proposes ways to change their influence.

The way that we finance election campaigns in this country cries out for change. The mushrooming influence of special-interest political action committees is beginning to threaten the basic concept of grassroots democracy.

In the most recent election, 163 successful candidates for Congress received more than half of their campaign contributions from special interest PACs instead of from individual contributors in their home states.

In the past ten years, PAC spending has grown at an explosive rate. In 1974, there were 600 PACs in existence. Today, there are more than 4,000. In 1972, PACs contributed only about $8 million to congressional campaigns. In 1984, they contributed more than $104 million. While contributions by PACs have been growing, the percentage of campaign funding provided by small donations of less than $100 has been cut in half.

In all of my election campaigns, I have followed a policy of not accepting PAC contributions. There are now only four senators left in the Senate who accept political contributions only from individual citizens.

It is frightening to consider the impact PAC contributions will have on the political system and the cost of campaigns if they continue to double every four years. When additional money is pumped into the system, it ends up being spent, and campaign costs soar. In just eight years, the average cost of winning a U.S. Senate campaign has risen from a little over $600,000 to more than $2.9 million, an increase of 385 percent!

The advantage that incumbents have over challengers is also a point of grave concern. For every $1 received by a challenger, an incumbent receives $4.50! Obviously, PACs are more interested in contributing to a member of Congress that will be around for a while—one whose vote they can influence by gaining access—than they are in contributing to an unknown challenger.

In addition, the growth in the influence of PACs further fragments our nation and its legislative bodies. It makes it increasingly difficult to reach a national consensus and holds our decisionmaking process hostage to the special interests that PACs represent.

PACs do not judge members of Congress on their overall record or personal integrity. PACs do not examine the candidate's record to see if it

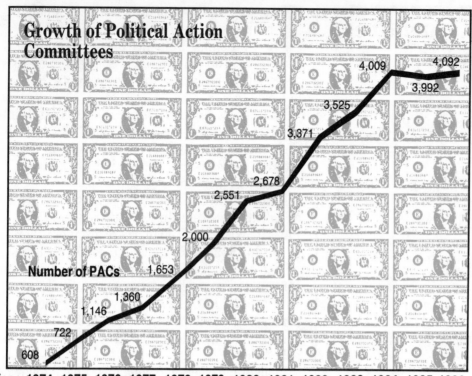

Growth of Political Action Committees

4,009
3,992
4,092
3,525
3,371
2,678
2,551
2,000
Number of PACs 1,653
1,360
1,146
722
608

Year 1974 1975 1976 1977 1978 1979 1980 1981 1982 1983 1984 1985 1986

Source: Congressional Quarterly

In 1974, Congress passed campaign finance laws which limited personal contribution to individual candidates seeking public office to $1,000 and allowed political action committees (PACs) to give up to $5,000. As a result, PACs are now a major source of campaign funds.

serves the national interest. Instead, PACs rate members of Congress solely on how they voted on bills affecting a particular interest group or single-issue constituency. Usually, the real decision about which candidate to support is made by the group's lobbyist and not by individual PAC contributors.

Interestingly, many PAC representatives have spoken with me privately about the need to limit PAC activities. The situation has become so bad that even the PACs are feeling victimized! Some members of Congress who are up for reelection now lobby PACs for as much money as possible. Indeed, some members of Congress send pointed letters to PACs asking for a contribution. They also pit one PAC against a competing PAC to assure contributions from both.

Ten senators from a broad political spectrum recently joined with me in a bipartisan effort to apply the brakes to the accelerating power of PACs. Our proposal has four main provisions:

First, it sets limits on the total amount of PAC funds that congressional candidates may receive. For House members, it would be $100,000 per election, or $125,000 if the member faced both a primary and a general election challenge. For Senate candidates, the maximum amount would range from $175,000 to $750,000, depending on the size of the state. This formula would cut in half the current amount of PAC spending.

Second, it puts contributions by PACs and by individuals on a more equal footing. Currently, PACs can contribute $5,000 per election, while individuals can contribute only $1,000. Our proposal sets the limit at $3,000 for PACs and $1,500 for individuals.

Third, it closes a loophole in the current election law that allows PACs to serve as a conduit for large individual contributions. Under the current law, it is possible for PACs to receive large individual contributions, bundle them together, and send them on to candidates without going over the $5,000 spending limit.

Fourth, it tightens the definition of what constitutes "independent" campaign spending. For example, under the current law, groups that are "independent" of a candidate are free to "attack" opponents without any spending limits. In fact, they are often staffed by former employees or consultants of a candidate's campaign committee. Under our proposal, the media would be required to provide free response time to candidates who are attacked in advertisements by these so-called independent groups.

I don't pretend that this proposal will solve all of the problems in our current election process. However, it is an important step in the right direction.

Former Solicitor General Archibald Cox stated his views very directly: "We must decide whether we want government of, by, and for the people, or government of the PACs, by the PACs, and for the PACs."

With every passing election, more and more candidates become dependent upon PACs as their principal source of campaign financing. The longer we wait to deal with the problem, the harder it will be to clean up the system.

Thomas Berglund

Thomas Berglund is chairman of AMPAC, the political action committee of the American Medical Association. Prior to his present position, he chaired the Michigan State Medical PAC. Dr. Berglund describes the many advantages that he thinks PACs give to our political system.

After an election, the nation lets out a collective sigh of relief as another frenetic campaign season comes to a close. It seems that each successive election involves more literature, more media advertis-

ing, and more television commercials. But apart from the constant barrage of candidate information (and promises), have you ever stopped to think there is something more behind all the hoopla?

Political action committees do. They recognize the need for people to band together so that they can be heard in the complex political world of today. More important, PACs encourage political participation far beyond listening to countless television spots or even casting a ballot on Election Day. PACs play a vital role in American democracy: they draw individuals into the system and enable citizens to be active in our political process.

The idea of groups of citizens joining together in political efforts goes back as far as the founding of the nation. James Madison, in writing his defense of the new Constitution, foresaw groups or "factions" as crucial to the balance of power in a representative democracy. He reasoned that if factions were encouraged to "multiply and grow," no single faction would gain too much power and remove the incentive for compromise

NEWS ITEM: NEW DANCE CRAZE SWEEPS WASHINGTON. LAWMAKERS IN RUSH TO CHOOSE PARTNERS.

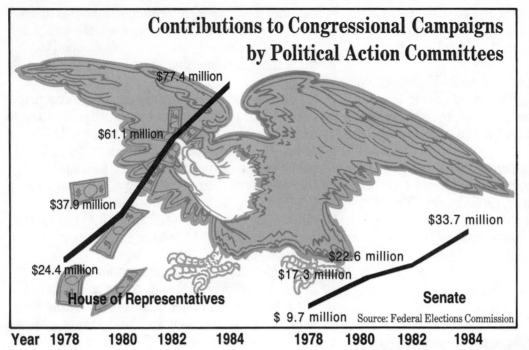

Contributions to Congressional Campaigns by Political Action Committees

$77.4 million

$61.1 million

$37.9 million

$24.4 million

House of Representatives

$33.7 million

$22.6 million

$17.3 million

$ 9.7 million   Source: Federal Elections Commission

Senate

Year   1978   1980   1982   1984   1978   1980   1982   1984

Since 1978, political action committees (PACs) have contributed more than $284 million to congressional campaigns. In the 1984 congresional campaign, the PAC that contributed the most to candidates seeking national office was the Realtors Political Action Committee, which gave more than $2 million to congressional campaign funds around the country.

with other factions in society. Political action committees are the modern-day version of Madison's 200-year-old political theory.

PACs themselves are not new to American politics. In fact, the first entry into the PAC community dates back to the 1940s, when labor unions formed political action committees on behalf of their members. In 1961, the American Medical Association created the first nonlabor PAC. However, it was the campaign reform laws of the early 1970s that provided the impetus for the growth of PACs over the past decade.

The proliferation of PACs has created political fallout far beyond what the original supporters of campaign reform ever imagined; but more often than not, the results have been exceedingly positive. First and foremost, more citizens than ever participate in the political process because PACs allow people of relatively limited means to compete on a more equal footing with people who have a lot of money. The Supreme Court has called the formation of PACs an "amplification" of the individual's political voice.

There is nothing inherently immoral or corrupting about contributing money to political campaigns. Yet, there always has been and always will be a fundamental suspicion on the part of the public of the role of money in politics. Congress has worked to alleviate some of the uneasiness by limiting the amount each PAC can

contribute to an individual candidate—thus, a candidate for public office can accept no more than $5,000 per PAC per election season.

This may seem like a lot of money until you realize that campaigns for congressional seats cost upwards of $500,000 and can run as high as $10 million for a Senate race. Even more important, however, is that very few PACs collect enough money to be able to contribute the maximum allowed in any political race. In fact, recent statistics show that the average PAC contribution amounts to only $687 per political campaign.

Given the figures and restraints, there can be no such thing as one PAC buying a legislator's vote. The fact is that when so many PACs are contributing money to so many candidates, the effect is to cancel each other out. Madison's many factions are at work.

And yet, PACs do have their critics. Many "PAC attacks" center upon the so-called relationship between the high cost of campaigning for elective office and PAC contributions, a charge with no foundation. Effective campaigning in America today requires large expenditures. It is each individual voter's decision to act independently—rather than allowing a political party or other institution to make the choice—that is responsible for rising campaign costs. One candidate must reach hundreds of thousands of independent-minded voters, and, in American society, the two most effective means of reaching those voters are also the two most expensive—television and direct mail.

One encouraging note is a study that uncovered a cause-and-effect relationship between campaign spending and voter awareness—the more money spent, the more informed the voter. However discomforting the large sums may be, who can argue with results that create a well-informed and knowledgeable American voting public?

Recent attempts to reform the current campaign financing laws raise the issue of fairness. Most proposals favor the incumbent, since a challenger would have to go to great lengths (i.e., vast amounts of personal income) to achieve recognition as a viable candidate. Two oft-mentioned proposals—limiting campaign expenditures and taxpayer financing—would actually favor incumbents, who begin reelection campaigns with the advantages of office: salary, staff, travel, communications, and free media attention.

Moreover, limits on campaign expenditures strike at the heart of our First Amendment rights. There is considerable question whether any proposal relating to expenditure limits could withstand a constitutional test. In one recent decision, the Supreme Court ruled that Congress cannot limit the amount PACs spend independently on presidential candidates without violating the First Amendment rights of freedom of speech and association.

However, there are some measures that would improve the current system. First, expanding the disclosure laws to include the hidden costs now often buried in campaign ledgers would enable the public to have the facts necessary to make informed voting decisions.

Second, increasing the limits and providing tax deductions for individual campaign contributions would further encourage people to become involved in the political process.

Third, encouraging radio and television stations to schedule debates and discussions of campaign issues would help reduce the costs of media exposure.

And, fourth, requiring that congressional candidates refund or donate to charity any campaign funds left 30 days after the election would eliminate the incentive to collect money for any purpose other than the current office at stake.

The most important fact remains: PAC contributions to congressional candidates do not represent a danger to the American political system. The diversity and large number of PACs are testimony to the health of democracy rather than to its sickness. PACs do not represent a monolith of business, health, trade, or any other special interests, but rather the interests of a pluralistic society.

Political action committees are an outgrowth of the American political process and offer an opportunity available to every American citizen—the right to have a voice in our government.

Questions to Consider

1. Do you think PACs encourage people to participate in the election process, or do they represent a danger to democracy? Why?

2. Do you think PAC contributions have caused the recent increase in campaign costs? Why or why not?

3. If you were running for Congress, would you accept campaign contributions from PACs? Why or why not?

The NRA:
A Legendary Lobbying Machine

James Madison, one of the founders of our country and proposer of the Bill of Rights, warned of the "mischiefs of faction" in *The Federalist Papers*. To counter-balance those mischiefs, a strong federal government was needed, he said. But Madison also wrote that removing the causes that led to special interests would require destroying liberty and homogenizing public opinion—creating a world of the sort characterized in George Orwell's *1984*. The right of special interest groups to lobby was made implicit in the First Amendment, which provides that "Congress shall make no law . . . abridging the freedom of speech or of the press; or the right of the people peaceably to assemble and to petition the govern ment for a redress of grievances."

Lobbying continues to be fre-quently equated with mischief. But the blatant vote-buying and bribery of the eighteenth and early nine-teenth centuries are long past. Techniques today are more sophisticated. Associations, organizations, coalitions, and cor-porations refer to their lobbying efforts as "government relations," "political affairs," and "legislative activities." Since the campaign law changes made in the 1970s, political action committees (PACs) are used to provide political support of all kinds.

Each lobby group has its own special interest, its own bias. Lob-byists are experts in their areas, capable of explaining complex sub-jects clearly and understandably. They provide statistics, analyses, position papers, and testimony to members of Congress and their staffs and to government officials. If they expect to be effective over a long period of time, the information

they provide must be honest and accurate.

Lobby groups serve as channels for information to as well as from their special-interest constituencies. To focus their efforts, lobbyists keep track of who votes for what and rate the members of Congress accord-ingly. They know what bills are com-ing up as well as the vulnerability of senators and representatives to pressure. The public may view inter-est groups with skepticism; never-theless, these groups do provide Americans with yet another way in which to gain access to and influ-ence the political system.

The National Rifle Association
One of the most effective special interest groups in recent years has been the National Rifle Association (NRA).

The NRA was founded in 1871 in New York by a group of former Union Army officers primarily to encourage competitive sport shoot-ing by persons who might have to serve in case of military emergency. Today, the NRA is the world's largest gun club with more than 3 million members and more than 12,000 affiliated local and state clubs and associations. Members come from all walks of life and include collectors as well as users of all types of firearms. Article II of the NRA's bylaws lists the following purposes and objectives:

1. To protect and defend the Con-stitution of the United States, especially with reference to the inalienable right of the indivi-dual American citizen guaranteed by such Constitu-tion to acquire, possess, transport, carry, transfer ownership of, and enjoy the

right to use arms, in order that the people may always be in a position to exercise their legitimate individual rights of self-preservation and defense of family, person, and prop-erty, as well as to serve effec-tively in the appropriate militia for the common defense of the Republic and the individual liberty of its citizens;

2. To promote public safety, law and order, and the national defense;

3. To train members of law enforcement agencies, the arm-ed forces, the militia, and the people of good repute in marksmanship and in the safe handling and efficient use of small arms;

4. To foster and promote the shooting sports, including the advancement of amateur com-petitions in marksmanship at the local, state, regional, national, and international levels;

5. To promote hunter safety, and to promote and defend hunting as a shooting sport and as a viable and necessary method of fostering the propagation, growth, conservation, and wise use of our renewable wildlife resources.

To accomplish these purposes and objectives, the NRA promotes marksmanship through a variety of programs that teach people (3 million annually) how to operate, care for, and store firearms properly and safely. Some programs, like those at summer camps, are for

The National Rifle Association was founded in 1871 to train people in the safe use of firearms and to defend the Constitution of the United States, especially with regard to Second Amendment rights. Here, NRA instructors teach the proper method of firing a handgun.

UPI/Bettmann Newsphotos

young people. Others are for women who want to protect themselves. Still others teach law enforcement and security firearms instructors (who in turn have trained nearly 1 million police officers). In addition to nationwide hunter safety programs (17 million trained), the NRA provides information to its members on all phases of hunting and wildlife management. The association also helps set up shooting ranges and conducts more than 10,000 tournaments in thirty-five shooting

disciplines each year. And the NRA selects and trains the U.S. Olympic teams.

Another service the NRA provides for its members is to staff the anti-gun-control barricades. Gun control was not a major consideration during the NRA's first fifty years. In the 1920s and 1930s, for example, when crime increased because of Prohibition and other economic and demographic changes, the NRA and its Office of Legislative Affairs supported uniform permit systems (for

purchasing and carrying firearms) for states. The association also worked with Congress on regulating possession of those kinds of weapons (such as sawed-off shotguns and machine guns) allegedly preferred by gangsters. Through the 1950s and 1960s, the NRA supported additional measures, such as waiting periods for purchase of firearms, again with the idea that such laws might keep guns out of the hands of criminals, but would not allow ordinary citizens access to

173

firearms. (The NRA has since withdrawn support for waiting periods.)

The most significant measure in which the association was involved was the Gun Control Act of 1968. With pressure from President Lyndon B. Johnson, this legislation was passed in response to the assassinations of Martin Luther King, Jr., and Robert F. Kennedy. The act:

- banned mail-order sales of firearms and ammunition;

- confined the purchase of firearms to the buyer's state of residence;

- prohibited certain classes of people (i.e., felons, fugitives, former mental patients, and drug addicts) from purchasing, receiving, or transporting firearms or ammuition in interstate commerce;

- required all persons engaged in the business of dealing with firearms to be federally licensed, to require proof of identity and residence from purchasers, and to keep records of all sales; and

- allowed importation only of firearms suitable for sporting purposes.

A major goal of the Gun Control Act was to keep people like Lee Harvey Oswald (accused killer of President John F. Kennedy) from ordering weapons by mail.

During the legislative process for the act, the NRA engineered one of its first outpourings of mail from members in protest of controls they saw as restricting their Second Amendment right to keep and bear arms. The effort was successful to some degree; opponents of the NRA saw the bill that passed as "watered down."

As the 1970s progressed, the NRA began to feel under siege. Gun-control proponents saw the act as having neither curbed crime nor mpaired criminal access to firearms. The association saw the act as having adversely affected the firearm freedoms of NRA members and other law-abiding citizens. For advocates of gun control, the answer was to pass more and tougher legislation. The NRA was seen not as a

compromiser on moderate legislation but as an obstructionist, negative lobby.

In 1975, the NRA's life members, who form the association's governing body, overturned the old guard leadership. A purely political arm—the Institute for Legislative Action (ILA) was set up. A year later, in 1976, the NRA's political action committee, the Political Victory Fund (PVF), was formed to raise money for election campaign contributions. In 1979, the Firearms Civil Rights Legal Defense Fund was established to assist members in taking legal action to protect their rights.

Thus, the NRA adopted a no-compromise position and began to acquire a reputation for legislative, political, and legal activism. It also acquired a great many more members. NRA membership rose from less than 1 million in early 1978 to 2.8 million in early 1984 and 3.1 million in early 1986.

Today, the ILA employs five full-time lobbyists and has a 65-member support and administrative staff that includes writers, researchers,

Most Americans are ambivalent about guns, particularly handguns. On the one hand, Americans want handguns controlled so criminals can't use them. On the other hand, Americans don't want them outlawed in case they need them to protect themselves and their families.

International Association of Chiefs of Police

and attorneys. Like all special-interest political units, the ILA works to influence government decisionmaking processes in such a way as to benefit NRA members by providing information, keeping track of legislation, and rating members of Congress. The ILA places particular emphasis on grassroots pressure, serving as a channel for information between NRA members and their senators and representatives in Congress. The ILA also assists NRA's local and state clubs and affiliates, providing advice and training for officers and members in legislative and political action.

The Constitutional Right to Keep and Bear Arms

The authors of the Constitution equated a standing army with tyranny and a militia with their freedom from tyranny. Thus, the Second Amendment states that "A well regulated militia, being necessary to the security of a free state, the right of the people to keep and bear arms, shall not be infringed." What the NRA stopped compromising on in 1975 was the Second Amendment right of the people to keep and bear arms.

According to proponents of gun control—for example, Handgun Control, Inc. (formerly the National Council to Control Handguns)—the right to keep and bear arms is not for each private individual, but instead relates to the purpose of a collective militia within the state. These proponents cite Supreme Court rulings in 1876, 1886, 1894, and 1934, which, they say, indicate that the Second Amendment is a guarantee to states that their militias would not be disbanded rather than a guarantee to individuals of the right to keep and bear arms in any and all instances. They quote the 1975 report of the American Bar Association, which says that, in addition to the Supreme Court decisions, "every federal court decision involving the amendment has given the amendment a collective, militia interpretation and/or held that firearms-

control laws enacted under a state's police power are constitutional. Thus arguments premised upon the federal Second Amendment, or the similar provision in the thirty-seven state constitutions, have never prevented regulation of firearms."

The NRA says that the first three cases (1876, 1886, and 1894) held only that the right to keep and bear arms "shall not be infringed by Congress" and that the first two are tainted with anti-black and anti-immigrant overtones. The association claims that the fourth case (1934) held that the National Firearms Act of 1934 was constitutional, but only because the Court did not hear evidence to the contrary. (The defendants did not appear and were not represented by counsel before the Supreme Court.)

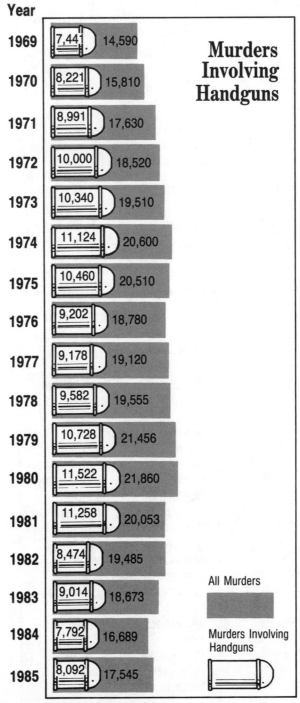

Murders Involving Handguns

Year	Murders Involving Handguns	All Murders
1969	7,441	14,590
1970	8,221	15,810
1971	8,991	17,630
1972	10,000	18,520
1973	10,340	19,510
1974	11,124	20,600
1975	10,460	20,510
1976	9,202	18,780
1977	9,178	19,120
1978	9,582	19,555
1979	10,728	21,456
1980	11,522	21,860
1981	11,258	20,053
1982	8,474	19,485
1983	9,014	18,673
1984	7,792	16,689
1985	8,092	17,545

Source: Handgun Control, Inc.

Gun control has been one of the most controversial issues of the past two decades. Supporters of gun control point out that in 1985 handguns were used to commit almost half of the murders in the United States. Opponents of gun control claim that 99.6 percent of all handguns will not be involved in any criminal activity.

175

In further supporting its view of the individual right to keep and bear arms, the NRA cites such founders as George Mason, who said, "Who are the militia? They consist of the whole people"; Patrick Henry, who said, "The militia is our ultimate safety . . . . The great object is that everyone who is able may have a gun"; and James Madison, who acknowledged an interpretation of the Second Amendment that confirmed the people "in their right to keep and bear their private arms."

What Makes a Lobby Successful?
Out of the 200 million firearms owned by Americans, approximately 60 million are handguns. The gun-control groups—spearheaded by Handgun Control, Inc., and the National Coalition to Ban Handguns—have been successful in publicizing that more than 10,000 Americans are killed with those handguns every year and that a handgun murder occurs approximately every 50 minutes. They tap the emotional responses of the American public to the victims of handguns, reminding us that handguns not only killed Martin Luther King, Jr., and Robert F. Kennedy, but also wounded President Ronald Reagan in 1981. They also tell us how handguns have killed average Americans such as a 51-year-old Las Vegas high school teacher whose student, afraid that the teacher might try to have him institutionalized, shot him to death with a small caliber pistol; an 18-year-old girl, who after being kidnapped and raped, was shot to death when she tried to get away; the son of the chair of Handgun Control, Inc., who was gunned down on the streets of San Francisco.

The NRA's message that more than 99.8 percent of U.S. firearms and 99.6 percent of U.S. handguns will not be involved in any criminal activity in any given year has not received such widespread coverage. The NRA also taps the emotional responses of the American public, pointing to survey research that says that about 350,000 Americans

every year use handguns to protect themselves from would-be burglars, robbers, rapists, assailants, and murderers. The association publicizes stories such as that of a 51-year-old Los Angeles woman who had been twice raped by the same man. He had not been apprehended, she bought a handgun, and when the man returned a third time, she ended his criminal career. Another NRA story tells of a housewife in Waco, Texas, who heard her front door window break and saw a man reach in and unlock the door. She ran to the bedroom, grabbed the handgun kept under the mattress, and when the intruder entered the bedroom and saw the gun aimed at him, he left.

The gun-control organizations have actively supported and lobbied for stricter gun-control legislation. Senator Edward M. Kennedy (D-Mass.) and Representative Peter W. Rodino, Jr. (D-N.J.), sponsored a bill that would: (1) ban the domestic manufacture of cheap handguns and the importation of parts that are used to assemble Saturday Night

---

Saturday Night Specials

Robert Sherrill explains the term "Saturday Night Specials" in his book by that name: "In the late 1950s and early 1960s, when mischievous residents of Detroit could not get their hands on guns in their hometown, they would simply hop in their cars and tool down to Toledo, Ohio, less than an hour away, where guns were sold in candy stores, flower shops, filling stations, shoeshine stands, anywhere at all. Since a great many of these purchases were made to satisfy the passions of Saturday night, Detroit lawmen began to refer to the weapons as Saturday Night Specials."

Specials (see box); (2) require a 21-day waiting period either to purchase a gun or to get a gun permit; (3) prohibit pawnshops from selling guns; and (4) mandate automatic prison sentences for anyone using a gun in the commission of a felony. But the legislation stalled.

The legislation proposed by Senator James A. McClure (R-Idaho) and Representative Harold L. Volkmer (D-Mo.) and supported by the NRA made it through the legislative process. The Firearms Owners' Protection Act, amending the Gun Control Act of 1968, had been held up in the House Judiciary Committee by its chair, Representative Rodino (one of the sponsors of the opposing legislation). It became the subject of a *discharge petition*, signed by two-thirds of the members of the House of Representatives. A discharge petition, which releases legislation from committees and brings it to the floor of the House for debate, is a rare event. Since 1800, only twenty-five out of 800 attempts have been successful in discharging legislation from committee, and only one out of twenty-five subsequently passed.

Representative Rodino released the bill just before being presented with the petition. Debate was extensive, and lobbying was heavy. Some representatives were reported to say that the NRA was so strong in their districts that they had no choice but to support the measure. Some police organizations opposed the act, saying that they believed the bill would increase the number of Americans killed by firearms each year. To demonstrate their opposition, uniformed officers stood silently outside the House doors while members entered to vote on the bill. Representative Robert Torricelli (D-N.J.) called the influence of the NRA "a genuine disgrace . . . a classic example of the power of big money and a well-orchestrated campaign by a narrow interest." Another Democrat was reported to say, "We made the hard political calculus. Do I want to spend the next five months debating one

The federal Bureau of Alcohol, Tobacco, and Firearms (BATF) is responsible for enforcing the nation's gun-control laws. The NRA charges that BATF agents violated the rights of gun owners through illegal search and seizure.

crummy vote on gun control? It's the kind of issue that could defeat me when nothing else could."

On April 10, 1986, the McClure-Volkmer bill passed the House of Representatives by a vote of 286 to 136. By May 6, a compromise bill—the compromise related to interstate traffic of concealable weapons—passed the Senate. On May 20, President Reagan signed it into law.

Dedicated Membership

Some credit for such a success is certainly due to NRA lobbyists, say NRA spokespersons. But in the end, the credit belongs to the NRA members who exercised their First Amendment freedoms and rights—freedom of speech, freedom of press, right to assemble, and right to petition the government for redress of grievances. The NRA sees the most important function of its lobbyists as acting as a channel for information between NRA

members and their representatives and senators in Congress.

When a matter of special interest to the NRA is being considered by a legislative body, the NRA informs its members so they can write their legislators. When time allows, the NRA uses its magazines, *American Rifleman* and *American Hunter*, as well as the ILA's biweekly tabloid, *Monitor*. With less time the NRA dispatches 1-page legislative alerts, telegrams, and mailgrams, and in some cases may even set up telephone trees. The NRA believes that successes depend on its having an active and involved membership.

An example of the NRA's utilization of this sort of political activism involved regulations proposed by the federal Bureau of Alcohol, Tobacco, and Firearms (BATF) in 1978. After the Gun Control Act of 1968 was passed, its enforcement was assigned to the BATF—an agency of the Department of

Treasury that formerly had the primary function of stamping out the illicit liquor trade. Problems quickly emerged with BATF interpretations of the law. For example, the law said that anyone engaged in the business of manufacturing, importing, or dealing in firearms or ammunition must be licensed, but failed to define what "engaged in the business" meant. The law further maintained that the BATF shall have access to the premises of a gun dealer during normal business hours. The BATF interpreted that to mean business premises must be separate from residences and that there should be ordinary posted business hours. The problem was that many gun dealers are actually collectors who got licenses so they could buy firearms wholesale and go to the various gun shows. Most operate from their homes. The BATF's method of enforcing the law was all too frequently seen to be

177

violating the rights of gun owners, collectors, and dealers. BATF agents often abused provisions for search and seizure, privacy rights, and warrant procedures and used techniques such as entrapment, harassment, and humiliation.

One such incident is described by author Barry Bruce-Briggs:

In Maryland, in 1971, a local pillar of the community—a boy scout leader, volunteer fireman, and gun collector—was in his bathtub when a group of armed men in beards and rough clothes—BATF agents—broke through the door. Understandably, he reached for a handy antique cap-and-ball pistol and was shot four times and left on the floor, while his wife, still in her underwear, was dragged screaming from the apartment. What had happened was that a local boy reported a hand grenade in the apartment. There was, but it was only the shell of a hand grenade. A simple records check would have been adequate to establish the resident as a gun collector, and if there was an interest in following up the matter, someone might have come and knocked on his door. He is now crippled for life.

Another such incident was related during 1980 hearings held by Senator Birch Bayh (D-Ind.) for the Senate Judiciary Committee's Subcommittee on the Constitution. Since 1960, a Virginia pharmacist, who was a long-time collector of high-quality antique guns and active in public affairs, had had the required federal firearm licenses so he could attend gun shows to display, buy, and sell. In 1966, a BATF agent made a surprise inspection of his gun collection and books. The agent complimented him on his neat books and told him he no longer needed a license. He turned his license in. The following year, four BATF agents and a police officer woke the pharmacist before dawn, announced they had a search warrant, read him his rights, and told

him they wouldn't tear up his house if he showed them where the guns were. His wife and daughter were in shock. He was advised he had been under surveillance for eighteen months and that this raid was part of a multistate raid. The agents forcefully confiscated his 70-gun collection. He was given a list of his guns, which contained no reference to their special engraving and value as antiques. Some weeks later, he was told that no charges would be pressed if he voluntarily gave up his collection. He refused. Several months later, the same offer was made if he would give up fifty of his pieces. The number dropped to nineteen, then to ten. In May 1979, three years after the raid and after further indignities but no charges, he got back all but four of the guns. As he testified in 1980, he was still hoping and working for the return of the four.

Also appearing at Senator Bayh's 1980 hearings was Richard J. Davis, the Treasury Department's assistant secretary for enforcement and operations, who oversaw the work of the BATF. It was clear from his testimony that work was still going on to ensure that BATF operations were conducted in a manner sensitive to constitutional and civil rights principles.

The proposed 1978 regulations appeared to NRA to compound the already existing problems. These regulations had been initiated by the National Council to Control Handguns—the forerunner of Handgun Control, Inc.—and required each gun manufactured to have a unique serial number, prompt reporting of thefts and losses, and reports to the Department of Treasury by each manufacturer and dealer as to the movement of guns within distribution channels (e.g., sales, receipts, transfers, losses, and inventories). Gun-control proponents saw this last requirement as giving the BATF the authority to audit the gun pipeline and see where guns were leaking out to criminals. They said that gun retailers—not the BATF—would keep the records

containing the names and addresses of individual buyers. The BATF computer would store the names of retailers, not individual owners, so the BATF could more easily trace firearms used in crimes.

The NRA activated its information channels and its all-member alert system. It warned its members that the proposed regulations would "establish a computerized national registration system" and "would set the groundwork for the stated goal of President Carter and the Justice Department: registration of all private firearms."

The National Council to Control Handguns solicited favorable comments among the media and among its then 50,000 supporters. The NRA solicited unfavorable comments from its then 1 million members. The BATF received 337,000 comments against the regulations, 7,000 for—numbers that suggest that NRA members were approximately twice as likely to comment. A year later, the proposed regulations were withdrawn.

The BATF abuses in enforcing the Gun Control Act of 1968 were one of the reasons that NRA members rose up so effectively for the McClure-Volkmer bill, which NRA members saw as reforming the 1968 Act and further protecting their Second Amendment rights. Among the changes (or "reforms") outlined by the Library of Congress Congressional Research Service are that the term "engaged in the business," which had been unevenly interpreted, is now defined as meaning the manufacture, import, or sale of firearms with "the principal objective of livelihood and profit." The bill also specifies that proof of profit is not to be required of a person who engages in the selling of firearms for criminal purposes or terrorism. The bill also relieves the problems incurred by the many gun collector/dealers who operate from their homes by allowing them to sell at temporary premises in connection with a show or event sponsored by a recognized organization interested in guns or gun use. In addition, the

registration system that was the red flag in the NRA's all-member alert for the 1978 BATF proposed regulations is now gone. The new bill prohibits the establishment of any system of registration.

Money and Volunteers
The NRA's ability to raise money and volunteers is another aspect of its success as a lobbying group. It is also another illustration of the dedication of its members. For example, Proposition 15, an initiative calling for a ban on new handgun sales and a freeze on the number of existing handguns, was on the ballot in California in 1982. Gun-control proponents saw the proposition, which guaranteed no further restrictions on rifles and shotguns, as a reasonable compromise in that it protected legitimate gun owners yet would slow handgun acquisition by criminals. The NRA saw such measures as ineffective in crime control and prevention and as a fresh assault on Second Amendment rights.

Gun-control proponents raised approximately $1 million in small contributions plus an additional $1 million from a small group of wealthy contributors. The coalition opposed to Proposition 15, Californians Against the Gun Initiative (in

which the NRA was an important element), raised approximately $3.5 million from small contributors, $3 million from the NRA, and $1 million from industry. In addition, volunteers turned out in large numbers—more of them working to defeat the initiative than in the campaigns for governor or senator. The proposition was defeated by a nearly 2-to-1 margin.

NRA members are equally involved in Senate and House races by way of their contributions to the NRA's political action committee, the Political Victory Fund (PVF). For example, PVF made contributions to twenty Senate campaigns in 1982. Seventeen of the NRA-supported candidates won, and PVF contributions were seen as the critical factor in three. In House campaigns, 80 percent of the PVF-assisted candidates were successful. The PVF is the fifth leading spender in independent campaigning. Usually the largest expenditures of PVF independent campaigns are for phone banks and bumper stickers. In 1980, Ronald Reagan was the first presidential candidate ever endorsed by the NRA.

Single Issue Purity
An important factor in keeping NRA members dedicated and active is that NRA avoids getting involved

in unrelated or peripherally related issues. The association rates candidates and participates in and contributes to election campaigns solely on the basis of candidates' stand on gun control. (If two opposing candidates are equally opposed to gun control, the NRA usually contributes to neither.) The NRA claims that the only "side" issues in which it will become involved are regulation of lobby and election activities. NRA members feel that the ability to protect Second Amendment rights might be impaired by restrictions on exercising the First Amendment freedoms of speech and press and the rights to assemble and petition the government for redress of grievances.

While the NRA is concerned about reducing the amount of violent and dangerous crime, its political activities related to crime reduction are generally tied to diminishing

Overleaf: **Since the passage of the Gun Control Act of 1968, supporters and opponents of gun control have engaged in massive advertising campaigns. Both sides seek to gain support for their position among members of the Congress and the public.**

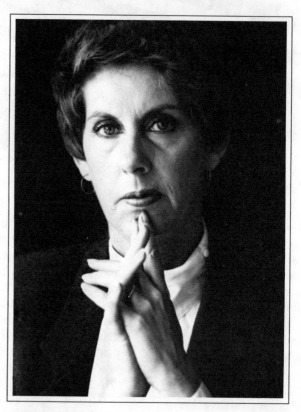

weapon-related crimes. The NRA gets involved only when it sees that the portions of an act relating to firearms and weapon-related crimes are beneficial or detrimental.

However, the NRA has become involved in pushing for speedy trials. It believes that speedy trials for career criminals—who are more likely to use firearms and commit violent crimes—decrease violent crime in the community and therefore diminish support for passage of restrictive gun-control laws.

Public Relations

Public relations efforts to keep and enlist additional members and support are essential to any lobby group. Publicity for the NRA has included an "I'm the NRA" campaign featuring a cross-section of NRA members—from a 9-year-old boy to Chuck Yeager, the first pilot to break the sound barrier. To supplement their national advertising campaigns, the NRA produces posters and bumper stickers—as it does for election campaigns—with such slogans as "Guns don't kill, people do" and "When guns are outlawed, only outlaws will have guns." Additional public relations efforts involve the member publications, *American Rifleman* and *American Hunter*. Others utilize the ILA's tabloid, *Monitor*, which focuses particularly on legislative and political matters such as a proposed gun freeze in Detroit and the NRA joint testimony with the National Wildlife Association on a bill requiring the U.S. military to promote and manage wildlife resources on its installations and reservations.

The ILA produces and distributes numerous pamphlets. Some of these are targeted on the Second Amendment right to keep and bear arms, some on protecting yourself from rape and criminal assault, and others on the use of firearms for personal security. Still others focus on debunking myths about gun control, on the failure of gun-control laws to reduce crime, and on the

ineffectiveness in preventing violence of waiting periods for gun purchase. Some have won awards for their design and effectiveness, for example, *Who Is the NRA?*, which has brief descriptions of NRA's programs and positions and features photographs of NRA members—males and females of all ages and ethnic backgrounds.

Other public-relations materials distributed by the NRA include wallet-sized yearly firearms fact cards and reprints of articles from the NRA and other periodicals. An example is an *American Rifleman* article on the Glock 17 plastic handgun that writers and columnists such as Jack Anderson say is undetectable by airport scanners, but that NRA technical staff say is detectable because the handgun also contains 19 ounces of steel.

Less Than Success

The NRA lobbying efforts sometimes meet with less than success. In 1979, for example, during debate on a bill regarding Alaska lands conservation, sponsored by Representative Morris K. Udall (D-Ariz.) and John B. Anderson (R-Ill.), Udall charged the NRA with "deliberate distortions" of his bill. Opposing the Udall-Anderson bill was legislation sponsored by Representative John B. Breaux (D-La.) and Representative John B. Dingell (D-Mich.). Dingell was an NRA board member.

The NRA executive director had sent a mailgram to NRA members saying, "The anti-gun, anti-hunting Carter administration and Congressman Udall are attempting to ramrod the Udall version of the Alaska lands bill through Congress, which will severely restrict hunting on all public lands." Another mailgram followed, saying, "Hunting on all public lands in U.S. at stake in Alaska lands bill now on the floor. Breaux-Dingell bill allows hunting and state management fish and game; Udall bill doesn't."

Even supporters of the Breaux-Dingell bill said the rhetoric was overreactive and counterproductive.

Udall put it this way in the debate: "If anybody can find anything in our bill that has any restriction on hunters or on the owners of guns or on carrying guns in any states of the union...I will eat a copy of my bill page by page without catsup or mustard....The National Rifle Association's legendary lobbying machine notwithstanding...Udall-Anderson is as neutral on control as it is on abortion, prayer in the schools, access to the notes of reporters, and ethical standards for lobbying organizations that spread deliberate distortions—as has the National Rifle Association."

An amendment to the Breaux-Dingell bill narrowed the difference with the Udall-Anderson bill to less than 1 percent in terms of Alaska lands open to sport hunting. The NRA effort was defused and deflated—except that the thousands of letters and phone calls to Capitol Hill had made the gun and hunting issue one of the most prominent issues in the debate. The "legendary lobbying machine" requires accurate targeting.

The NRA has also lost on the Second Amendment issue, most notably in Morton Grove, Illinois, where the village board passed an ordinance banning possession of handguns within the village. The ordinance took effect in February 1982. A year later, the Supreme Court let stand the appeal court ruling that the local ordinance did not violate the constitutional right to keep and bear arms. Morton Grove voters continued to support the ordinance in the spring of 1984, rejecting village board candidates who promised to rescind the pistol ordinance, despite intense campaigning. In the fall, the Illinois Supreme Court again upheld its ruling, maintaining that the village did have the authority to impose such an ordinance in order to reduce weapon-related injuries and accidents. In 1986, the Supreme Court refused to hear a further appeal, again letting the Illinois ruling stand.

Lobbying: Vital for the Legislative Process

Special interest groups like the NRA, which work to influence public opinion through public relations campaigns, direct contacts with members of Congress, and organizing grassroot responses to issues, perform important functions. Among these are informing both the public at large as well as Congress about issues and problems, causing public debate, providing people who feel they have been wronged or who need access to Congress, and making members of Congress aware of some of the practical aspects of proposed legislation (i.e., who would be helped, who would be hurt, who is for, who is against).

The NRA has performed these functions and raised passions while doing so. The association has alerted Congress and the public to the dangers of possible infringements on the constitutional right to keep and bear arms. It has produced debate on the most effective methods of controlling crime, pointing out that gun control is most often not the most effective method, provoking and producing research.

The efforts and counterefforts of the NRA and gun-control advocates have revealed the ambivalence of most Americans concerning guns, particularly handguns. Handguns are frightening, handguns are necessary for protection; Americans want handguns controlled so criminals won't use them, Americans don't want them banned in case they need them to protect themselves and their families. Such a debate keeps Americans aware of the need to accommodate their traditional diversity. As President Reagan suggested in a speech to the NRA in May 1983, the divisions in gun-control positions seem to lie not between liberals and conservatives, but between urban and rural. To urban dwellers, guns most often mean crime and danger; to suburban and rural dwellers, hunting and sport.

The NRA has also provided access to members of Congress for people who need help and feel they have been wronged—both for those abused by BATF agents during the 1970s and for its membership as a whole, which strenuously supports and defends the right to keep and bear arms. The NRA has made Congress aware of the practical aspects of proposed legislation, for example, by monitoring studies on the relation of gun controls to handgun-related crimes.

Despite the positive results arising from interest-group lobbying, critics often note some serious problems. Congress may be led into making decisions that benefit only the special interest group. The special interest group's influence can be based less on its arguments than on the number of its members, the funds at its disposal for lobbying activities, and the ability of its officers and lobbyists. Special interest groups that oppose the NRA certainly see the legendary lobbying machine as directly related to the size of the NRA's membership and the funds it generates. Nevertheless, the exploration of many points of view is important for the public and vital for the legislative process on which American democracy is based.

Activities

1. Reading Between the Lines

In this chapter, Nancy Neuman and Michael Ware discuss the differences between a special-interest lobby and a public-interest lobby. Skim through both articles, and locate the author's definition of each type. In what ways do the authors agree? disagree? Why do you think some organizations prefer to be called "public interest" lobbyists?

2. Developing Your Own Perspective

Campaign contributions from political action committees (PACs) have increased dramatically over the past decade. In 1984, nearly three-fourths of the money spent on congressional campaigns came from PACs. The role of PACs in the election process is under hot debate. See if you can find out if PACs have an impact on elections in your district.

Call or write the district office of the winner of the last congressional election. Ask for a detailed list of campaign contributions. Next, write the Federal Election Commission (FEC) at 1325 K Street, N.W., Washington,

D.C., 20463, or call (800) 424-9530. Ask the FEC for the same information, but this time for the loser in the election. Compare the two lists. Did either candidate receive PAC contributions? Who received more—the incumbent or the challenger? Do you think PAC money made a difference in the eventual outcome of the election?

If your member of Congress received PAC money, follow the voting record of your representative. Try to determine if he or she supports the views of the PACs who contributed to their campaign.

3. Becoming an Active Citizen

Not all lobby organizations are located in Washington, D.C. Many companies or groups in your local community are involved with lobbying. To find out more about lobbying and the influence these groups exert on state and national legislators, make a list of any organizations in your area that you think are involved in a lobbying effort. Interview representatives from the organization, and find out more about their lobbying activities. Some questions to ask:

- What issues concern your organization?

- Does your organization lobby at the local, state, or national level?

- What techniques does your organization use to lobby legislators? the public?

- How much money does your organization spend on lobbying?

- Does your organization have a political action committee? If so, which candidates or parties does your group support with campaign contributions?·

Remember that the more you know about interest groups and lobbying, the more informed you will be about the political process.

★★★★★★★★★★

THE MEDIA

7. The Media

In This Chapter

It is never more clear than during election time that the media are a powerful political force. Television and the press heavily influence how we see politicians and which issues we think are important. In fact, the media have often been labeled another branch of government, rivaling the three official branches in political power. Although probably not this powerful, the media can exert tremendous influence on our attitudes toward the institutions of government and the people who make decisions on our behalf.

A Free and Responsible Press
Freedom of the press is guaranteed in the Bill of Rights and was considered by the authors of the Constitution to be imperative to making democracy work. The founders of the nation viewed the press as a vital link between public officials and the people.

While the First Amendment generally protects the media from limitations on its freedom of expression, that right is not absolute. Since the early years of the nation, the United States has had laws against libel. And the Supreme Court has held that the constitutional freedoms of speech and press may be curtailed if there is a clear and present danger to the nation. Also, the right to a fair trial may limit media access to criminal trials. And recently the courts have attempted to force reporters to reveal their sources of information when a judge considers it necessary. Thus, while the press in the United States is free, it must also be held responsible for what it reports.

The Media and the Public
The nation depends on the media for virtually all news and information about government. Everyone can't be in Washington to observe our

In our political system, the media are a vital link between the government and the public. The media keep the public informed about the problems facing the nation and what public officials are doing to solve them.

government officials firsthand. Thus, the news media serve as our "window" on government, providing the people with information on the decisions being made daily.

In its daily reporting, the media must make decisions as to which stories receive the most attention. Media coverage can give status to people and events. For these reasons, the media can actually set the national agenda—what we should take seriously, what we should take lightly, and what we should ignore.

The Media and Government

While sometimes at odds with each other, the media depend on our public officials to provide them with news, while public officials in turn rely on the media for publicity. Public officials benefit from the publicity media exposure gives them by

gaining support for their campaigns and programs among the voters. However, some politicians think that journalists are overzealous.

High government officials are concerned about "leaks" to the media, especially those that might compromise our nation's security. From the government's point of view, certain facts, if made public, would damage the country's ability to defend itself. Also, politicians—like most people—do not enjoy being continually watched by the media. Most politicians feel that they are entitled to a certain amount of privacy—both in their private as well as their professional lives. They do not enjoy seeing their mistakes broadcast to millions of Americans.

Journalists, on the other hand, see their job as a "watchdog" of the government. Their obligation is to give the public a balanced report of what the government is doing. No part of the government is immune from scrutiny. Most journalists believe that the public's right to know far outweighs the claims of public officials to withhold information because of national security or personal privacy.

Media and Politics

During elections, the relationship among the media, the government, and the public comes into sharp focus. The public relies on the media to tell them who and what is news. To some extent, the media control a political campaign by deciding which candidates receive the most coverage and which issues make "front-page news." To make the most of their media exposure, candidates hire expensive public relations experts to develop elaborate campaign strategies. The modern-day politician's reliance on Madison Avenue techniques has led some analysts to wonder if a candidate's image has become more important than the campaign issues.

Keeping the Public Informed

Sarah McClendon

Sarah McClendon is a veteran journalist. A native of Tyler, Texas, she worked as a journalist on several Texas dailies before joining the Philadelphia News *as a Washington correspondent. She also worked as a public affairs officer in the Army during World War II. In 1946, she started her own news service. Her pieces appear in newspapers across the country. In her article, Ms. McClendon discusses the importance of a free press in a democratic society.*

A free press informs the people about their government and educates them as to what should be its structure in the future. As President John F. Kennedy was fond of saying, "The people cannot make a judgment if they are not informed." There can be no freedom without a free press. Without it, special interests would flourish at the expense of the majority. Injustice would prevail. Dictators could take over.

A free press enables the people "to make a judgment." When the people have the facts, they are able to make balanced judgments, for the good of our nation and our society. An informed public is the backbone of democracy.

In writing the Constitution, our nation's founders expected that the people would watch their government carefully. But they could not do this without a free press. People cannot see everything that happens in government. It is when the public does not know what is going on that politicians and officials of unscrupulous habits defraud the people.

Currently the press is being attacked on many fronts. When the press is critical of their views, politicians often use the excuse that "the press took their comments out of context." Officials from the National Aeronautics and Space Administration—when charged with negligence—said it was pressure from the press that caused them to launch the space shuttle *Challenger* in early 1986 to avoid further delays. In fact, the more skilled reporters become at investigative journalism and the more facts they uncover, the more politicians cry that the press is unfair, unjust, and carrying on a campaign against them.

The free press is also threatened by public officials who, fearing criticism, attempt to shut off sources of information while claiming to conduct an open government. Some officials do not want the public to know how much money they are spending, despite the fact that it is the people's money. But most bureaucrats want to produce an excellent record. They do not necessarily want reporters prying into their affairs. I believe that billions of dollars are being spent annually to keep taxpayers from knowing what some agencies are doing.

There is another bar to public knowledge. Ironically, it may lie within the press itself. Censorship by editors, publishers, and broadcast executives is increasing. At times, this is a judg-

ment on the part of one individual. For example, an editor may censor a story because of a dislike for a particular subject. At times, whole areas of information are kept out of public view because writers are not covering a news story or editors are keeping the story out of the media. The problems of millions of people are ignored because reporters and editors decide to keep the public from being informed.

Some people ask me if I believe that everything ought to be printed. I reply that very little should be left out of the press, only matters of national security. Who am I to say that you should not be told that taxpayers' money is going to paint an individual's barn, or that a politician is being paid for his vote in Congress, or that special interest groups are contributing huge sums of money to political campaigns? Why shouldn't the public be told that certain defense contractors are receiving more money from the government than their original contract provided? Why shouldn't the

public understand who is causing the delay in the delivery of a new weapons system—the contractor or an inefficient government planner?

Some people ask me why they cannot have only the good news. In reply, I ask if they would rather not be warned of a hurricane threat. Bad news may seem spectacular and distasteful, but its airing may in time outweigh the bad if society learns from the experience. With knowledge, society may be able to correct safety hazards, inefficiency, or carelessness.

Some people ask if I would expose the private lives of public officials. I reply that I would. I would tell the public because I feel they need to understand the full character and personality of officials before entrusting them with political office, the public treasury, or the nation's leadership.

I wish that more people were united in educating the public as to the benefits of a free press, the most notable benefit being the success

Diversity is one of the strengths of a free press. The nation's 1,600 daily newspapers not only report the news, but also represent many different political viewpoints.

of the U.S. government, the greatest experiment in freedom that has ever been.

I believe that the need for a free press is best expressed by the late Walter Williams, founder of the first school of journalism at the University of Missouri in 1908.

Writing a creed for journalists, he said:

"I believe that the public journal is a public trust, that all connected with it are, to the full measure of their responsibility, trustees for the public; that acceptance of a lesser service than the public service is betrayal of that trust.

"I believe that clear thinking and clear statement, accuracy and fairness, are fundamental to good journalism.

"I believe that any suppression of the news, for any consideration other than the welfare of society, is indefensible...

"I believe that the journalism which succeeds best...is respectful of its readers but always unafraid, is quickly indignant of injustice, and seeks to give every man an equal chance."

Questions to Consider

1. Do you agree with the author that everything about a politician's life—even personal matters—should be reported? Why or why not?

2. Do you think one of the responsibilities of a free press is to uncover wrongdoing in government?

3. Why does the author believe that "a public journal is a public trust"?

Freedom of the Press and the Law

Lyle Denniston

Lyle Denniston covers the Supreme Court for the Baltimore Sun. *Prior to his present position, he covered the Supreme Court for the* Washington Star *for eighteen years. Mr. Denniston also contributes a monthly column on the news media and the law to the* Washington Journalism Review *and is a regular contributor to* American Lawyer. *In his article, Mr. Denniston discusses the limits of a free press.*

In the First Amendment, the founding fathers gave the free press the protection it must have to fulfill its essential role in our democracy. The press was to serve the governed, not the governors. The government's power to censor the press was abolished so that the press would remain forever free to censure the government. The press was protected so that it could bare the secrets of government and inform the people.

Justice Hugo L. Black,
New York Times Company v.
United States, 1971

The press in America—newspapers, magazines, radio and television stations and networks—is free primarily because the United States Constitution provides in the First Amendment that government may pass "no law" that takes away that freedom. Because almost any form of government regulation or control of the press has the potential of interfering with that freedom, the press as well as the general public often tends to think of press freedom as mainly an issue for the courts, judges, and lawyers. However, the press enjoys wide freedom that seldom turns into a legal question. Hour after hour, day after day, broadcast and print journalists write and distribute news and feature stories that no one seeks to censor or even to challenge. The press enjoys as much "freedom of expression" as do individual citizens. It does so because America is an open society, one in which ideas—even controversial ideas—are found to be interesting. Communication of those ideas goes on most of the time without the slightest hint of government interference.

Because the press spends so much of its effort and time in writing and distributing news about what the government—federal, state, county, and city—is doing, there is a tendency to view its freedom as something that exists mainly to communicate ideas about official policy and action. When the press seeks to defend its rights under the First Amendment, it often does so by arguing that those rights are necessary to ensure that the people of America receive the information they need about their government. Judges in all courts, including the justices of the U.S. Supreme Court, tend to view the First Amendment in that way, too. The Supreme Court has issued many decisions interpreting press freedom under the First Amendment. Most of those have been based on the theory that the First Amendment was written in order to assure that the press would assist the people of America in monitoring their government, so that the people may decide whether to elect new officials, to demand changes in the laws, or to insist that the form of government itself be altered.

It is a mistake, however, to conclude that the press has a need for freedom only to communicate information about the government. Much of what is published or broadcast as news deals with the activities of private individuals or organizations and with social and cultural events or trends. The press expects to be left free from restraint when it publishes nonofficial stories. Most of the time, the First Amendment has been interpreted so as to assure press freedom.

But whether the press is issuing stories about the government or about private lives and activities, it does not expect—and it has not been given—*absolute* freedom to broadcast or print anything that it wishes. The First Amendment has never been interpreted by the courts to say that "anything goes" in the press.

Although from time to time government officials and the courts may provide some measure of restraint or some form of punishment for stories that have been in the press, the press in America has its own internal form of self-control. It considers itself to be restricted by a series of ethical rules or understandings, most of which operate on the premise that the press should not publish stories that are inaccurate, that do needless harm, or that violate the "good taste" of most of their readers or listeners.

The ethical norms of the press, however, are not rules of law; they are voluntary acts of self-restraint. Courts generally do not consider press ethics when issues arise as to whether the press must be restrained or punished for its conduct. A story may be entirely ethical from the point of view of reporters and editors, but still not fully satisfy all legal requirements.

When the press is confronted with challenges in court, it generally knows that it will be allowed to publish a story without the government first censoring its content. The Supreme Court has been very strict in forbidding the government, including the courts, to impose "prior restraints" on the press: that is, orders not to publish or broadcast a story.

Most of the legal issues surrounding press freedom involve actions that are taken after a story has appeared in print or on the air. If a story causes harm to the reputation of a private person, the press may be sued for libel and, if it loses, may be required to pay heavy money damages. If a story invades the privacy of a private person, the press may be sued for that, too, and again may have to pay heavy money damages. If a story harms the reputation of a public official or a celebrity, such as a movie star, the press may be sued for libel, but the First Amendment, as interpreted by the courts, provides the press with much more protection from that kind of lawsuit.

If the press publishes sexually explicit material in photographs or in stories, it runs the risk of being prosecuted for the crime of obscenity. Most such cases, however, are brought against publications that are mainly devoted to "x-rated" material, not against what might be considered part of the "ordinary" media.

Government is generally forbidden from trying to censor or prohibit stories in advance, but government officials have tried to stop the publication of stories, films, or photographs that would disclose classified information or military and diplomatic secrets. These cases happen rarely, however, and few have been successful.

In modern times, there has emerged a number of new legal issues dealing with the rights of the press to gather news—that is, the entire process

of finding out about a story, doing research, and reporting about it—before the story is written for publication or broadcast. Most of the time, legal questions arise about whether reporters are to be allowed to sit in on government proceedings such as court trials and legislative committee meetings or hearings. The Supreme Court is slowly developing broad theories about the right of the press to have access to what occurs in government. State and local governments also have provided press access through "open meetings" or "open records" laws, or so-called "sunshine acts," that put limits on when government activities may be carried on in secret. There also is the Freedom of Information Act, passed by Congress in 1966, that assures press and public access to federal government files.

Another legal issue involving news gathering deals with the authority of government officials to require the press to disclose the identity of individuals or organizations that provide confidential information that the press uses in developing a story. The press generally relies on secret sources only when it is investigating corruption or scandal in government or in private organizations, or when it is investigating the intelligence, military, or diplomatic agencies of the United States or of other nations. In general, reporters argue that they must be able to assure their sources that their identities will not be revealed in order to persuade those sources to provide important information that the press otherwise would not be able to obtain.

Most of the time, demands for disclosure of reporters' sources occur in criminal investigations or in lawsuits where the press has been sued for libel or for invasion of privacy. The Supreme Court has ruled that the press has no constitutional right under the First Amendment to keep its sources secret if the identity of those sources has been demanded in a legitimate criminal investigation by the government. The Supreme Court has not clarified whether the press has any right to keep its sources secret when their identity has been demanded in a libel or privacy lawsuit. However, many states have passed so-called "shield laws" to protect the press from forced disclosure to the government of its confidential sources.

Overall, the actual exercise of freedom by the press in America seldom conflicts seriously with the operation of the government or with the rights of individuals. More often, press freedom is likely to assist the democratic system by disclosing information that the public may need or want to know. It is more likely to protect, rather than inhibit, individual rights by acting as a check upon arbitrary police or government power. When the press's exercise of its freedom does conflict with government operations or the rights of individuals, legal principles impose some limits, but those limits are to remain sensitive to the basic commitment of the society and of the Constitution itself to openness in communication.

Questions to Consider

1. What are some of the limits of the free press in the United States?

2. Do you think reporters should be required to reveal the identity of individuals who provide them with confidential information? Why or why not?

3. Is there too much freedom of the press in the United States? Why or why not?

The Media and Government: Two Views

Is the press really free in the United States, or does the government control what the media report? CLOSE UP asked two political commentators to examine the tension that exists between the press and the government.

Jody Powell

Jody Powell served as President Jimmy Carter's press secretary from 1976 to 1980. He is the author of The Other Side of the Story, *a book about his years with the Carter administration. Mr. Powell is currently a syndicated columnist for the* Los Angeles Times *and a political commentator for ABC News. His unique experience allows him to view the relationship between the media and the government from both perspectives.*

Having spent almost a decade as a press secretary and six years as a journalist, there is one thing of which I am certain—politicians and journalists will continue to abuse, and use, each other because neither profession would be much of a challenge, or much fun, were it otherwise.

From the politician's perspective, a good bit of the animosity between the media and the government stems from the fact that few of us, whatever our profession, enjoy having someone looking over our shoulder always asking why we did what we did—particularly on those occasions when things didn't work out the way we'd hoped. And the more difficult and frustrating the task, the greater the distaste for that critical, questioning onlooker who seems to delight in exaggerating our failures, ignoring our successes, and generally making the job more difficult and frustrating than it was to begin with.

Most of us resent being told that we made a mistake, particularly if it's true, and especially if the telling takes place in front of 40 million of our fellow citizens (an average audience for the networks' evening news broadcasts).

This source of resentment is absolutely unavoidable. And there is nothing that journalists or anyone else can or should do about it.

Nor should journalists or the public worry too much about charges that media reports are partisan or philosophically biased. Most of these allegations come from critics who are themselves more ideological than analytical, and they just won't stand up in court.

The vast majority of the reporters I have known, from both sides of the fence, are primarily concerned about getting an interesting story, not promoting a point of view. The thing that most frequently leads journalists astray is not ideology but ambition, the temptation to cut corners to make a story more interesting and exciting than the facts justify.

However, some criticisms from public officials are worthy of attention. First is the charge that journalists tend to be arrogant and self-righteous, based on the erroneous assumption that journalism is somehow a more noble and idealistic vocation than public service.

The main problem with this "holier-than-thou" attitude is that it makes it too easy to dismiss all public officials as a "bunch of crooks" with few redeeming virtues. What this creates is a self-fulfilling prophecy. Because it is easier to deal

with being treated like a rascal if you really are one, this attitude tends to drive decent people away from public service in the long run.

The truth is that both politicians and journalists can be powerful and inspirational leaders at their best and positively disgusting criminals at their worst. Most of us, whether we are asking or answering the questions, fall somewhere in between. We make our daily compromises between what we know to be right and what we think is possible and hope that the balance of a life's work will be judged more selfless than selfish.

A second criticism of the media that has some justification is the charge that journalists are not held sufficiently accountable for their mistakes. Politicians are held accountable primarily through the efforts of those nosy, irritating, second-guessing journalists—and by criticism from their opponents, who get most of their material from news reports.

Journalists, however, are notoriously reluctant to criticize, second-guess, or otherwise look over

the shoulder of other journalists. Journalists will, and should, go headlong after business executives, labor leaders, county commissioners, and presidents when we catch them outside the bounds of propriety. But we turn meek and mild when it comes time to point the finger at shoddy practices in our own profession.

It's not that editors don't edit or that news organizations never penalize their reporters for their mistakes. The problem is that it makes no more sense to leave the managers of newspapers and networks solely responsible for calling the fouls on their own team than it does to leave the president or his chief of staff solely in charge of keeping White House staff on the straight and narrow. Both institutions, indeed all powerful institutions with great capacity for good or ill, need someone from the outside to look over shoulders, ask hard questions, and point fingers.

For example, if a newspaper makes an accusation of wrongdoing based on questionable information, why shouldn't other newspapers feel a responsibility to look into the controversy, determine the truth to the best of their ability, and set the record straight?

If a television network misinforms its viewers about an important matter of public policy, why shouldn't the other networks feel an obligation to answer the public's legitimate questions about what happened and why and what is being done to see that it doesn't happen again?

If a reporter or columnist is known by his or her colleagues to be promoting a politician or special interest, why should that information be withheld from the rest of the country?

The good news is that journalists do criticize other journalists more frequently than they once did. And news organizations have become a bit more willing to investigate one another. The bad news is that much more of this sort of finger pointing needs to be done. It won't make journalists more popular with politicians, but it might make for better journalism—and a better informed public.

Jim Dickenson

Jim Dickenson is currently a national political reporter for the Washington Post. *Previously, he was a political reporter and columnist at the* Washington Star, *the* National Observer, *and* United Press International. *Mr. Dickenson sees the relationship between the media and the government as adversarial, but beneficial, to the American people.*

It is obvious that the press in a democracy must be free. That is what we mean when we say that the crucial question is not whether the press is responsible or competent or honest or patriotic, but that it's free. Who determines whether we're responsible or competent? Democrats? Republicans? Liberals? Conservatives? If the press is free, the people decide—as they have for more than 200 years.

We enjoy, more than we realize, a free press in this country, which is a major reason why our two-century experiment in democracy has worked so well. That freedom isn't absolute, however, for a very good reason.

None of the freedoms and rights laid out in the Bill of Rights is absolute because often they are in direct conflict. Freedom of information often collides with an individual's right to privacy or the security of the nation and so on.

But for the most part, the press in the United States is free from government control, although the struggle to control the information that gets to the people is a day-in, day-out struggle. And the struggle is as often between conflicting factions within the government as it is between the government and the media.

We in the press obviously depend on sources of information within the government for our news stories. Finding sources on Capitol Hill isn't difficult because there are 535 members of Congress plus several thousand staff members.

However, covering the White House is more difficult because the number of people there who really know what is happening narrows down to six or twelve. Before the Watergate scandal, the executive branch frequently used "national security" as a cover for almost everything, including minor errors and embarrassments as well as legitimate security concerns. After the Watergate scandal broke, this practice became less prevalent, although the temptation to revert back to it is enormous and takes unrelenting effort to combat it.

Primarily because of the way the Vietnam War was covered, I think many people both in and out of government believe that the press has a liberal, and to some even anti-American, bias. They conclude that the press has an influence, probably malign, over government and the political system.

As a political reporter for twenty years, I have heard the media blamed many times for the failure of a losing campaign or an unsuccessful

Thoughts on Freedom of the Press

"The freedom of the press is one of the great bulwarks of liberty, and can never be restrained but by despotic governments."

George Mason
(1725–92),
Virginia statesman

"A free press is not a privilege, but an organic necessity in a great society."

Walter Lippmann
(1889–1974),
writer and political
commentator

"The press is a sort of wild animal in our midst—restless, gigantic, always seeking new ways to use its strength."

Zechariah Chafee, Jr.
(1885–1957),
American lawyer, historian,
and teacher

"A free press can, of course, be good or bad, but most certainly, without freedom it will never be anything but bad."

Albert Camus
(1913–60),
French essayist and
playwright

"I do not seek to intimidate the press, the networks, or anyone else from speaking out. But the time for blind acceptance of their opinions is past. And the time for naive belief in their neutrality is gone."

Spiro T. Agnew
(1918–),
Vice president under
Richard Nixon

"The hand that rules the press, the radio, the screen, and the far-spread magazine, rules the country."

Learned Hand
(1872–1961),
federal judge

"In America, the president reigns for four years, and journalism governs forever and ever."

Oscar Wilde
(1854–1900),
English writer and wit

"If the American press is to remain free—even in the somewhat limited sense that results from the conflict of this freedom with the other guaranteed freedoms in the Constitution—it cannot have responsibility imposed on it by legislation, judicial interpretation, or any other process."

Tom Wicker
(1926–),
political columnist

---

governmental policy. However, I have never heard us credited with a winning campaign or successful policy, and I think the charge that we somehow control the selection of candidates—particularly for the presidency—and their subsequent election is sheer rubbish. The fact is that we report on politicians who make things happen in their campaigns and respond—often overrespond—when politicians "make news."

The relationship between the media and the government is often described as an adversarial one, and that's the way it should be. Critics often ask us, "Who elected you?" when we presume to criticize our political leaders, and our proper response is, "No one. That's exactly the point."

The country has an adequate number of elected representatives, and the role of the media is to be an independent, outside observer. This arrangement doesn't work perfectly, but then nothing does work perfectly, even in a democracy.

Many people in government and politics view us as shameless opportunists who care nothing for the public good. Granted, we sometimes are overaggressive, particularly since Watergate, but like most politicians, we assume that our practices also contribute to the common good. Our aggressiveness and competitiveness help maintain freedom of the press; you can't have freedom if you don't exercise it.

Moreover, the people are well served by the adversarial relationship between the media and the government, and they have a surprising degree of awareness of it. A recent survey of the public's attitudes toward the press showed that people do appreciate our "watchdog" function, and some believe that we aren't aggressive enough in pursuing it. A remarkably large majority of those interviewed think that we in the media are competent, decent, honest, and even patriotic. However, an equally large number think that we are influenced too much by big government, big business, and big labor—the "establishment"—and want us to be even more independent than we are.

There is no question that people in the media, along with many other Americans, are more skeptical and suspicious of government since Vietnam and Watergate. In Vietnam, we learned that the federal government—which many Americans for decades had viewed as a benign factor in society because of the New Deal and federal support of the civil rights movement—

198

was lying to us about nothing less than life and death. Under successive administrations, the government was stealthily escalating a war in Southeast Asia.

There are bad policies and bad public servants, but there are many good ones as well. Our job is not to make blanket conclusions or condemnations, but to distinguish the good from the bad. Once the people have this knowledge, the democratic system and process can take care of the rest.

Questions to Consider

1. What "checks and balances" are there over the media?

2. In what ways does the government exert control over what the media report? Do you think the government should have more or less control?

3. Do you think the media have a bias? Why or why not?

A Political Cartoonist Looks at His Work

Bob Gorrell

Bob Gorrell is the political cartoonist for the Richmond News Leader. *Prior to joining the* News Leader *in 1983, he was the cartoonist for the* Charlotte News. *He draws five cartoons a week and is distributed through News America Syndicate. In his article, Mr. Gorrell explains the art of political cartooning.*

As much as anything else, the job of modern political cartoonists is that of exciting reader interest in the issues of the day. Very rarely will a political cartoon actually shift an unsympathetic reader's point of view to that of the artist, but it often does serve to polarize opinion, increase debate, and mobilize support both for and against the cartoonist's position on any given issue. When a cartoonist does alter public opinion directly through his work, it is most often by way of a long "war of attrition," through many cartoons on a single issue rather than through one single, potent masterpiece of satire. No one cartoon leveled Richard Nixon's image with the voters, but many cartoons of Nixon crawling from sewers wearing his notorious five o'clock shadow over many years of relentless attack finally changed the public's perception. Nixon the president came to be viewed as Nixon the sleazy cartoon caricature, and this as much as any political intrigue precipitated Nixon's downfall.

Such effectiveness is the ideal to which all editorial cartoonists aspire. It is a dream inspired by political cartoonist Thomas Nast and his battles against Tammany Hall in the 1870s. But more often than not, the cartoonist falls short of that perfection and must settle for the consolation prize of giving some editorial insight and motivating his readers to thinking about and discussing the issues.

Even in this limited capacity, editorial cartoons have a unique power. An island of art surrounded by a sea of grey text, they naturally attract the reader's attention and are generally the first item studied in their section of the newspaper. The old cliche holds that one picture is worth a thousand words, but when carefully crafted, a

1986 THE RICHMOND NEWS LEADER
NEWS AMERICA SYNDICATE
GORRELL

political cartoon might be worth much more. The visual character of the cartoon is its strength; simplicity of form and content make it stand out on a page of convoluted analysis of complex issues. In these days of maze-like budgetary considerations and confusing foreign policy options, it is a luxury for readers to find editorial commentary that is direct and unequivocating. While a cartoonist lacks the writer's tools for making fine distinctions of fact and precise expressions of thought, his visual vocabulary is just as effective. The editorial writer manipulates a verbal scalpel, but the cartoonist wields a visual hatchet.

The cartoon form is most useful for making broad editorial points in a relatively direct fashion. Because cartoons are generally more emotive than written editorials, they tend to carry more immediate impact. Reading a cartoon is a quick experience. What takes the artist hours to produce is usually consumed by the audience in a few brief seconds. That short time, though, is sufficient to convey the cartoonist's message, and the cartoon image imprints itself on the reader's mind as no long-winded editorial can.

Artwork is the cartoonist's vocabulary, and, as any writer would, he selects and arranges his "words" in any way desired. The term "cartoon" implies humor, and that is the mode in which many modern cartoonists choose to operate. Laughter takes the hard edge off of serious commentary, and even the most acidic humorous satire is easier for the reader to digest than dry pontification and somber messages of political doom. Rather than alienating their readers with editorial browbeating, most cartoonists prefer making their points while chuckling with the audience.

The best cartoons use humor only as a means and not as an end in itself. Humor is merely a vessel in which commentary is conveyed, and the cartoonist must recognize that not every situation or event can be treated in a lighthearted manner. Masters of the cartoon craft can control many moods and create many variations of tone in their work. They employ all aspects of argumentative style—from pathos to irony to pure logic—in their approach to various subjects. One of the signs of a top cartoonist is his ability

to keep the reader a bit off balance from day to day. His political and social philosophy remains basically constant throughout his work, but his mode of expression is always fresh and unexpected.

Because his imagery is based upon exaggeration of fact and can be very biting, the cartoonist is constantly faced with the question of fairness in his work. Each individual cartoonist and his editor establish their own unique working environment and set their own rules and guidelines as to how outrageous a cartoon may become. Many cartoonists believe that they should be "free agents" on the editorial page and that they should be allowed to voice whatever opinion in whatever fashion they desire. Others are more inclined to consider themselves employees of the newspaper whose duty is to illustrate that journal's editorial philosophy. Perhaps the ideal situation for a cartoonist lies somewhere in between those extremes, with the artist finding employ-

ment with an editor who is in broad agreement with his political beliefs and who will exercise subtle and unobtrusive authority in limited cases of taste.

Fairness usually enters into the cartoonist's work during its early formative stages, while he is deciding his position on any given issue. It is at this point that the artist weighs all the facts at hand, listening carefully to both sides of a question before arriving at his position. Once that point is reached, however, fairness becomes a secondary consideration. Within the limits of taste, the cartoonist utilizes whichever imagery or metaphor makes his point most effectively.

Comic strip artist Bill Keane jokes that editorial cartoonists work out of a "deep hatred for mankind." That is, of course, an overstatement, but it is impossible for the editorial car-

toonist to worry about the sensitivity of his subjects and remain effective. To some degree at least, the cartoonist must view politicians and public figures in the abstract. His role as political and social critic is essentially a negative enterprise, and it would be impossible to point out politicians' many faults if he viewed them as friends.

The inherent negativism of his craft sometimes brings criticism raining down on the cartoonist himself. Usually, outraged reaction to cartoons originates with readers rather than politicians. It seems that those holding public office are less inclined toward indignation than their supporters, subscribing to the old theory that a newspaper can say whatever they want about the

politician, as long as they spell his name correctly.

Much of the condemnation directed at cartoonists is the result of his opinions on social issues such as abortion or school prayer rather than his political beliefs. The volume of response received by a cartoonist on any given drawing can be viewed as an index of its effectiveness. It is on those days when the phone keeps ringing and the mail keeps coming that the cartoonist knows he has done his job. He has awakened the politically lazy and made the reader take notice.

Questions to Consider

1. How effective do you think political cartoons are in shaping public opinion about a government official or an issue?

2. Why do you think the author describes his work as "essentially a negative enterprise"?

3. How do you react to the author's statement that once the artist has taken a position on an issue, "fairness becomes a secondary consideration"?

The U.S. Government, the Media, and the Invasion of Grenada

In the complicated business of defending this great nation, we have a very real need to maintain secrecy over a wide variety of information.

> Caspar W. Weinberger
> Defense 85

The free press in our society performs the important role of reporting on the actions of the government. That reporting cannot be silenced when the nation commits its citizens to fight in military campaigns.

> Jack Smith
> Columbia Brocasting
> System (CBS)

In times of national emergency, the issues of freedom of the press can become cloudy. On the one hand, it is in the country's interest to see that certain information is kept confidential; it is obviously important not to alert or assist the enemy. On the other hand, the American public has a right to be kept informed about the nation's activities.

War correspondents have long risked their lives to keep the public informed in times of war. The presence of news reporters on the battlefield is a fighting tradition, as the more than 140 correspondents killed during World War II demonstrate. The reporter's independent perspective provides the public with a different viewpoint from official military statistics and reports. But do reporters have a right to be on the battlefield when the military does not want them there? Are they a necessary part of a military campaign, or a hindrance to the effective pursuit of duty by the soldiers?

On October 25, 1983, President Ronald Reagan sent the U.S. Marines to the tiny Caribbean island of Grenada. His stated purposes were "to protect innocent lives . . . to forestall further chaos . . . and to assist in the restoration of conditions of law and order and of governmental institutions to the island of Grenada."

The brief conflict, initiated and planned in secret, was carried out under a news blackout. No members of the civilian media landed with the first invasion forces, and no correspondents were officially allowed on the island until two days after the marines landed. U.S. military camera crews and staff provided almost all of the on site battle coverage of the war.

Did the Department of Defense try to conceal essential information from the public by banning the media from Grenada? Or was the Pentagon merely protecting a sensitive military operation? Did news reporters have a right to be on the island as soon as the troops landed? How important is independent civilian coverage of a military attack, particularly one as controversial as the invasion of Grenada?

A study of the history of news reporting in wartime and a look at the Grenada campaign sheds some light on these questions.

Journalists and War

The struggle between the press and the military goes back more than a century. During the American Civil War, reporters were commonplace on the battlefield. Photographer Mathew Brady followed the Union Army with his cartload of cameras, taking pictures of soldiers, officers, and tent encampments as he went. He moved behind Union lines with almost complete freedom, often on the heels of the attacking soldiers.

Union General William Tecumseh Sherman became famous for his spats with newspaper reporters, saying, "We don't want the enemy any better informed than he [the enemy] is." Sherman even threatened to shoot one correspondent as a spy until President Abraham Lincoln intervened. In retaliation for such treatment, northern newspapers began reporting that Sherman was insane. However, Sherman's strong-arm tactics may have stood to his benefit; his devastating "march to the sea" through Georgia—in which he captured Atlanta and Savannah—was over before any mention of it appeared in print.

In subsequent American military involvements, the role of the press

Photographer Mathew Brady was the first journalist to go to the battlefield to cover a war. Brady's photographs of the Civil War document what soldiers on both side had to endure.

UPI/Bettmann Newsphotos

was equally controversial. Sometimes press coverage worked in reverse. In 1898, newspaper mogul William Randolph Hearst sent artist Frederick Remington to Cuba to report on the war there. Remington wired Hearst that there was no war. Hearst cabled in return, "You provide the pictures, and I'll provide the war." Hearst's paper, the *New York Journal*, then inflamed popular opinion toward a war with Spain. During the Spanish-American War, Lieutenant Theodore Roosevelt realized that his prestige would grow stronger if he handled the press properly and was hailed as a hero on his return to the United States.

However, every government recognizes the need for strict censorship during times of war. During the First World War, the United States entered the conflict on the side of England and France. Press reports of the fighting passed through British and French censors before reaching America. Again, during the Second World War, American reporters could write what they wished, but army censors had to review all dispatches.

As an example of how wartime censorship could be conducted in the age of live radio, when German planes bombed London during World War II, Edward R. Murrow broadcast reports of the bombing from a rooftop. At his elbow was a censor; as soon as Murrow began to talk about any sensitive topic, the censor would tap his wrist and Murrow would change the subject.

Similarly, the press participated in the D-Day landings of Normandy, France, on June 6, 1944, under censored conditions. Some correspondents parachuted into the war zone with the first troops, bearing typewriters instead of the standard M-1 rifles. Others, such as Walter Cronkite, landed with the assault troops on French beaches. All were able to write what they saw as they saw it, but military censors reviewed their stories for any information that might aid the enemy.

UPI/Bettmann Newsphotos

During World War II, radio broadcasts from Europe kept Americans informed about the allies' progress. Perhaps the most famous of all radio journalists, Edward R. Murrow, made broadcasts daily from London during the Battle of Britain.

Despite its censorship, the military in World War II gained the cooperation of the news media. The war was a popular one with the clear purpose of stopping Nazi leader Adolph Hitler. The press joined with the military in keeping vital facts secret and willingly delayed news reports until the events they described were no longer important to the enemy. This "self-censorship" by the press created a sense of trust between the military and the news media.

The Media and Vietnam
During the 1950s, President Dwight Eisenhower sent military advisors to Vietnam to help create a democracy in the southern half of the country. France, the former colonial power in Vietnam, had pulled out, and the stability of Vietnam was seen as an important link in preventing the spread of communism in Southeast Asia.

Early American press reports from Vietnam were few and reflected the Eisenhower administration's optimism about its policies there. Most American jour-

nalists did not arrive until after 1961, when a popular movement against the corrupt regime of Ngo Dinh Diem grew into a civil war between government troops and the Viet Cong, or Vietnamese Communists. When President John Kennedy increased the number of U.S. "advisors" from 500 to 10,000, press coverage of the country increased proportionately. In mid-1964, about 20 American and foreign correspondents reported from Saigon, the capital of South Vietnam. The number of reporters grew to 131 by late 1965 and to 634 by 1968 when American involvement peaked.

Perhaps the most important aspect of the coverage of the Vietnam War was its vividness. Vietnam was America's first televised war. Instead of reading about battles, body counts, and bombings, Americans actually saw these events happening every evening on the news. War was no longer newsprint or black-and-white newsreels in a movie theater. The war thrust itself into the nation's living rooms in living color.

The media brought back graphic images of human suffering, of bleeding soldiers and destroyed homes. Many military officers believed that television coverage of the war focused on the negative side of combat, which eroded popular support. American officers felt that the stories that came out of Vietnam were slanted against the army and did not present a balanced view of the fighting. They felt that television made them look like vicious killers, minimizing the importance of their mission and their accomplishments. As a result, relations between the military and the media became strained even though, according to one historian, no tactical military operation was jeopardized by premature disclosure in the press.

Instead, the threat perceived by the army was the misrepresentation of the army's purpose and image. Many military officials wanted stronger control over what the people back home saw about the war.

This attitude was shared by the British government during the 1982 conflict over the Falkland Islands.

The Falkland Islands Campaign
The Falklands, known in Argentina as Islas Malvinas, are a rocky outcrop of islands in the south Atlantic Ocean. Although Argentina claims sovereignty over the islands, the 1,800 native Falklanders speak English, grant allegiance to the queen of England, and are legally British citizens.

On April 2, 1982, the president of Argentina, General Leopoldo Galtieri, ordered his troops to invade the islands and bring them under Argentine control. The small British garrison on the islands surrendered with no casualties and little resistance. The Argentines thought that the lack of bloodshed would appease the British and that the Falklands were theirs.

But the Argentine invasion brought screams of protest from the British government and people. Great Britain called the takeover an act of international aggression, and in the words of British Foreign Secretary Lord Carrington, "a national humiliation." Britain quickly assembled its naval fleet and immediately sent it to the

Falklands. One month later, the Argentines and the British met in battle. Although a full-scale naval campaign never materialized, a series of air strikes by British Harrier jets destroyed several Argentine planes. The British blockaded the islands by sea and air and landed on the islands on May 27. Three weeks later on June 14, the Argentine forces surrendered.

During the war, the British government severely limited press coverage of the conflict. The military high command censored all reports and sharply curtailed the number of reporters with access to the fighting. Stories were checked at the point where they were filed and again at the Ministry of Defence before being released to the public. Only 28 reporters were allowed to cover the entire force of 28,000 soldiers.

In spite of its strict censorship, the British military still had problems with the media coverage. Lacking full access to the battle area and hungry for information, the British press relied on reports from Argentina (which issued its own version of

Many American military officers felt that the graphic coverage of the fighting in Vietnam turned public opinion against our involvement there. Relations between the military and the media have been strained ever since.

UPI/Bettmann Newsphotos

206

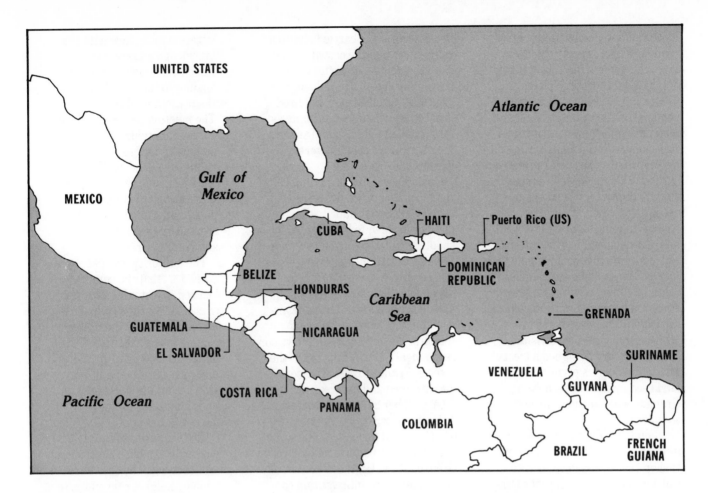

events), interviews with British military experts, and speculation. The speculation created special problems when it proved to be correct and, vital information was inadvertently published. The press also published reports of unexploded bombs hitting British vessels, thus alerting the Argentines that their fuses were inadequate.

Even with strict censorship, Prime Minister Margaret Thatcher attacked the British Broadcasting Company in the House of Commons as presenting a biased picture of the Falklands situation.

Supporters of the media ban say that the British public continued to favor the war throughout its admittedly brief duration. British viewers were spared the graphic visions of gore that characterized American coverage of the Vietnam War because news stories avoided the human suffering of war. As a consequence, the overall objective—to retrieve a British possession and avenge a wrong—dominated popular

British sentiment, unclouded by photographs of bloody faces and mangled limbs.

In June 1983, the *Naval War College Review*, a popular American military publication, printed an article by Lieutenant Commander Arthur A. Humphries. Humphries held up the Falklands campaign as an example of effective news management by a country at war. He stated:

> The Falklands war shows us how to make certain that government policy is not undermined by the way a war is reported....If you don't want to erode the public's confidence in the government's war aims, then you cannot allow that public's sons to be wounded or maimed right in front of them via their TV sets; you must, therefore, control correspondents' access to the fighting....The news media can be a useful tool, or even a

weapon, in prosecuting a war psychologically....To maintain popular support for a war, your side must not be seen as ruthless barbarians.

Humphries's article, published five months before the U.S. invasion of Grenada, was later seen by some news people as a blueprint for how the American military would handle the media's coverage of that conflict.

Grenada: The Political Background

At first glance, Grenada does not seem to be worth exchanging shots over. With fewer than 100,000 people and a land area about twice the size of Washington, D.C., Grenada is the smallest independent nation in the Western Hemisphere. Its chief contribution to international trade is that it supplies nearly a third of the world's supply of nutmeg.

In 1979, Grenada's government was overthrown in a nearly

bloodless coup led by Maurice Bishop. Bishop's party, the New Jewel Movement (an acronym for Joint Endeavour for Welfare, Education, and Liberation) soon reneged on its promises of general elections and a new constitution. Relations with the United States deteriorated as the new regime turned to Cuban-style "revolutionary democracy" and began accepting Cuban aid. In 1980, Bishop announced that Cuba would help Grenada build a new international airport that could handle both tourist jets and long-range military aircraft. Cuban advisors and construction workers began to pour into the island. Then Deputy Prime Minister Bernard Coard visited Moscow, where he signed a treaty giving the Soviets permission to land reconnaissance planes on Grenada when the new airport was completed.

When Ronald Reagan took office in 1981, his administration informed Bishop that Grenada's ties with Cuba posed a serious threat to the peace of the Caribbean. The threat deepened when Bishop visited Moscow in 1982 and announced that the Soviet Union would help Grenada construct an earth station linked to a Soviet satellite.

In June 1983, however, Bishop's outlook appeared to change. He visited Washington, D.C., and talked of improving relations with the United States. He also announced the formation of a commission to write a new Grenadian constitution.

The slackening of Bishop's anti-American posture may have angered his Cuban and Soviet advisors. On October 13, 1983, Deputy Prime Minister Coard staged a coup, arresting Bishop and several cabinet ministers. Over the next few days, more cabinet ministers were arrested. Shops were closed, the airport shut down, and Radio Free Grenada, the island's only radio station, went off the air.

On October 19, several thousand Bishop supporters rushed the gates of his residence, freed him from

house arrest, and carried him to a rally. But when the crowd moved to Fort Rupert, headquarters of the Grenadian army, troops loyal to Coard captured Bishop and fired into the crowd, killing as many as forty civilians. Bishop and several members of his cabinet were executed.

Radio Free Grenada announced the formation of a new Revolutionary Military Council and a 24-hour curfew, to be enforced by shooting violators on sight. Conditions on the island were dangerous, and reports were few and unreliable. Several foreign journalists arrived at the Grenada airport, but were turned away by soldiers. The only resident news correspondent, Alister Hughes of the Agence France Presse wire service, was arrested and imprisoned.

On October 21, the Organization of Eastern Caribbean States (OECS) voted formally and unanimously to intervene by force in Grenada if the United States would assist them. The intervention conformed to the provision in the OECS charter that the heads of government could collectively agree to take whatever measures deemed necessary to defend the region and preserve the peace.

On October 23, the United States received an official letter from the OECS, which stated:

The authority of the Organization of Eastern Caribbean States is aware...that the overthrow of the Bishop admin-

istration took place with the knowledge and connivance of forces unfriendly to the OECS leading to the establishment of the present military regime. The meeting took note of the current anarchic conditions, the serious violations of human rights and bloodshed that has occurred, and the consequent unprecedented threat to the peace and security of the region created by the vacuum of authority in Grenada.

The authority was deeply concerned...that the country can be used as a staging post for acts of aggression against its members...that the present regime in Grenada has demonstrated by its brutality and ruthlessness that it will stop at nothing to achieve its ends and to secure its power....

The Authority of the OECS wishes to establish a peacekeeping force with the assistance of friendly neighboring states to restore on Grenada conditions of tranquility and order.

The Invasion of Grenada

The weekend of October 23 and 24 was to be a relaxing golf outing for President Reagan at the Augusta National Golf Club in Georgia. Early in the morning of Saturday, October 23, Secretary of State George Shultz received word that the OECS wanted the United States to invade Grenada. In Washington, Vice President George Bush met with

In 1983, President Reagan ordered U.S. armed forces to invade the small island nation of Grenada to prevent a possible communist takeover and to rescue American medical students. American forces gained control of the island within a few days.

Defense Secretary Caspar Weinberger, Joint Chiefs of Staff chairman John Vessey, and several key White House aides.

Their consensus was that a strike against Grenada was justified. If nothing else, ensuring the safety of 600 American medical students studying there provided an incentive. Memories of the recent Iranian crisis, in which American hostages were held captive for 444 days, were still fresh, and the conferees wished to avoid any chance of a similar episode in Grenada. (On October 22, two U.S. consular officials had gone to Grenada to check on the American students. The officials were not allowed to see the students, but were assured by the government that all Americans were safe. The officials were alarmed at the lack of governmental authority on the island, and reported their concern back to President Reagan.)

Prior to the invasion itself, numerous "storm warnings" appeared in the media. On October 21, the *New York Times* reported that a 10-ship U.S. task force that had been headed for Lebanon was being sent to Grenada. The paper reported the move as a "precautionary measure." On Monday, October 25, the *Times* reported that Radio Free Grenada had warned that an invasion by forces from neighboring Caribbean states was expected. All militia units in Grenada were activated for duty. That same day, about fifty U.S. Marines landed in Barbados, supposedly on their way to evacuate Americans from Grenada. Again, the *Times* reported: "Just what was going on was not clear. United States spokesmen both here and in Washington maintained that they did not know why the fifty marines had made their brief stopover here and where they had gone."

In Washington, Bill Plante of CBS News asked Principal Deputy Press Secretary Larry Speakes point blank if U.S. Marines would invade Grenada the next day. Speakes replied, "No."

Department of Defense

When the marines first landed on Grenada, American journalists were prohibited from traveling to the island to cover the story. The military said that it could not guarantee the correspondents' safety. However, many news organizations protested the press ban, calling it censorship.

Early the following morning, U.S. Marines invaded Grenada.

At a 9 a.m. news conference on October 25, President Reagan said that the United States "had no choice but to act strongly and decisively" in response to the OECS request. However, the Soviet Union called the invasion an "act of undisguised banditry and international terrorism." And Great Britain protested that it had urged President Reagan not to invade and stated that no British troops had taken part in the event. However, the British did not condemn the invasion.

In the attack group led by U.S. Seals, a specially trained navy sealand tactical squad, soldiers from the OECS countries accompanied the Americans. More than 300 soldiers from the Caribbean nations of Antigua, Barbados, Dominica, Jamaica, St. Kitts-Nevis, St. Lucia, and St. Vincent's participated in the invasion. U.S. troops included the army's First and Second Ranger Battalions, the Eighty-second Airborne Division, and the marines.

The attack focused initially on the southwest corner of the island, the location of the uncompleted airport. Marines also secured Pearls Airport, in the northeast corner of the island, and attacked the Governor's House and the Richmond Hill Prison.

On October 26, the first American students were evacuated from Grenada. By late in the day of October 27, Atlantic Fleet Commander Admiral Wesley McDonald

reported, "All major military objectives in the island were secured," but "scattered pockets of resistance" remained and "fighting was still in progress." By then, the United States had more than 6,000 troops on the island.

The invading forces captured 638 Cubans; many more may have escaped in small boats or fled to the island's mountainous interior. American troops also found warehouses stacked with Soviet and Cuban arms "far above what any island this size needs for self-defense," according to the Department of Defense.

While the media dutifully reported the military's account of the invasion, it could not confirm the facts. The press was miles away, prohibited by the military from nearing Grenada.

The Press in Grenada
Although the conflict had lasted less than a week, echoes of protest in the U.S. news community took a long time to die down. Yes, the marines had landed, but the war correspondents were not there to record them. All media coverage for the invasion was handled from the nearby island of Barbados.

For the first two days of the invasion, the restrictions on independent reporting from Grenada continued. No outside journalists accompanied the U.S. military, and no correspondents were allowed on or near the island. The Department of Defense cited protection of the correspondents' safety as a significant factor in this decision. Small craft were being shot at, and the marines could not be responsible for Americans who might be aboard.

A team of seven American journalists did reach Grenada on a chartered boat on the first day of the invasion, but they could not send out stories because all local communications were dead. They spent the night on the island, and the next day, three reporters met American troops and were taken to the USS *Guam*. The other reporters stayed on the island, taking photographs and notes but unable to communicate until the military lifted the press ban on October 27. On that day, the military flew in a small pool of reporters, who took their stories back to Barbados to share with the news media there. The reports were the first independent, civilian stories to emerge from Grenada. A regular transport of reporters then began; eventually more than 600 reporters reached the island and were able to file stories.

Media reaction to the initial news restriction was strong. Protests came from some of the country's major news organizations, including CBS News, the *Washington Post*, and other news groups. In newspaper and television editorials, reporters rejected the military's concern for their welfare, pointing to the hundreds of combat correspondents who had willingly risked their lives in the past to bring back the news.

The October 28 edition of the *New York Times* carried the story, "U.S. Bars Coverage of Grenada Action; News Groups Protest." The article stated: "Reporters here and elsewhere had found themselves relying heavily on ham radio operators and Radio Havana for reports on conditions on the island. . . . Defense Department officials who spoke on the condition that they not be named said that Britain's tight control over press coverage of its war with Argentina . . . had made an impression on some military com-

manders." The *Times* quoted General John Vessey as saying, "We needed surprise," but also cited a Defense Department official who called the press blockade very unusual.

At the White House, harsh words passed between Principal Deputy Press Secretary Speakes and reporters asking for explanations of the press ban. But the exclusion of media and public relations people from the Grenada invasion had extended to the highest levels. White House press officers had been taken by surprise at news of the invasion. Speakes's previous denial of invasion plans was the truth: he did not know of any. Les Janka, Deputy White House Press Secretary for Foreign Affairs, resigned over the issue. He pointed out that "the twin decisions of excluding its own press officers from the pre-invasion planning and denying/delaying media access to the island were not only a serious breach of constitutional responsibil-

Before invading Grenada, U.S. military leaders decided to bar journalists from covering the invasion, feeling that extensive press coverage might eliminate the element of surprise from their plan. Here, Larry Speakes, President Reagan's spokesman, holds a briefing with the White House press corps to explain the military's decision.

ity toward informing the public, they were also acts of political stupidity for the most practical of reasons: Our military forces performed superbly and the overall operation was a domestic political success. But the positive results were underobserved and ultimately tarnished by the controversy over media access."

When U.S. reporters saw the first televised pictures of the invasion in film shot by a U.S. military cameraman, *Newsday's* Thomas Collins said:

> The 8-minute film was more notable for what it did not show than what it did. There were no combat scenes, no shots were heard, and there were no pictures of terrorized civilians; no evidence that a war was going on. It was the kind of reporting one gets when the government is behind the camera.

Collins also claimed, "The truth is that Defense Secretary Caspar Weinberger is not a very good reporter."

Public opinion surveys tended to support the press. A majority of Americans said in a Harris poll in December 1983 that they felt the administration was wrong in not allowing reporters into Grenada. However, a majority agreed with the statement: "If the President and the military feel that the press and TV should not be allowed to cover an invasion . . . then their right to make that decision should not be questioned."

In another study, researchers from George Washington University (GWU) found that 64 percent of the American students on Grenada "felt the reporters should not have been permitted to accompany U.S. troops as they arrived." According to one researcher, "Just under 40 percent [of the medical students] said the press that had covered them did not behave in a responsible way."

Another GWU researcher added, "Respondents were twelve times as likely to complain about the behavior of our press as they were likely to complain about the behavior of our soldiers."

The Sidle Panel

In early 1984, the Reagan administration appointed a commission to study the issue of media coverage in Grenada and in future military engagements. The Joint Chiefs of Staff Media–Military Relations Panel (known as the Sidle Panel after its chair, Major General Winant Sidle) met from February 6 to February 10, 1984, in Washington, D.C. Military officers involved in media relations and prominent media figures testified before the panel.

A statement from the Joint Chiefs of Staff regarding "Operation Urgent Fury," as the Grenada invasion was code-named, maintained that:

> It was felt by all parties that secrecy had to be maintained to insure safety of not only the American citizens in Grenada but also our military forces. In order to maintain this level of secrecy, only those persons with an absolute need to know were involved in the planning of the operation. No members of the press were deemed to have this need.
>
> From the beginning, our plans called for media from Barbados to be placed on the ground in Grenada not later than the morning of the second day of the operation. Unfortunately, resistance was more determined than expected . . .
>
> On the third day of the operation, we were able to reserve fifteen seats on tactical aircraft and move a pool of reporters . . . On October 28, we moved twenty-seven additional reporters and on the 29, forty-seven more. All of these reporters went on a pool basis and upon return briefed the 400-plus reporters remaining in

Barbados. All film and photography were also pooled. In this way, we were able to provide all agencies with media-developed coverage . . .
> All told, through November 2, 606 reporters, some of them repeaters, representing 152 separate domestic and foreign news agencies, were transported to Grenada via U.S. military aircraft. . . . Given the very short notice of this operation and the secrecy and operational constraints, the efforts of the DOD [Department of Defense] public affairs officials represent no small achievement. . . .
>
> We often hear the word "censorship" used regarding this operation. There was no censorship. . . . Our laws don't permit it, and we don't desire it. . . .
>
> To have told newsmen in advance of the operation . . . could have risked the lives of the students and of our military personnel.
>
> It was a risk we were unwilling to take.

Media representatives also gave their views on the military's control over media access to the battle area. Jack Smith, Washington bureau chief for CBS News, said:

> It is clear to us that the press must be able to cover military operations so that the public can have the benefit of independent reporting and not be dependent on government handouts for its information. It is also clear that in covering military operations, the press must recognize the importance of mission security and troop safety. . . .
>
> The important issue, however, must be to assure that print and broadcast reporters and cameramen be allowed to cover these events. Once that principle is met, there is clearly

a willingness on the part of the press to be flexible enough to work out the appropriate arrangements.

We at CBS News believe this panel can well serve the public if it makes clear that in future military operations the interests of our democratic society demand that the press be permitted to cover military operations from their inception.

Edward M. Fouhy of the National Broadcasting System (NBC) said:

What we fear is the exercise of censorship for political reasons.... We in TV news would be particularly vulnerable to a government tempted to manipulate reality.... We do not, for example, feel we must have a correspondent-camera crew on the first helicopter or landing barge. We *are* asking, indeed insisting, on reasonable access in timely fashion to the troops engaged in a military operation.

But the opinion about the military's decision to bar the media was not unanimous. A letter from

Henry A. Grunwald of *Time* magazine addressed the constitutional issues:

We do not believe that there is a clear-cut right under the First Amendment for the media to cover military operations.... There is, however, a strong and clear tradition of coverage of military operations throughout our history.

The Sidle Panel reviewed all the testimony and in August 1984 issued a statement of principle and a series of recommendations. The panel stated:

The American people must be informed about U.S. military operations, and this information can best be provided through both the news media and the government. Therefore, the panel believes it is essential that the U.S. news media cover U.S. military operations to the maximum degree possible consistent with mission security and the safety of U.S. forces.

The panel issued eight recommendations for improving the working

relationship between the media and the military. These recommendations included:

- The military should plan for press access as part of its operational planning.

- When pooling of the news media is the only feasible means of coverage, the military should provide for the largest practical press pool and provide full press access as soon as possible.

- A study should be made of whether to use a pre-established list of reporters for pools or whether to accept reporters selected by a news agency.

- Members of the media who are granted access to military operations should voluntarily comply with security guidelines. Violators would be excluded from further coverage of the operation.

- The military should provide sufficient equipment and personnel to assist correspondents in covering the operation.

- The military should carefully consider the media's communications needs. But these communications must not interfere with combat and combat-support operations.

In its report to the president, the Sidle Panel recommended that the media be allowed to cover U.S. military operations to the maximum degree possible. The panel also recommended that the military allow the press some access to its planning meetings.

- The military should try to provide transportation for the media during a military operation.

- To improve understanding and cooperation between the media and the military, both sides should participate in programs of instruction, in meetings, and in visits by military personnel to news organizations.

Since the recommendations of the Sidle Panel, the military and the press have had several opportunities to practice the media pool type of coverage of military operations. These have been held during strategic exercises and practice drills, such as an amphibious assault drill conducted off the coast of California. During that exercise, a pool of twelve correspondents, accompanied by two Department of Defense escorts, accompanied the marines as they staged the assault. Their stories were released to the media through the Office of the Assistant Secretary of Defense for Public Affairs.

Whether or not such pooling will work during actual combat remains to be seen. Neither the military nor the press is completely satisfied with the pooling arrangement. If the media believe that they need more information about military actions or that the military is deliberately hiding information, they will work to reduce limits on reporters. But the Department of Defense will also try to deny information to the media that might jeopardize military actions. The Pentagon will have to weigh the concerns of a free society with its military objectives in allowing access to and reports from the battlefield.

Activities

1. Reading Between the Lines

Some people complain that the media are biased and do not present the news fairly. Critics of the press say that newspapers especially take sides on the issues. Read either a local or national newspaper for a week, and see if you can determine that paper's political leaning. The editorial page of the newspaper is a good place to begin.

Read the editorial cartoon. What is the subject of the cartoon? What is the view of the cartoonist? Would you associate the cartoon with a liberal or conservative? Read the editorials, and try to determine if the newspaper has a liberal or conservative point of view. Do you think the newspaper is likely to be conservative or liberal in its presentation of the news?

Now read the rest of the paper to see if you find stories that show a particular point of view. Compare your paper to others on the same day. Did both papers present the same stories in the same way?

2. Developing Your Own Perspective

In a typical 30-minute network news program, only about 20 to 22 minutes are allotted for news reporting. The rest of the time is reserved for commercials or political commentary. In fact, only about one-third of a page from a national newspaper can be read on the air during a television newscast. Out of the hundreds of news events that happen every day, producers must decide which stories will receive airtime. Deciding what to include in a news show is not an easy task. See if you can do it.

Read a major newspaper (*Washington Post, New York Times, Los Angeles Times*, etc.), and use it as a basis for writing a news show. Remember that you have only a limited amount of time to report the news of the day. Some questions to consider:

- What criteria will you use to determine if a story is important enough to be aired?
- How many minutes will you spend on each story?
- Which elements will you emphasize in each story?
- What will be your lead story?

After you have written your news program, examine it carefully. Do you think your own political beliefs are reflected in what you decided to broadcast? Is the amount of time you spent on each story also a reflection of your political beliefs?

3. Becoming an Active Citizen

Staying informed is the key to active citizenship. Try to read your local newspaper every day and a major newsmagazine every week. Watch television news programs as often as possible. To learn more about a particular subject, watch for news specials on that topic. The media—in all its forms—are a valuable educator of all citizens.

Besides being an educator, however, the media present many avenues for political participation. For example, you can write a letter to your local newspaper editor and express your views on local or national issues. If you are a member of a club or organization, you can contact local newspapers and the news department of your local television stations and ask them to cover any events you are sponsoring. You can also get involved with your school or community newspapers by writing articles. Remember, if you are involved in the political process in any way, the media are an important ally in getting your message across to others.

★★★★★★★★★★ THE PEOPLE

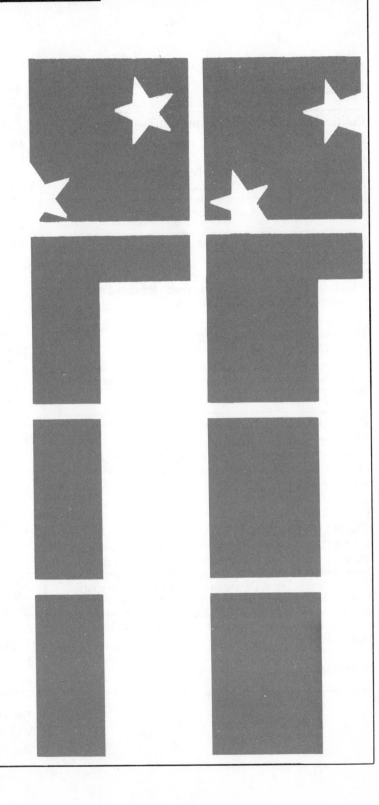

8. The People

In the United States, we have a government of the people, by the people, and for the people. Our political system works because it relies on the involvement of citizens. As Americans, we have a responsibility to participate so that our views and desires are heard. Our choice is not *whether* to participate, but *how* to participate.

Voting

The most basic way for a person to participate in a democracy is to vote. Citizens who are age eighteen or older and who satisfy the residency requirements of their states are eligible to vote; but unfortunately, an increasing number of Americans do not. Despite the efforts of both parties to register new voters, the number has only slightly increased since 1980, and voter turnout in presidential and other elections remains low. Past studies have shown that nonvoters were most often less educated, rural, or poor. But today, nonvoters come from all segments of society, including the college-educated, urban, affluent, and white-collar groups.

There are several reasons for the increase in nonvoting. Americans in general are not well informed about politics. For example, surveys show that only about half the voters in the country know the name of their representative in Congress. Also, the people's trust in their government has been low since the Vietnam War and the Watergate scandal, and has only recently begun to rebound. In addition, many people believe that they have no influence over government, that one vote does not make a difference.

But the reasons to vote far outweigh the reasons not to. When only a few people vote, the will of a small minority can take over. The potential for a dictator to gain political power becomes greater. The health of our democracy depends on all the people exercising their right to vote.

Political Parties

Citizens can also participate in our system of government through political parties. During an election, the parties develop positions on the issues, nominate candidates, conduct voter registration drives, and educate the voters. Political parties provide people with a choice among candidates. However, many people question whether there is a real difference between the two major parties. Increasingly, voters are giving up their membership in a political party and are voting as independents. They base their decisions not on a candidate's party, but rather on the candidate's position on the issues.

But political leaders see an active role for the parties in the electoral process. They claim that there are strong differences between the two major parties and that the parties still offer voters a choice. Parties give the people a way to tell the government how they think it should operate and provide an avenue for active participation in American politics.

Modern Campaigns and the Voter

The recent increase in nonvoters and independent voters has changed election campaigns. Today's campaigns are often run by media and public relations experts who attempt to create the image of a forceful, dynamic, highly professional candidate. Campaigns rely on expensive television ads that emphasize image over issue. Somehow, the candidate's viewpoints seem to get lost. Critics say that many people have come to mistrust the slick advertising campaigns and thus refuse to vote.

However, most campaign consultants agree that it would be impossible to create a false image of a candidate. They can only communicate the personality and views that truly belong to the candidate. Campaign consultants also believe that they actually increase voter interest in a campaign by exposing a candidate to more people.

Activism

The issues currently facing our nation are varied and complex. Every day our nation's leaders discuss how best to solve the deficit crisis, ensure a strong and healthy economy, and protect the nation's security. As citizens, we have a responsibility—and a right—to enter the national debate.

Our nation's history is filled with examples of citizens participating in their government and having an impact. In the 1800s, abolitionists fought to abolish slavery in the United States. In the 1900s, suffragists worked to secure the right to vote for women. And in the 1950s, advocates for civil rights marched to end racial discrimination. These citizens exercised their right to have their voices heard. Citizen activism is—and remains—an important aspect of our democracy and our culture.

218

The strength of the American government resides in the involvement of the people. Each year, millions of Americans across the country participate in our political system as voters, campaign volunteers, and candidates.

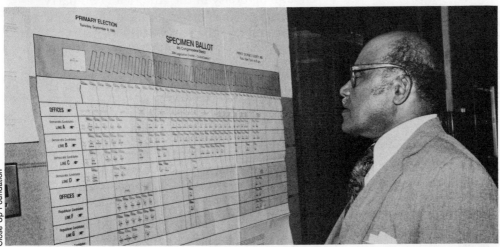

Political Parties and Participation: Two Views

Participation in a political party is an excellent way for people to get involved in the electoral process. CLOSE UP asked the heads of both major parties to describe their parties' goals and the methods they use to attract new members.

Frank Fahrenkopf, Jr.

Frank Fahrenkopf, Jr., chairs the Republican National Committee. He has served as national chair of the Republican State Chairmen's Association, chair of the Western States Republican Chairmen's Association, and state chair of the Nevada Republican Party. Mr. Fahrenkopf presents the Republican party's plans for attracting new members in the future.

A political party is a coalition of like-minded citizens. In a sense, it is like a corporation, but with this difference: you don't have to own stock to be a member. You merely have to exercise your birthright as an American and vote.

Both the Republican and the Democratic parties are truly national "corporations," composed of fifty state organizations, half a dozen local parties in the District of Columbia and the U.S. territories, thousands of county organizations, and millions of individual voters. In times past, a lot of third parties have come and gone, e.g., Know-Nothings, Free-Soilers, Progressives, and Socialists. But for the last 120 years, Americans have chosen their elected representatives almost exclusively from the ranks of Republicans and Democrats.

Skeptics often question whether there is enough diversity in the American two-party system. People sometimes ask if there isn't really just one party—the party of the rich and powerful—and if political labels really mean anything. Others question why we don't have as many parties as Great Britain, which has the Conservative, Labour, Liberal, and Social Democratic parties.

I don't share the skeptics' concern. As chair of the Republican National Committee, I have seen the parties up close. I see a diversity between the two parties that is as keen as any in democracy on earth.

The Republican party today is experiencing a revival of party spirit, thanks largely to President Reagan's bold leadership. But the challenge for Republicans is to maintain this enthusiasm and attract new members. We are doing this in several ways.

First, the Republican party is organizing a nationwide effort to register new voters, including Independents and Democrats as well as Republicans. And as more Democrats seem to become dissatisfied with their party, we intend to register many more as Republicans.

Second, the Republican party is reaching out to youth. In a poll of high school students in 1975, 37 percent of those polled called themselves Democrats and only 24 percent considered themselves to be Republicans. Last year, the same poll showed that Republicans are now the overwhelming majority among high school students. Fifty percent of those polled called themselves Republicans, while only 24 percent said they were Democrats.

Most young Americans want their political party to provide them with a wealth of opportunities. I believe the Republican party is reaching young America because we provide those opportunities. But our success also has a lot to do with getting people involved in the party at a young age. The Republican party has taken the time and effort to organize high school and college students into groups such as the Teenage Republicans, College Republicans, and the Young Republicans.

Third, the Republican party is reaching out to different ethnic and social groups. For example, in the state election in New Jersey in 1985, the Republican party took a majority of the traditionally Democratic, black, blue-collar, Catholic, and Hispanic vote. This is evidence that the Republican party can break down the tradition of party identification along ethnic, religious, and economic lines. Now, more than ever, Americans are joining political parties because of what they *believe*, not because of tradition.

Fourth, the Republican party is rebuilding the party organization. One of the historic weaknesses of the Republican party has been its top-heaviness. Republicans are adept at electing presidents and senators. (A Republican has won the presidency in four out of the last five presidential elections.) But we have not done a good job at electing county judges, city council members, and state legislators.

This is more important than it may first seem. A national political party must be built just like a house, on a sturdy foundation from the bottom up. The Democrats were successful because they did an excellent job of electing their candidates to state and local offices.

A party with support among city and county voters will increase its chances to elect candidates for the state legislatures. This task requires a new emphasis on county Republican offices. The Republican "1991 Plan," which is already well underway, is a national plan to reorganize all 3,304 county parties in the country, through the use of talent and money.

I believe the competition between the two parties is intense and wide open. And it is intense because the two parties really do offer different visions of the future. America has a two-party system because it doesn't need a third party.

There is enough competition between the two parties, and enough diversity within each party, that every credible interest of American society can express itself politically.

Regardless of whether a person decides to become a Republican or a Democrat, my hope is that they will participate. Both parties are in need of new talent and ideas.

Paul Kirk

Paul Kirk chairs the Democratic National Committee. Previously, he served as treasurer of the Democratic National Committee, special counsel to Senator Edward Kennedy (D-Mass.), and assistant counsel to the Senate Judiciary Committee. Mr. Kirk says that the Democrats encourage participation through voter registration and public education.

In his classic work, *Democracy in America*, the French historian Alexis de Tocqueville commented on the difference between the New World and Europe.

The emigrants who colonized the shores of America. . .somehow separated the democratic principle from all [others]. . .and transplanted it in the New World.

221

I HAD SHOCKING NEWS TODAY. JENNY, MY MAID, TOLD ME SHE'S A REGISTERED REPUBLICAN.

No!

IT HAD TO HAPPEN!

COUNTRY CLUB AFTERNOON TEA

Once transplanted, the seeds of democracy soon flourished. Perhaps no single development better illustrates this transformation than the emergence of the American party system.

Although our nation's two-party system is almost 200 years old, there was a time in U.S. history when political parties did not exist. It was not until 1790, a full twenty-three years after the Revolutionary War, that political parties began to evolve. Voters began to align themselves with well-known legislators who supported their views on a variety of issues. Candidates, in turn, sought to respond to the will of the people. Alliances were formed, and the final pieces of democratic government were put into place. The party system was born.

In the years that followed, political parties have undergone many changes. The Democratic party, which is the oldest political party in the world, has become more than a vehicle through which voters choose their elected officials. As the government has grown in size and complexity, the Democratic party has followed. At our national headquarters in Washington, D.C., the Democratic National Committee (DNC) provides service to state, county, and local party organizations across the country. Each of these organizations is headed by a chairman, who works to coordinate various party activities. Chief among

these activities are voter registration and mobilization, fundraising, and public education.

What Does the Democratic Party Do?
One of the most important tasks the Democratic party engages in is that of voter registration. In order for a democracy to work effectively, citizens must be active participants in the electoral process. Upon reaching the age of eighteen, every U.S. citizen has an obligation to register as a voter and exercise their constitutional right to choose the members of their government. Unfortunately, close to half of those individuals who are eligible to vote do not. In each of the fifty states, the Democratic party tries to solve this problem by organizing voter registration drives.

But, registering voters is only half the battle. Once voters are registered, they must be encouraged to cast their ballots on Election Day. The Democratic party, with the aid of state and local party activists, organizes "get-out-the-vote" drives, which encourage people to participate in their democracy. Without participation, our nation's ability to function would be severely hampered.

The Democratic party's efforts to encourage participation in the electoral process do not end here though. We also educate and inform the American public about the party's fundamental philosophy as well as our candidates' positions on critical issues. Without the proper information, voters would be unable to make an informed choice among candidates.

Who Are the Democrats?
In my tenure as chairman of the Democratic party, I have been asked frequently to describe the typical Democratic voter. The question is a difficult one. In their long histories, the two political parties have contained the entire ideological spectrum. Because the American political system is open to all who choose to participate, America's political parties have been similarly void of restrictions. A voter can become a Democrat or a Republican simply by declaring himself that. A person who votes for a Democratic candidate might be a lifelong member of the Democratic party or might simply be attracted to that particular candidate, rather than the entire Democratic philosophy. Throughout our history, the Democratic party has come to represent many things to many people. For the nation's elderly, we are the party of

Franklin Roosevelt, the Democratic president who initiated the social security system on which so many Americans depend. For many others, we are the party of John F. Kennedy and Lyndon Johnson, two presidents who stood strongly against the threat of communism, and for civil rights and social and economic justice. Still other Americans view the Democratic party as the embodiment of social values—such as equal education and ending poverty—which are so important to our nation.

Today, one issue that divides Democrats and Republicans is the role of the federal government. The Democratic party views government as a vehicle for investment in America's future. Republicans usually oppose use of the tool of government.

The Democratic party believes that government can at once be pragmatic and compassionate—that we can, for example, maintain a low inflation rate, while also protecting our nation's environment. For Democrats, compassion and pragmatism are not mutually exclusive. That is the essence of democratic government. And as the Democratic party moves into the future, we will continue to prove that compassion and pragmatism, together, form the cornerstone of successful government.

Questions to Consider

1. What are the similarities between how the Republican and Democratic parties attract new members? What are the differences?

2. According to Mr. Fahrenkopf, between 1975 and 1985, the number of high school students calling themselves Republicans more than doubled. What do you think accounts for this trend?

3. Do you agree with Mr. Kirk that the main difference between the Democrats and Republicans is their view of the role of the federal government?

Campaigning in the Eighties

Steve Allen

Steve Allen is assistant to the president of the Viguerie Company, a direct marketing and advertising agency that handles political advertising. Previously, he was senior editor of the Conservative Digest *and served as press secretary to Senator Jeremiah Denton (R-Ala.). In his article, Mr. Allen describes how modern campaign technology (i.e., television and direct mail) aids voters.*

The 1840 presidential contest went down in history as the first election in which the outcome was determined largely by campaign technology, but it would not be the last.

Using buttons, lithographs, transparencies, and whiskey bottles shaped like log cabins, the Whig party elected its candidate, 67-year-old William Henry Harrison, as president of the United States, upsetting the incumbent Democrat, Martin van Buren. The Whig victory of 1840 was the first political campaign in the modern sense—the first mass use of banners and other paraphernalia to generate excitement for a political candidate.

In 1980, the Republican party used computer-written letters, telephone banks, television commercials, and "media events" staged for the evening news to elect its candidate, 69-year-old Ronald Reagan, as president of the United States, upsetting the incumbent Democrat, Jimmy Carter.

In politics, like warfare, the advantage often goes to the side that uses the most modern weapons. If two candidates are otherwise evenly matched, the winner will be the one with the most up-to-date campaign technology. New methods of communication are constantly being invented, and a candidate or party cannot afford to fall behind.

Nevertheless, every time someone comes up with a new way of reaching the voters, the cynics repeat the old stories: that behind every successful political candidate, there is a clever image maker—a mastermind who can take a mediocre office seeker and mold him into a matinee idol or a paragon of statesmanship. This mastermind (a political consultant) creates an image for the politician that is wholly at odds with reality. He pulls the politician's strings, telling him to do whatever is necessary to win the next election, because winning is the only thing that matters.

None of this is true. In the long run, new campaign technology helps voters more than politicians and political consultants.

Occasionally, political consultants can be helpful to a campaign, and a good consultant can help win a race that would otherwise be lost. But most of the time, elections are decided on the basis of ideology, issues, and qualifications. In other words, usually the person who deserves to win does.

It is nearly impossible for a political consultant to craft an image that is different from a can-

In the 1960 election campaign, Richard Nixon and John Kennedy participated in the first televised presidential debate. Their debate served as a model for subsequent debates among presidential candidates.

didate's background and views on the issues. The best a consultant can do is help the candidate communicate those qualities to the voters in the most favorable light. For example, if a candidate is seeking to clean up state government, the consultant might suggest that the candidate carry a mop as a symbol. If the candidate is running on a "get-tough-on-crime" platform, the consultant might create a TV commercial in which the candidate slams a jail door shut with a loud clang. An especially clever consultant can make his point memorable by using humor. One Senate campaign commercial ridiculed excessive government regulation by showing a cowboy on his horse being required to drag a portable toilet behind him.

With a few rare exceptions, slogans, gimmicks, and clever commercials work only to the extent that they reflect reality. If a candidate is completely unknown to the voters, it is possible for a false image to be created. But in almost all cases, the truth about the candidate comes out before the election.

Of course, modern campaign technology can have an impact on politics. Many people believe that John Kennedy defeated Richard Nixon for the presidency in 1960 because Nixon looked tired and sick during his televised debate with Kennedy. However, voters who listened to the two candidates on the radio thought Nixon had won the debate.

Does television turn elections into beauty contests in which the candidate with the best smile or the cutest dimples wins? I don't think so. Neither Lyndon Johnson, winner in the 1964 presidential election, nor Richard Nixon, winner in 1968 and 1972, could be considered especially attractive. Jimmy Carter, winner in 1976, was

thought to be handsome, but his southern accent was a handicap. Among recent presidents, only Ronald Reagan, a former actor, had the right "look" and the right voice for television, but he didn't get elected until he was nearly 70 years old!

A candidate's looks can be an important factor in winning an election—but so can his voice, the strength of his handshake, the familiar sound of his name, or his position on the issues. An examination of hundreds of national, state, and local elections over the years would show that political

I MUST ADMIT WHEN I MADE "ROAD TO THE PRESIDENCY" FOR OUR NEW PRESIDENT-ELECT, I NEVER FIGURED THE FILM WOULD WIN AN ACADEMY AWARD FOR BEST ORIGINAL FICTION.

NEWS ITEM: PRESIDENTIAL CAMPAIGN FILM WINS OSCAR. ACADEMY SAYS IT CAN NO LONGER OVERLOOK THE FINE CREATIVITY IN CAMPAIGN PROMOS.

225

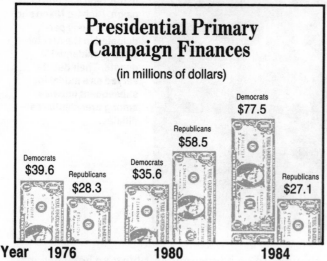

Presidential Primary Campaign Finances

(in millions of dollars)

Democrats
$39.6

Republicans
$28.3

Democrats
$35.6

Republicans
$58.5

Democrats
$77.5

Republicans
$27.1

| Year | 1976 | 1980 | 1984 |

Source: Federal Election Commission

In recent years, spending for presidential campaigns—especially by challengers—has increased. Most campaign funds are spent on television advertising, but funds are also needed for campaign staff salaries, literature, transportation, and food.

victory goes almost as often to the unattractive person as it does to the matinee idol.

The real impact of television on the electoral process is not that it puts a premium on makeup artists and plastic surgeons. Rather, it is that television spreads information faster, to more people, than ever before. Only a handful of people attended the Lincoln-Douglas debates in the 1850s, but hundreds of thousands might watch a modern-day debate between two Senate candidates. Tens of millions watch the presidential debates and political conventions. And, with overnight polling (another example of new technology), people can talk back to the politicians immediately. Future innovations, such as two-way cable hookups, will bring the political process even closer to home. In a similar way, the development of direct mail as a political tool has made it easier for average citizens to participate in and support the political process by supporting the candidate of their choice.

Direct mail is now a vital part of most political campaigns, especially those that are based on strongly held beliefs, such as nuclear disarmament, the environment, abortion, and taxes. Using computers, political organizers are able to identify the people most likely to give money to particular candidates and causes. Over a period of time, they can generate lists with millions of names and addresses and can use the lists over and over again.

Today, because of developments like television and direct mail, people rely less on political parties to provide them with information about candidates. They are more free to vote their own convictions based on the information they can obtain on their own. They are more likely to vote for the person, not the party. In the last twenty years, the number of independent voters has grown significantly, and even persons who identify themselves as Republicans and Democrats cross party lines far more often in their voting.

The founders of this country hoped that political parties would never arise in the United States. But the ink on the Constitution wasn't even dry before the Federalists and Republicans were at each other's throats. Strangely enough, it took twentieth-century technology to bring us closer than ever before to the partyless politics the founders envisioned.

Questions to Consider

1. Do you think television has turned campaigns into beauty contests? Why or why not?

2. Do you think campaign techniques such as television ads and direct mail efforts help voters make a decision in an election? Why or why not?

3. Do you think politicians rely too heavily on campaign advertising in order to win an election?

The Dangers of Voter Apathy

Curtis Gans

Curtis Gans directs the Committee for the Study of the American Electorate, a nonpartisan research organization that looks into the causes and cures of declining voter participation. In his article, Mr. Gans explains why voting in the United States has declined and offers his ideas for improving participation in the electoral process.

When the followers of right-wing activist Lyndon LaRouche won the Illinois Democratic primary nominations for lieutenant governor and secretary of state in spring 1986, the results were greeted with public concern. Yet, this result is the logical outgrowth of an electorate in which a smaller percentage of citizens vote and an even smaller percentage is paying attention.

When few people vote, the candidates of a militant few can win.

When few people vote, the forces of an organized special interest have the opportunity to dominate the nation's political dialogue.

When few people vote, the potential for a demagogue to come to power becomes ever greater.

For the past two decades (with the notable exception of 1982 and 1984), an ever smaller percentage of eligible Americans have been casting their ballots. In each presidential election, more than 80 million eligible Americans fail to vote. In congressional elections, the number rises to more than 100 million eligible Americans who reject the ballot box.

Over these two decades, the percentage of eligible Americans who vote has declined by 10 percent in both presidential and off-year elections. More than 20 million Americans who used to vote frequently have ceased participating altogether. The United States—with voter turnouts of around 50 percent in presidential elections and 40 percent in off-year elections—now has the lowest rate of voter participation of any democracy in the world.

More than half of America's nonparticipants are chronic nonvoters—people who have never or hardly ever vote, whose families have never voted, and who are poorer, less educated, and less involved participants in American society. But a growing number of the Americans are simply dropping out of political process—many of whom are educated, white-collar professionals. In addition, a growing number of younger Americans are failing to enter the political process. Both of these trends constitute a major national concern, for there is a very real danger that the habits of good citizenship will die and that government of the people, for the people, and by the people will become government of, for, and by the few.

There is no predetermined optimal level of voter participation. American democracy has

Reflections on the People

"The health of a democratic society may be measured by the quality of functions performed by private citizens."

Alexis de Tocqueville
(1805-59),
French politician
and philosopher

"I know no safe depository of the powers of society but the people themselves."

Thomas Jefferson
(1743-1826),
president of the
United States—1801-09

"You cannot possibly have a broader basis for any government than that which includes all the people, with all their rights in their hands, and with an equal power to maintain their rights."

William Lloyd Garrison
(1805-79),
abolitionist writer and editor

"Why should there not be confidence in the ultimate justice of the people? Is there any better or equal hope in the world?"

Abraham Lincoln
(1809-65),
president of the
United States—1860-65

"There is no group in America that can withstand the force of an aroused public opinion."

Franklin D. Roosevelt
(1882-1945),
president of the
United States—1932-45

"We hold the view that the people make the best judgment in the long run."

John F. Kennedy
(1917-63),
president of the
United States—1960-63

"There can be no daily democracy without daily citizenship."

Ralph Nader
(1934-   ),
lawyer and consumer
advocate

"Government must be kept open. If we intend to rebuild confidence in the government process, policy must be shaped through the participation of the American people."

Jimmy Carter
(1924-   ),
president of the
United States—1976-80

"The most important power of the people is this: they will endure."

Carl Sandburg
(1878-1967),
poet and historian

both survived and prospered despite rates of voting lower than many other democracies. But the continuing and sharp decline in the level of voting and citizen involvement cannot help but adversely affect the health of American politics.

Much of the decline in voter participation has occurred during a time when the procedures governing voting have been liberalized. In 1963, shortly before he died, President Kennedy established a commission to investigate the low rate of American voter participation. That commission, reporting shortly after his death, made a series of recommendations, including the abolition of poll taxes and literacy tests, the enfranchisement of blacks and the young, the establishment of voter outreach programs and bilingual ballots, and the shortening of the time between the close of registration and elections.

All of these recommendations were enacted either nationally or by a large number of states, but voter participation has continued to go down. Which is to suggest that it is not the *procedures* governing American politics but rather the *substance* of American politics which is at the heart of declining rates of voter participation and public disaffection with the political process.

This is not to suggest that procedural questions are irrelevant to the low rates of American participation. Of all the democracies, the United States stands alone in making voting a two-step act by making the citizen qualify himself for

I HAVEN'T VOTED SINCE I WAS 18. IT'S BEEN A PERSONAL PROTEST AGAINST BAD GOVERNMENT BUT I'M NOT SURE HOW EFFECTIVE IT'S BEEN.

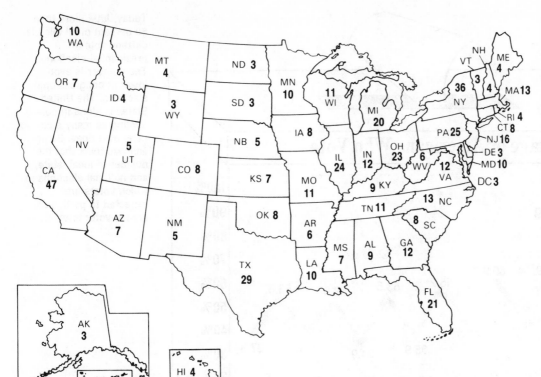

voting through registration. In almost every other nation with elections, the government conducts registration and all the citizen has to do is vote.

Similarly, the United States is almost alone in conducting as many elections as it does. Almost every year, citizens are called upon to vote for school board or county commissioner while other offices are elected in separate elections, a procedure that seems designed to wear out citizen interest and insure low turnout. And the amount of information a citizen, who depends on television for his news, gets in order to make an informed decision tends to be limited to those offices at the top of the ballot.

The United States also tends to have polling and registration hours that are too short, ballots that are too long, and procedures that are often too difficult for the average citizen to understand. But these impediments have always been with us and, in general, have been made somewhat easier. Yet, voter participation has continued to decline.

It has become fashionable in recent years for those in the media to exhort the citizenry to vote and then berate them for the failure to do so. This is, it seems, blame misplaced.

The scars of the Vietnam War and the Watergate scandal run deep. To many Americans, politics seems to be characterized by poor public leadership, increasingly complex issues, and an ever-growing and inflexible government with few successes in meeting public needs. The public has been called upon to vote in a series of negative elections—*against* Barry Goldwater in 1964, *against* the policies of Lyndon Johnson in 1968, *against* George McGovern in 1972, *against* Gerald Ford in 1976, *against* Jimmy Carter in 1980, and *against* Walter Mondale in 1984.

The people have been forced to choose between two competing parties, one of which is associated with right-wing populism and big business greed and the other a cacophony of competing interests whose whole is less than the sum of its parts. And it gets its information in 1-1/2 minute blips from a medium that highlights the visually exciting at the expense of the substantively important.

Sadly, for the average citizen, nonparticipation is becoming an increasingly rational act.

Reversing this trend and instilling both hope and vigor among American voters will not be an easy task. But I think a few steps will help improve participation in America. We need to:

■ increase the amount and sophistication of civic education in our homes and schools;

■ develop policies that address the central concerns of the electorate;

229

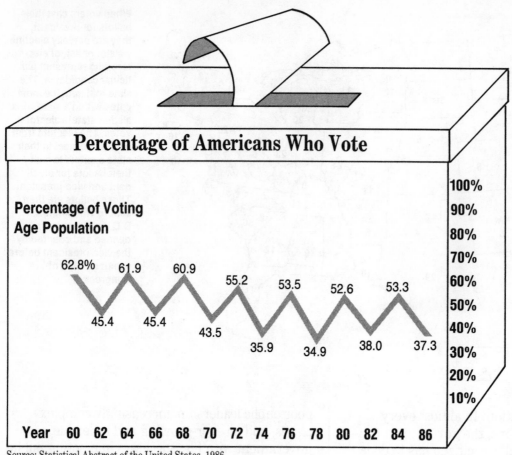

Percentage of Americans Who Vote

Percentage of Voting Age Population

Year	Percentage
60	62.8%
62	45.4
64	61.9
66	45.4
68	60.9
70	43.5
72	55.2
74	35.9
76	53.5
78	34.9
80	52.6
82	38.0
84	53.3
86	37.3

100%
90%
80%
70%
60%
50%
40%
30%
20%
10%

Source: Statistical Abstract of the United States, 1986

Today, little more than 50 percent of all eligible citizens vote in presidential elections. The number is even lower in congressional elections. The United States is alone in conducting as many elections as it does. Some analysts think that the number of local, state, and national elections in which voters are expected to participate erodes voter interest.

■ realign and strengthen the two-party system so that its advocacy is relevant to the electorate and its performance in government is improved;

■ supplement the information we receive from television with deeper and more adequate information from other sources;

■ instill in our young people a sense of values that emphasizes something larger than the self and something more enduring than today; and

■ develop a standard for leadership that makes the term "not unfit to serve" inadequate for public service.

In the end, voting is a religious act. Citizens must come to believe that—despite the thousands of elections that are not decided by one vote—his or her vote *does* make a difference. It is that faith that needs to be restored.

Questions to Consider

1. What are the dangers of low voter turnouts?

2. Why do you think a growing number of young Americans are choosing not to vote?

3. How would you go about implementing the author's suggestions for improving voter participation?

Political Activism in America

The Reverend Robert Drinan, S.J.

Father Robert Drinan is a professor of law at Georgetown University specializing in international human rights, constitutional law, and civil liberties. He was a U.S. representative for Massachusetts from 1971 to 1981. Father Drinan is the former president of Americans for Democratic Action and is a member of the board of numerous organizations including Common Cause, the Legal Defense and Education Fund of the National Association for the Advancement of Colored People (NAACP), and the National Conference of Christians and Jews. In his article, Father Drinan describes how the roots of political activism date back to the founding of the nation and remain a key element of democracy in America.

For veterans of the days of activism on civil rights and the war in Vietnam, the recent campus demonstrations over South Africa come as a welcome reminder. The protests against apartheid are encouraging because, unlike black activists working for the enforcement of civil rights or young people likely to be drafted to go to Vietnam, the demonstrators against segregation in South Africa have no self-interest in the issue. They march or protest out of sheer dismay that some 3 million white people control the lives of 25 million black people. In that sense, the crusade against apartheid can be compared to the fundraising activities undertaken on behalf of the hungry in Africa.

America has always believed in people's movements. Indeed, one could say that citizens who care have to some extent been the architects of America's public morality. It was citizens who around the year 1800 began the movement to abolish slavery. The abolitionist movement is the forerunner of and prototype for every citizen group that has come into existence since then. The courageous men and women who proclaimed that they could not live in a nation that held slaves probably did not realize in the year 1800 that their crusade would take sixty-five years to accomplish. But their victory in the Emancipation Proclamation established a standard that has emboldened all of the moral movements since that time. The abolitionist movement made it clear that in America the government does not decide the morality of the nation; rather, America's morality comes from a delicate consensus among all types of citizens. At its best, citizen activism is the articulation of what the people of America want their nation to be.

Those who claim that citizen activism is futile do not know American history. That history demonstrates that a well-informed and determined group—even a small minority—can have a significant impact. Clearly the women and men who worked to obtain the vote for women in America demonstrated that militancy on behalf of an unpopular cause can succeed. The suffragists chained themselves to hydrants and engaged in countless other attention-getting devices before their objective was finally realized in 1920.

In more recent times, thousands of individuals made possible the enactment of the Civil Rights Act of 1964 and the Voting Rights Act of 1965. In 1963, President Kennedy signed the Nuclear

1...2...3...4... WE DON'T WANT YOUR CRUMMY WAR!

STUDENTS AGAINST THE WAR!

1972

1...2...3...4... FLAME-BROILED'S WHAT WE'RE FIGHT'N FOR.

STUDENTS FOR FLAME-BROILED BURGERS VS. FRIED IN THE CAF.

PETER ©1986

1986?

Test Ban Treaty eliminating all atomic tests in the atmosphere and in the ocean. That treaty was brought about not by the politicians but by the millions of people who protested the emission into the atmosphere of radioactive substances. A decade later, the people had another victory when, largely because of a broadly based citizen protest against the construction of antiballistic missiles, President Nixon agreed in SALT I (first Strategic Arms Limitation Talks) with the Soviets to renounce the construction of the anti-ballistic missile that was designed to protect America's land-based ICBMs (intercontinental ballistic missiles). And possibly the largest and most persistent people's movement in American history—at least since the abolitionist movement—ended the war in Vietnam in 1974.

In our own decade, some observers say that the level of caring for others has gone down in America. They criticize the self-centeredness and widespread apathy, especially among young people. But I see as much political activism and caring among Americans today as at almost any moment in American history. People are still concerned about:

■ passage of the the Equal Rights Amendment;

■ giving the citizens of the District of Columbia voting representation in the Congress;

■ the rights of the physically handicapped to have access to public facilities;

■ the legality of handgun control in the United States;

Throughout American history, many citizens have disagreed with the policies and decisions of our political leaders. To publicize their differences, citizen groups conduct marches, hold rallies, and organize other activities to attract public attention.

■ the amount of money that political action committees (PACs) should be allowed to give to election campaigns; and

■ the nuclear arms race and national security.

These examples of citizen activism are but a few of the many causes in which citizens of all kinds—singly and collectively—are seeking to improve life in America. The moral zeal of these groups is just as intense as similar groups who worked in the 1960s and 1970s. Indeed, it could be argued that activists in the 1980s are more sophisticated in their approach and in their techniques than those who preceded them.

In any event, all of these groups represent the best of American tradition and American culture. They know that people in America who care about public morality have a right and a duty to speak out, to work, to lobby, to demonstrate, and, sometimes, to try to insist on the acceptance of their point of view. When people have failed to follow this tradition, America has been the loser.

The outspoken, the activists, the people who demonstrate that they care—these are the moral architects of America and the real heroes and heroines of the republic. The question that confronts everyone is an ancient one: "Am I my brother's keeper?" The answer to that question is yes, I am my brother's keeper because I am my brother's brother.

Questions to Consider

1. Do you think political activism is inseparable from citizenship? Why or why not?

2. Do you think public protests are an effective way to participate in the political process? Why or why not?

3. Do you agree with the author that Americans should be concerned about the plight of people around the world? Why or why not?

The MADD Crusade

"The anti-drunk-driving movement is a cause that has enlisted the support of the young and the old, liberal and conservative, drinker and non-drinker," says Gerard Murphy, president of the Automotive Trade Association. "For the first time, large numbers of Americans are thinking about the horror and waste drunk driving produces through thousands upon thousands of injuries and deaths each year on the nation's highways."

The movement against drunk driving is also a crusade set in motion in part by one citizen activist. It began as a personal need to do something about a child who fell victim to a drunk driver and quickly grew into a national organization. This crusade has been responsible for a ground swell of public awareness and outrage against drunk driving as well as passage of new legislation and stricter enforcement of existing legislation.

A Mother's Grief

In May 1980, 13-year-old Cari Lightner was walking in a bicycle lane on her way to a school carnival in Fair Oaks, California. She was hit by a swerving car and thrown forty yards. She was dead within the hour. The driver never stopped.

Cari's mother, Candy Lightner, was a divorced, real-estate businesswoman with two other children—Cari's twin sister and a younger son. Her reaction at first, Lightner said, was "anger, grief, revenge." On her way to dinner with family and friends a few days later, she passed the place where her daughter was killed. There she saw two police officers investigating the site and stopped.

She learned from the police officers that the man who killed her daughter, Clarence Busch, was a repeat-offender drunk driver. He had been convicted of drunk driving three times in the past four years

and was just out on bail on another hit-and-run drunk-driving charge. She asked the police how much time Busch would get in prison. "Lady," they said, "you'll be lucky if this guy gets *any* jail time, much less prison. That's how the system works."

At dinner, she spoke of her shock, anger, and frustration. "Start an organization," one friend said. "Call it Mothers Against Drunk Driving," said another. "I thought for ten seconds," Lightner reported later, "before saying 'I will.'" The next morning she went downtown and filed for incorporation of Mothers Against Drunk Driving (MADD). Her crusade against drunk driving was under way.

The Road to Activism

"You begin," says Lightner, "by asking people if they know someone who can help. This leads to others, and you develop a network of individuals you can turn to as time goes

In May 1980, Candy Lightner's 13-year-old daughter was killed by a hit-and-run drunk driver. Lightner's anger at a judicial system that was lenient on repeat offenders led her to form Mothers Against Drunk Driving.

on." But the beginning was not easy. As Lightner said later, "I wasn't even a registered voter. I had never read a law in my life, never spoken in public, never formed a corporation. I'd never been to court, never spoken to a judge." When she asked who she should talk to first, the answer was the attorney general. Lightner had to find out who the attorney general was. She also had to learn who represented her in the state assembly and what that representative did and could do. "Everywhere I went," Lightner recalled, "people said, 'You won't get anywhere. It'll take years.' I was so bitter. But I just kept plugging along."

With her father and her friend Sue LeBrun, Lightner plunged into research on what other counties and states were doing about drunk drivers. They talked to police, lobbyists, lawyers, and judges. They even visited courtrooms and found some judges much too lenient. For example, Clarence Busch, who killed Cari Lightner, was allowed to plead *nolo contendere* on the single count of vehicular manslaughter even though he had three felony counts in Cari's death and two additional charges hanging over him from the earlier hit-and-run accident. (*Nolo contendere* is a plea made by a defendant in which the defendant is subject to conviction, but without having to admit guilt.) As a result, although Busch was sentenced to two years in prison, he went to a work camp for only three months and then was transferred to a halfway house.

One judge told Lightner, "If you don't like the law, little lady, change it." Lightner answered by expanding MADD's focus from public education to include affecting the legislative process. She worked with her representative in the state assembly and a lobbyist in the attorney general's office, and she continued to release information to the press as she obtained it. In August 1980, three months after her

daughter's death, she planned her first press conference to apply pressure.

"Before you go public with what it is you're going to do," advises Lightner, "know the issue well, research it carefully, and understand both sides of the issue." At the press conference, held in the governor's press room on the first floor of the state capitol building in Sacramento, Lightner announced a statewide petition drive aimed at getting drunk drivers off the road. She also asked then Governor Jerry Brown to appoint a task force to develop solutions to the state's drunk-driving problem. Outside the building, a group of twenty teenage friends of Cari's—calling themselves SADD (Students Against Drunk Driving)—picketed to support the call for the task force and to focus attention on the needless death of their friend. Inside, at the press conference, Cari's twin sister broke down as she tried to describe what it was like to lose a sister to a drunk driver. Her mother comforted her. Widely publicized photos of their moment of grief, and of the students marching outside, told the consequences of drunk driving.

The governor did not act. Lightner continued to lobby state officials. She also lobbied the press. More and more stories were written. Other women who had lost children to drunk drivers called her. She asked them to start chapters of MADD.

By October 1980, five months after her daughter Cari's death, there were three chapters of MADD in California and one in Maryland. Lightner took a trip to Washington, D.C., to participate in a press conference with U.S. Representative Michael Barnes (D-Md.) and Cindi Lamb, founder of the Maryland chapter of MADD. Lamb's 5-month-old daughter, Laura, was permanently paralyzed from the neck down because of a repeat-offender drunk driver—a tragedy that had been covered in detail by a local television station. Also participating

in the press conference was Senator Claiborne Pell (D-R.I.), who had lost two of his staff members to drunk driving. Afterwards, Lightner picketed the White House in her first attempt to get President Ronald Reagan to appoint a commission to study alcohol-related deaths.

One immediate result of the national publicity was a meeting with California Governor Brown and his appointment of a task force to study the problem in California, with Lightner as a member. When Brown informed Lightner of his decision, she "just started crying right there in his office."

During the first year of her crusade, Lightner went without salary. She also contributed 60 percent of MADD's $41,000 budget from her personal savings and from the insurance money she collected when Cari died. Her commitment to MADD was total. "If you have a drinking problem, it's your problem," she said. "But once you get behind the wheel of a car, it's my problem." Her mission was to make citizens and local, state, and national government officials recognize that traffic accidents that involve alcohol should be seen not as "accidents," but as violent crimes. As people called and wrote to her from all over the country, Lightner sent them press kits and resource lists and urged them to form their own chapters. She personalized the issue, speaking of the "horrors" done to individuals, to families, and to the nation. "You kick a few pebbles," she said, "you turn over a few stones, and eventually an avalanche begins."

The avalanche was well under way by the summer of 1981, just one year after Cari's death. MADD had twenty-four chapters in four states—fourteen in California, eight in Maryland, and one each in Pennsylvania and Virginia. Officials no longer thought of Lightner as a "hysterical mother leading a fly-by-night organization." A formal membership drive had been launched. More than 50,000 people

Close Up Foundation

had signed MADD petitions urging federal action.

At the end of 1981, California passed the toughest law against drunk driving in the nation thus far, imposing minimum fines of $375 and mandatory imprisonment of up to four years for repeat offenders. "That law was due solely to us," said Lightner. Federal legislation related to drunk driving had also been introduced into Congress, which granted additional funding to states that adopted regulations to deter drunk driving. (This provision, part of Public Law 97-364, was signed into law in October 1982.)

In April 1982, President Reagan appointed the Presidential Commission on Drunk Driving and charged it "to encourage state and local governments, as well as the private sector, to implement programs that will reduce the carnage caused by the drinking drivers on our highways." Lightner was among the thirty-two members appointed. The final report, issued in November 1983 after extensive hearings, contained thirty-nine recommendations, ranging from the development of public awareness and education campaigns to alcoholic beverage regulation, enforcement, prosecution, and rehabilitation. The report emphasized that "no one is in favor of drunk driving, not even drunk drivers." It spoke of a national outcry that demanded immediate action. What was new was that the intensity, extent, and drama of that national outcry were directly related to one woman's grief.

Joining the Outcry

MADD calls itself "a body of people who are enraged over the failure of our legislators and courts to pass and enforce laws that will protect us from the death and injury that occurs daily at the hands of drunk drivers in America." The personal nature of the cause has been a key to the organization's success, although MADD members echo the feelings of Cari Lightner's twin sister Serena, who said, "What bothers me is that all this came about because of children who have died." Yet her mother's anger, which inspired others to channel their feelings of anger and outrage, is what has made MADD grow.

For example, the Milwaukee County, Wisconsin, chapter of MADD was started by Micky Sadoff, who with her husband, was a victim of an accident involving a drunk driver in 1982. The San Diego, California, chapter of MADD was started by Norma Phillips, whose son Dean and his girlfriend were killed by a drunk driver on Thanksgiving Day in 1981. And Virginia MADD was started by Susan Midgett, who lost her 14-year-old son when a drunk driver ran off the road and onto her front lawn. Midgett's outrage was part of a larger movement that forced the Virginia General Assembly to strengthen the state's drunk-driving laws in March 1982. It was to be one of the most emotional debates of the 1982 Virginia session. Virginia MADD had set up a network of parents, who phoned legislators, testified at committee hearings, held press conferences, and finally, on the night the bill was voted on, maintained a candlelight vigil on the state capitol grounds in honor of the tragic losses their families had suffered at the hands of drunk drivers. "Passage of the bill," reported the *Washington Post*, "concluded one of the more effective grassroots lobbying campaigns to hit the capital in years." The bill—one of thirty-eight pieces of legislation in twenty-five states enacted in 1982—would never have passed without the MADD campaign.

Much of the material that MADD distributes personalizes the outrage by describing the results of drunk driving, as with Cari Lightner's death and Laura Lamb's paralysis. Materials also describe the anguish of drunk drivers. High school student Kevin Tunell admits, "I sit up in bed all night long thinking about how I killed somebody. You're always condemning yourself." Seventeen-year-old Hector Del Valle regrets, "One good time is not worth sitting in a wheelchair for the rest of my life."

What MADD finds out, it makes public—as it has since its beginning. Such statistics as the following (compiled from the records of the National Highway Traffic Safety Administration, the National Safety Council, and the Insurance Institute for Highway Safety) make an eloquent case.

■ Over the last ten years, an average of 23,500 people a year have been killed in drunk-driving crashes. This figure represents sixty-four dead every day; one life ended by a drunk driver every twenty-three minutes.

■ On the average weekend night, one of every ten drivers on the road is legally drunk.

■ Only one in every 2,000 drunk drivers will ever be arrested for driving under the influence of alcohol.

■ Of those who die in single-car wrecks, 65 percent are drunk.

■ Eighty percent of all fatal alcohol-related auto crashes occur between 6 p.m. and 6 a.m.

■ Forty-four percent of all fatal, alcohol-related crashes that occur at night are caused by drivers age 16 to 24, yet this group accounts for only 22 percent of all licensed drivers.

■ More than 75 percent of American youths are drinking alcoholic beverages by the age of 16.

■ Between 1974 and 1978, the number of male alcohol abusers rose by 3 percent to 38 percent; during the same period, female misusers rose by 5 percent to 26 percent.

■ Fifty-nine percent of high school males have had problems with drinking and driving; 42 percent of high school females had trouble with drinking and driving.

■ A study released recently by the Insurance Institute for Highway Safety confirms the beneficial effects of raising the legal drinking age. Based on the experience of twenty-six states that had raised the minimum purchasing age during the study period, the result was a 13-percent decrease in fatalities among young drivers from nighttime crashes.

■ Each year 8,000 teens and young adults are killed, and 40,000 are injured in crashes involving drinking and driving.

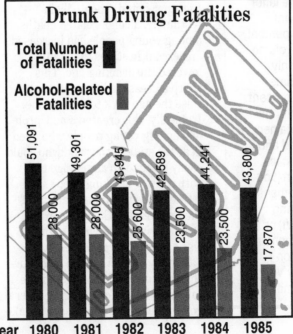

Since 1980, the number of people killed by drunk drivers on our nation's highways has decreased. Thirty-seven states have passed laws that increase the power of the police to identify drunk drivers, improve state legal systems to aid in the prosecution of drunk drivers, and establish victim restitution funds.

Drunk Driving Fatalities

Total Number of Fatalities ■
Alcohol-Related Fatalities ■

Year	1980	1981	1982	1983	1984	1985
Total Number of Fatalities	51,091	49,301	43,945	42,589	44,241	43,800
Alcohol-Related Fatalities	28,000	28,000	25,600	23,500	23,500	17,870

Source: National Highway Transportation Safety Administration, National Center for Statistics and Analysis

How Much Is Too Much

What is a "drink"? A drink can be a 12-ounce can of beer, a 4-ounce glass of wine, or a 1.5-ounce shot glass of 80-proof liquor. How much is "too much" depends upon the drinker's weight and how much time has elapsed between drinking and driving. People weighing between 110 pounds and 129 pounds are five times as likely to have an accident if they drive within two hours of drinking and twenty-five times as likely if they drive within three hours of having four drinks. Heavier people, weighing between 170 pounds and 189 pounds, are five times as likely to have an accident if they drive within an hour of consuming two drinks and twenty-five times as likely within two hours of having five drinks.

Whether a person is legally drunk can be determined in different ways—by walking a line, a by taking a breathalyzer test, or by measuring a person's blood alcohol content. In the latter case, the measurement is given in terms of the percent of alcohol in a given volume of blood. The commonly accepted maximum safe level is less than .10 percent. Unfortunately, this information is most easily obtained from the fatally injured and not from the driver. Police often rely on their own judgment in deciding whether a person has been driving while intoxicated (DWI) or driving under the influence.

Too often people don't even know when they've reached their legal limit.

Another example of the kind of information MADD publicizes is "How Much Is Too Much?" (see box) which explains how the effects of one drink can be estimated. MADD also furthers public awareness through a speaker bureau, direct-mail campaigns, public service announcements, press releases, pamphlets, films, and commemorative candlelight vigils. Lightner and other MADD representatives appear often on network news and other television shows such as *Donahue, PM Magazine,* and *Nightline.* Lightner's own personal story was made into a movie for television, which aired in March 1983.

New Directions

One group of drivers—young adults—was overrepresented in the statistics for drunk driving. In testimony and activities, Lightner began to focus particularly on drivers under age twenty-one who represented 8 percent of the nation's drivers, but who had 20 percent of the alcohol-related fatalities. After the Twenty-sixth Amendment gave 18-year-olds the right to vote, many states lowered their drinking age, based on the assumption that a person old enough to vote was also old enough to buy a drink. But as Lightner noted repeatedly in testimony, alcohol-related deaths among young people had increased 25 percent in states that had lowered the drinking age. This sharp increase led some states to raise the age back to twenty-one. Ironically, this created a new problem among young people who lived near the state border and who could easily drive to an adjoining state with a lower drinking age.

One of the recommendations of the Presidential Commission on Drunk Driving, of which Lightner was a member, was to raise nationally the "minimum legal purchasing and public possession age" to twenty-one. However, the federal government felt it necessary to take a "carrot-and-stick" approach, by tying the drinking age to federal highway funds. The "carrot"—in Public Law 98-363 and Public Law 99-272 (see box)—was an increase in highway funds. The "stick" was no increase and, later, reductions in highway funds if states chose not to conform to the requirement for new and stricter state laws against drunk drivers and for stricter enforcement of laws already in effect. Lightner stood beside President Reagan in July 1984 as he signed the first new law containing a provision withholding federal highway construction funds for states that failed to raise the drinking age to twenty-one.

Related to the push for a national drinking age of twenty-one is MADD's program aimed at young people between the ages of sixteen and twenty-four—the only age group in which death rates are increasing while others decline. Many activities are organized in cooperation with SADD, which has been closely allied with MADD since its picketing of Governor Brown's office in 1980. Other cooperative groups are BACCHUS (Boost Alcohol Consciousness Concerning the Health of University Students) and STOPP (Students to Organize Participative Prevention). Local MADD chapters also work with business and civic organizations. For example, Project Graduation works with local media in publicizing a telephone number for free rides to imbibers, and tuxedo-rental and flower shops are asked to distribute cards urging wearers not to drink and drive.

Another area in which MADD has increased its efforts is victim assistance. In many ways, MADD has been a victim-assistance organization since the beginning. Lightner began MADD to make sure that her daughter's death had "meaning." No one knew better than Lightner that victims and survivors of alcohol-related crashes have to live with the nightmare of

Federal Laws to Combat Drunk Driving

Public Law 97-364—
Contains a provision that grants additional funding to states that adopt penalties to deter intoxicated driving (e.g., prompt and automatic license suspension for drivers who fail breathalyzer tests and mandatory incarceration for repeat offenders). Signed into law on October 25, 1982.

Public Law 98-353—
Contains a provision that prevents drunk drivers from escaping damage judgments by taking refuge in bankruptcy. Signed into law on July 10, 1984.

Public Law 98-363—
Contains a provision that withholds federal highway construction funds (5 percent in fiscal year 1987 and 10 percent in fiscal year 1988) for states that do not enact a drinking age of twenty-one and provides additional funding for states that computerize their traffic-record systems for the purpose of tracing repeat offenders. Also included are additional incentives to encourage states to address drugged driving and minimum sentencing standards. Signed into law July 17, 1984. By November 1986, forty-two states were in compliance.

Public Law 99-272—
Contains a provision that prevents states from lowering their drinking ages after 1988 by making permanent a 10-percent withholding of highway construction funds from states that do not enact a minimum drinking age. Signed into law April 7, 1986.

these tragedies for the rest of their lives. MADD provides victim advocates—usually other victims—who visit the family promptly, accompany the family to court, and follow up on sentencing after the case has been decided. MADD also makes sure that victims have information on victim-assistance programs and provides materials to help families and friends deal with grief. MADD has also prepared an educational video, "Only You Can Share My Pain," to heighten awareness of victim and survivor needs. The video is narrated by actress Rita Moreno, whose brother was killed in a drunk-driving crash.

By the end of 1984, MADD had 320 chapters. Today MADD has grown into an even larger national organization with close to 400 chapters and three-quarters of a million volunteers and donors. Since September 1983, its headquarters has been in Texas. Norma Phillips, who founded the San Diego County chapter and who has concentrated her work with MADD on improving communications with chapters, became president of the organization in late 1985. Lightner is still the organization's official spokesperson.

However, calling up and wanting to start a chapter is no longer enough. The national headquarters considers the organization of a new chapter to be a "significant learning experience" for applicants. A possible new group is required to conduct extensive research on local affairs, demonstrate they know how the local system works and where its strengths and weaknesses are regarding the arrest and prosecution of drunk drivers, and be prepared to monitor court cases. The process is not easy. Of 657 requests for applications in 1985-86, only 136 were completed and returned, and of the 136, the requirements were fulfilled by 82.

Future Prospects
The National Commission Against Drunk Driving, appointed to monitor progress made on the 1983 recommendations of the Presidential Commission Against Drunk Driving, issued a report in December 1985. (Lightner is again a member of the commission.) One of the best indications of "the remarkable work of citizen action groups," the report notes in its introduction, is the 1984 Louis Harris poll, which found that the public's number-one health and safety priority had become the avoidance of driving after drinking. Just two years earlier, a Gallup poll had found that "80 percent of American drivers would not hesitate to drive after drinking." In 1985, according to the Harris poll, the number had dropped to 65 percent.

Another important change is that from 1981 to 1985 the states enacted 478 new laws relating to alcohol and highway safety. This is in addition to the four federal laws. Furthermore, enforcement has been stepped up, and arrests have increased 27 percent. By January 1985, twenty-four states had raised the minimum drinking age to twenty-one. By November 1986, eighteen more states had raised their legal drinking age. The National Highway Traffic Safety Administration estimates that 475 fewer fatalities occurred in 1984 as a result of the higher drinking age laws. About 515 additional lives could have been saved if all states had raised their minimum drinking age to twenty-one.

Other changes noted by the National Highway Traffic Safety Administration are that the percentage of fatally injured legally intoxicated drivers dropped from 50 to 43 percent and that in 1984 total fatalities increased 3 percent but alcohol involvement in those fatalities decreased 3 percent.

But the goal is to eliminate drunk driving and to make drunk driving socially unacceptable. Progress made needs to be maintained and increased. If Lightner has her way, it will. Since she founded MADD in 1980, she seems to have lost little of her determination to work for that goal. In the fifth anniversary edition of the MADD newsletter, Lightner's

Every year during December, MADD members gather in communities across the country to mourn the victims of drunk drivers. The candlelight vigils dramatize the pain and anger experienced by the families of the killed and injured.

zeal was sharp and fresh over a newscast that reported that although traffic fatalities were on the rise, drunk-driving "accidents" were decreasing. To Lightner, they will never be "accidents." Said Lightner, "My daughter's obituary said 'Cari Lightner, 13, was the victim of a traffic accident.' Cari was not the victim of a traffic 'accident.' She was the innocent victim of a violent crime—a crime that kills more than sixty-eight people daily in the United States and injures more than 650,000 annually. It is a crime that kills more than homicides; creates more property damage than robbers, burglars, and forgers combined; and costs society approximately $20 billion each year . . . Crimes involving impaired drivers are not 'accidents.' They are heinous crimes . . ."

The organization Lightner founded has expanded dramatically and raised public consciousness enormously. "MADD is so well known," the head of the Klamath, California, chapter pointed out, "that its name alone is a deterrent. Just knowing that there is a MADD group in the area makes people more cautious." When she was featured as one of the "Seven Who Succeeded" in *Time* magazine's January 1985 issue, Lightner said, "I believe that for every problem there is a solution. We are changing the way people think about drinking and driving. But more than that, we have caused people to change their behavior, and that is saving lives. I believe in the rights of victims. And I do feel that if you believe in something badly enough, you can make a difference."

Activities

1. Reading Between the Lines

In this chapter, Father Robert Drinan argues that citizen protest against a government policy is a vital part of American democracy. Do you agree with his position? Do some research on the history of protest movements in this country. Historically, in what ways have citizens made their voices heard? Do those who protest express the desires of the majority or only a few? What impact do you think protest movements have on our political system?

2. Developing Your Own Perspective

Campaign advertising has become a multimillion-dollar business in the United States. Any candidate who wants to win an election must spend thousands of dollars for television and radio ads. In fact, television advertising has become the major expense of most political campaigns.

During an election year, try to watch, read, and listen to as many campaign ads as you can. What methods do the candidates use to try to influence your decision to vote for them? What message do the ads impart? How do the opponent's ads compare? From what you observe, do you think political advertising is an effective way for candidates to publicize their stands on the issues? What other methods do you think they can use?

3. Becoming an Active Citizen

Participation is essential to American democracy. A government such as ours must have an active, involved, and interested citizenry if it is to remain responsive to the needs of the people. Being an active citizen really means participating in the political process and making the government work for you. Here are just a few of the many ways to participate:

■ Register to vote, and then *vote!* Some political commentators have said that people who do not vote get what they deserve. Your vote is more than just your support for a particular candidate or point of view. When you vote, you are exercising your right as an American to have your voice heard.

■ Join a political party. Political parties provide people with a way to collectively express one point of view. Being a member of a party puts you in touch with others who share your views and can help you to get involved in a campaign.

■ Participate in local government. Attend meetings of local governing boards such as the school board, city council, or county board. Stay informed on the issues that affect your community and offer your views or assistance when appropriate.

■ Join an interest group. Thousands of interest groups support a wide variety of causes and concerns. Find a group that supports your views, and get involved.

You can probably think of many other ways to participate in government. Remember, if American democracy is to work, it needs the involvement of *all* its citizens.

★ ★ ★ ★ ★ ★ ★ ★ ★ ★

The Constitution of the United States

The Constitution of the United States

Portions of the text printed in italics have been changed by amendment or have gone out of date.

Preamble

We, the people of the United States, in order to form a more perfect Union, establish justice, insure domestic tranquility, provide for the common defense, promote the general welfare, and secure the blessings of liberty to ourselves and our posterity, do ordain and establish this Constitution for the United States of America.

Article 1. The Legislative Branch

Section 1. Congress

All legislative powers herein granted shall be vested in a Congress of the United States, which shall consist of a Senate and House of Representatives.

Section 2. House of Representatives

1. Election and Term of Members. The House of Representatives shall be composed of members chosen every second year by the people of the several states, and the electors in each state shall have the qualifications requisite for electors of the most numerous branch of the state legislature.

2. Qualifications. No person shall be a Representative who shall not have attained to the age of twenty-five years, and been seven years a citizen of the United States, and who shall not, when elected, be an inhabitant of that state in which he shall be chosen.

3. Apportionment of Representatives. Representatives *and direct taxes* shall be apportioned among the several states which may be included within this Union, according to their respective numbers *which shall be determined by adding the whole number of free persons, including those bound to service for a term of years, and excluding Indians not taxed, three-fifths of all other persons.* The actual enumeration shall be made within three years after the first meeting of the Congress of the United States, and within every subsequent term of ten years, in such manner as they shall by law direct. The number of Representatives shall not exceed one for every 30,000, but each state shall have at least 1 Representative; *and until such enumeration shall be made, the state of New*

Hampshire shall be entitled to choose 3; Massachusetts, 8; Rhode Island and Providence Plantations, 1; Connecticut, 5; New York, 6; New Jersey, 4; Pennsylvania, 8; Delaware, 1; Maryland, 6; Virginia, 10; North Carolina, 5; South Carolina, 5; and Georgia, 3.

4. Vacancies. When vacancies happen in the representation from any state, the executive authority thereof shall issue writs of election to fill such vacancies.

5. Impeachment. The House of Representatives shall choose their Speaker and other officers; and shall have the sole power of impeachment.

Section 3. Senate

1. Number of Members and Terms of Office. The Senate of the United States shall be composed of two Senators from each state *chosen by the legislatures thereof,* for six years, and each Senator shall have one vote.

2. Classification; Vacancies. *Immediately after they shall be assembled in consequence of the first election, they shall be divided as equally as may be into three classes. The seats of the Senators of the first class shall be vacated at the Expiration of the second year, of the second class at the expiration of the fourth year, and of the third class at the expiration of the sixth year, so that one-third may be chosen every second year; and if vacancies happen by resignation, or otherwise, during the recess of the legislature of any state, the executive thereof may make temporary appointments until the next meeting of the legislature, which shall then fill such vacancies.*

3. Qualifications. No person shall be a Senator who shall not have attained the age of thirty years, and been nine years a citizen of the United States, and who shall not, when elected, be an inhabitant of that state for which he shall be chosen.

4. The President of the Senate. The Vice-President of the United States shall be president of the Senate, but shall have no vote, unless they be equally divided.

5. Other Officers. The Senate shall choose their other officers, and also a president pro tempore, in the absence of the Vice-President, or when he shall exercise the office of the President of the United States.

6. Impeachments. The Senate shall have the sole power to try all impeachments. When sitting for that purpose, they shall be on oath or affirmation. When the President of the United States is tried, the Chief Justice shall preside; and no person shall be convicted without the concurrence of two-thirds of the members present.

7. Penalty for Conviction. Judgment in cases of impeachment shall not extend further than to removal from office, and disqualification to hold and enjoy any office of honor, trust, or profit under the United States; but the party convicted shall nevertheless be liable and subject to indictment, trial, judgment, and punishment, according to law.

Section 4. Elections and Meetings

1. Holding elections. The times, places, and manner of holding elections for Senators and Representatives shall be prescribed in each state by the legislature thereof; but the Congress may at any time by law make or alter such regulations, except as to the places of choosing senators.

2. Meetings. The Congress shall assemble at least once in every year, *and such meeting shall be on the first Monday in December,* unless they shall by law appoint a different day.

Section 5. Procedure

1. Organization. Each house shall be the judge of the elections, returns, and qualifications of its own members, and a majority of each shall constitute a quorum to do business; but a smaller number may adjourn from day to day, and may be authorized to compel the attendance of absent members, in such manner, and under such penalties, as each house may provide.

2. Proceedings. Each house may determine the rules of its proceedings, punish its members for disorderly behavior, and with the concurrence of two-thirds, expel a member.

3. The Journal. Each house shall keep a journal of its proceedings, and from time to time publish the same, excepting such parts as may in their judgment require secrecy; and the yeas and nays of the members of either house on any question shall, at the desire of one-fifth of those present, be entered on the journal.

4. Adjournment. Neither house, during the session of Congress, shall, without the consent of the other, adjourn for more than three days, nor to any other place than that in which the two houses shall be sitting.

Section 6. Privileges and Restrictions

1. Pay and Privileges. The Senators and Representatives shall receive a compensation for their services, to be ascertained by law and paid out of the Treasury of the United States. They shall in all cases, except treason, felony, and breach of the peace, be privileged from arrest during their attendance at the session of their respective houses, and in going to and returning home from same; and for any speech or debate in either house, they shall not be questioned in any other place.

2. Restrictions. No Senator or Representative shall, during the time for which he was elected, be appointed to any civil office under the authority of the United States, which shall have been created, or the emoluments whereof shall have been increased, during such time, and no person holding any office under the United States shall be a member of either house during his continuance in office.

Section 7. Passing Laws

1. Revenue Bills. All bills for raising revenue shall originate in the House of Representatives; but the Senate may propose or concur with amendments as on other bills.

2. How a Bill Becomes a Law. Every bill which shall have passed the House of Representatives and the Senate shall, before it becomes a law, be presented to the President of the United States; if he approves, he shall sign it, but if not, he shall return it, with his objections, to that house in which it shall have originated, who shall enter the objections at large on their journal, and proceed to reconsider it. If after such reconsideration two-thirds of that house shall agree to pass the bill, it shall be sent, together with the objections, to the other house, by which it shall likewise be reconsidered, and, if approved by two-thirds of that house, it shall become a law. But in all such cases the votes of both houses shall be determined by yeas and nays, and the names of the persons voting for and against the bill shall be entered on the journal of each house respectively. If any bill shall not be returned by the President within ten days (Sundays excepted) after it shall have been presented to him, the same bill shall be a law, in like manner as if he had signed it, unless the Congress by their adjournment prevent its return, in which case it shall not be a law.

3. Presidential Approval or Veto. Every order, resolution, or vote to which the concurrence of the Senate and House of Representatives may be necessary (except on a question of adjournment) shall be presented to the President of the United States; and before the same shall take effect, shall be approved by him, or being disapproved by him, shall be repassed by two-thirds of the Senate and House of Representatives, according to the rules and limitations in the case of a bill.

Section 8. Powers Delegated to Congress

The Congress shall have power
   1. To lay and collect taxes, duties, imposts, and excis-

es, to pay the debts and provide for the common defense and general welfare of the United States; but all duties, imposts, and excises shall be uniform throughout the United States;

2. To borrow money on the credit of the United States;

3. To regulate commerce with foreign nations, and among the several states, *and with the Indian tribes;*

4. To establish a uniform rule of naturalization, and uniform laws on the subject of bankruptcies throughout the United States;

5. To coin money, regulate the value thereof, and of foreign coin, and fix the standards of weights and measures;

6. To provide for the punishment of counterfeiting the securities and current coin of the United States;

7. To establish post offices and post roads;

8. To promote the progress of science and useful arts by securing for limited times to authors and inventors the exclusive right to their respective writings and discoveries;

9. To constitute tribunals inferior to the Supreme Court;

10. To define and punish piracies and felonies committed on the high seas and offenses against the law of nations;

11. To declare war, *grant letters of marque and reprisal,* and make rules concerning captures on land and water;

12. To raise and support armies, but no appropriation of money to that use shall be for a longer term than two years;

13. To provide and maintain a navy;

14. To make rules for the government and regulation of the land and naval forces;

15. To provide for calling forth the militia to execute the laws of the Union, suppress insurrections, and repel invasions;

16. To provide for organizing, arming, and disciplining the militia, and for governing such part of them as may be employed in the service of the United States, reserving to the states, respectively, the appointment of the officers, and the authority of training the militia according to the discipline prescribed by Congress;

17. To exercise exclusive legislation in all cases whatsoever, over such district (not exceeding ten miles square) as may, by cession of particular states, and the acceptance of Congress, become the seat of government of the United States, and to exercise like authority over all places purchased by the consent of the legislature of the state in which the same shall be, for the erection of forts, magazines, arsenals, dock-yards, and other needful buildings;—and

18. To make all laws which shall be necessary and proper for carrying into execution the foregoing powers, and all other powers vested by this Constitution in the government of the United States, or in any department or officer thereof.

Section 9. Powers Denied to the Federal Government

1. *The migration or importation of such persons as any of the states now existing shall think proper to admit shall not be prohibited by the Congress prior to the year 1808; but a tax or duty may be imposed on such importation, not exceeding $10 for each person.*

2. The privilege of the writ of habeas corpus shall not be suspended, unless when in cases of rebellion or invasion the public safety may require it.

3. No bill of attainder or ex post facto law shall be passed.

4. *No capitation or other direct tax shall be laid, unless in proportion to the census herein before directed to be taken.*

5. No tax or duty shall be laid on articles exported from any state.

6. No preference shall be given any regulation of commerce or revenue to the ports of one state over those of another; nor shall vessels bound to, or from, one state, be obliged to enter, clear or pay duties in another.

7. No money shall be drawn from the Treasury, but in consequence of appropriations made by law; and a regular statement and account of the receipts and expenditures of all public money shall be published from time to time.

8. No title of nobility shall be granted by the United States; and no person holding any office of profit or trust under them, shall, without the consent of the Congress, accept of any present, emolument, office, or title, of any kind whatever, from any king, prince, or foreign state.

Section 10. Powers Denied to the States

1. No state shall enter into any treaty, alliance, or confederation; grant letters of marque and reprisal; coin money; emit bills of credit; make anything but gold and silver coin a tender in payment of debts; pass any bill of attainder, ex post facto law, or law impairing the obligation of contracts, or grant any title of nobility.

2. No state shall, without the consent of the Congress, lay any imposts or duties on imports or exports, except what may be absolutely necessary for executing its inspection laws; and the net produce of all duties and imposts, laid by any state on imports or exports, shall be for the use of the Treasury of the United States; and such laws shall be subject to the revision and control of the Congress.

3. No state shall, without consent of Congress, lay any duty of tonnage, keep troops, or ships of war in time of peace, enter into any agreement or compact with another state, or with a foreign power, or engage in a war, unless actually invaded, or in such imminent danger as will not admit of delay.

Article 2. The Executive Branch

Section 1. President and Vice-President

1. Term of Office. The executive power shall be vested in a President of the United States of America. He shall hold his office during the term of four years, and together with the Vice-President, chosen for the same term, be elected as follows:

2. Electoral System. Each state shall appoint, in such manner as the legislature thereof may direct, a number of electors, equal to the whole number of Senators and Representatives to which the state may be entitled in the Congress; but no Senator or Representative, or person holding an office of trust or profit under the United States, shall be appointed an elector.

3. Former Method of the Electoral System. *The electors shall meet in their respective states, and vote by ballot for two persons, of whom one at least shall not be an inhabitant of the same state with themselves. And they shall make a list of all the persons voted for, and of the number of votes for each; which list they shall sign and certify, and transmit sealed to the seat of the government of the United States, directed to the president of the Senate. The president of the Senate shall, in the presence of the Senate and House of Representatives, open all the certificates, and the votes shall then be counted. The person having the greatest number of votes shall be the President, if such number be a majority of the whole number of electors appointed; and if there be more than one who have such majority, and have an equal number of votes, then the House of Representatives shall immediately choose by ballot one of them for President; and if no person have a majority, then from the five highest on the list the said House shall in like manner choose the President. But in choosing the President the votes shall be taken by states, the representation from each state having one vote. A quorum for this purpose shall consist of a member or members from two-thirds of the states, and a majority of all the states shall be necessary to a choice. In every case, after the choice of the President, the person having the greatest number of votes of the electors shall be the Vice-President. But if there should remain two or more who have equal votes, the Senate shall choose from them by ballot the Vice-President.*

4. Time of Elections. The Congress may determine the time of choosing the electors, and the day on which they shall give their votes; which day shall be the same throughout the United States.

5. Qualifications for President. No person except a natural-born citizen *or a citizen of the United States, at the time of the adoption of this Constitution,* shall be eligible to the office of the President; neither shall any person be eligible to that office who shall not have attained to the age of thirty-five years, and been fourteen years a resident within the United States.

6. Filling Vacancies. In the case of the removal of the President from office, or of his death, resignation, or inability to discharge the powers and duties of the said office, the same shall devolve on the Vice-President, and the Congress may by law provide for the case of removal, death, resignation, or inability, both of the President and Vice-President, declaring what officer shall then act as President, and such officer shall act accordingly, until the disability be removed, or a President shall be elected.

7. Salary. The President shall, at stated times, receive for his services, a compensation, which shall neither be increased nor diminished during the period for which he shall have been elected, and he shall not receive within that period any other emolument from the United States, or any of them.

8. Oath of Office. Before he enter on the execution of his office, he shall take the following oath or affirmation;—"I do solemnly swear (or affirm) that I will faithfully execute the office of President of the United States, and will to the best of my ability, preserve, protect, and defend the Constitution of the United States."

Section 2. Powers of the President

1. Military Powers. The President shall be Commander in Chief of the Army and Navy of the United States, and of the militia of the several states, when called into the actual service of the United States; he may require the opinion, in writing, of the principal officer in each of the executive departments, upon any subject relating to the duties of their respective offices, and he shall have power to grant reprieves and pardons for offenses against the United States, except in cases of impeachment.

2. Treaties and Appointments. He shall have power, by and with the advice and consent of the Senate, to make treaties, provided two-thirds of the Senators present concur; and he shall nominate, and by and with the advice and consent of the Senate, shall appoint ambassadors, other public ministers and consuls, judges of the Supreme Court, and all other officers of the United States, whose appointments are not herein otherwise provided for, and which shall be established by law; but the Congress may by law vest the appointment of such inferior officers, as they think proper, in the President alone, in the courts of law, or in the heads of departments.

3. Filling Vacancies. The President shall have power to fill up all vacancies that may happen during the recess of the Senate, by granting commissions which shall expire at the end of their next session.

Section 3. Duties of the President

He shall from time to time give to the Congress information of the state of the Union, and recommend to their consideration such measures as he shall judge necessary and expedient; he may, on extraordinary occasions, convene both houses, or either of them, and in case of disagreement between them, with respect to the time of adjournment, he may adjourn them to such time as he shall think proper; he shall receive ambassadors and other public ministers; he shall take care that the laws be faithfully executed, and shall commission all of the officers of the United States.

Section 4. Impeachment

The President, Vice-President, and all civil officers of the United States, shall be removed from office on impeachment for, and conviction of, treason, bribery, or other high crimes and misdemeanors.

Article 3. The Judicial Branch

Section 1. Federal Courts

The judicial power of the United States shall be vested in one Supreme Court, and in such inferior courts as the Congress may from time to time ordain and establish. The judges, both of the Supreme and inferior courts, shall hold their offices during good behavior, and shall, at stated times, receive for their services a compensation, which shall not be diminished during their continuance in office.

Section 2. Jurisdiction of Federal Courts

1. General Jurisdiction. The judicial power shall extend to all cases, in law and equity, arising under this Constitution, the laws of the United States, and treaties made or which shall be made, under their authority; to all cases affecting ambassadors, other public ministers and consuls; to all cases of admiralty and maritime jurisdiction; to controversies to which the United States shall be a party; to controversies between two or more states; *between a state and citizens of another state;* between citizens of different states; between citizens of the same state claiming lands under grants of different states, and between a state or the citizens thereof, and foreign states, citizens, or subjects.

2. Supreme Court. In all cases affecting ambassadors, other public ministers and consuls, and those in which a state shall be a party, the Supreme Court shall have original jurisdiction. In all the other cases before mentioned,

the Supreme Court shall have appellate jurisdiction, both as to law and fact, with such exceptions, and under such regulations as the Congress shall make.

3. Conduct of Trials. The trial of all crimes, except in cases of impeachment, shall be by jury; and such trial shall be held in the state where the said crimes shall have been committed; but when not committed within any state, the trial shall be at such place or places as the Congress may by law have directed.

Section 3. Treason

1. Definition. Treason against the United States shall consist only in levying war against them, or in adhering to their enemies, giving them aid and comfort. No person shall be convicted of treason unless on the testimony of two witnesses to the same overt act, or on confession in open court.

2. Punishment. The Congress shall have power to declare the punishment of treason, but no attainder of treason shall work corruption of blood or forfeiture except during the life of the person attainted.

Article 4. Relations Among States

Section 1. Official Acts

Full faith and credit shall be given in each state to the public acts, records, and judicial proceedings of every other state. And the Congress may by general laws prescribe the manner in which such acts, records, and proceedings shall be proved, and the effect thereof.

Section 2. Privileges of Citizens

1. Privileges. The citizens of each state shall be entitled to all privileges and immunities of citizens in the several states.

2. Extradition. A person charged in any state with treason, felony, or other crime, who shall flee from justice, and be found in another state, shall on demand of the executive authority of the state from which he fled, be delivered up, to be removed to the state having jurisdiction of the crime.

3. Fugitive Slaves. *No person held in service or labor in one state, under the laws thereof, escaping into another, shall in consequence of any law or regulation therein, be discharged from such service or labor, but shall be delivered up on claim of the party to whom such service or labor may be due.*

Section 3. New States and Territories

1. Admission of New States. New states may be admitted by the Congress into this Union; but no new state shall be formed or erected within the jurisdiction of any other state; nor any state be formed by the junction of two or more states, or parts of states, without the consent of the legislatures of the states concerned as well as of the Congress.

2. Powers of Congress Over Territories and Other Property. The Congress shall have power to dispose of and make all needful rules and regulations respecting the territory or other property belonging to the United States; and nothing in this Constitution shall be so construed as to prejudice any claims of the United States, or of any particular state.

Section 4. Guarantees to the States

The United States shall guarantee to every state in this Union a republican form of government, and shall protect each of them against invasion; and on application of the legislature or of the executive (when the legislature cannot be convened) against domestic violence.

Article 5. Methods of Amendment

The Congress, whenever two-thirds of both houses shall deem it necessary, shall propose amendments to this Constitution, or, on the application of the legislatures of two-thirds of the several states, shall call a convention for proposing amendments, which, in either case, shall be valid to all intents and purposes, as part of this Constitution, when ratified by the legislatures of three-fourths of the several states, or by conventions in three-fourths thereof, as the one or the other mode of ratification may be proposed by the Congress; provided that *(no amendments which may be made prior to the year 1808 shall in any manner affect the first and fourth clauses in the Ninth Section of the First Article; and that)* no state, without its consent, shall be deprived of its equal suffrage in the Senate.

Article 6. General Provisions

1. Public Debts. All debts contracted and engagements entered into, before the adoption of this Constitution, shall be as valid against the United States under this Constitution, as under the Confederation.

2. The Supreme Law. This Constitution, and the laws of the United States which shall be made in pursuance thereof, and all treaties made, or which shall be made, under the authority of the United States, shall be the supreme law of the land; and the judges in every state shall be bound thereby, anything in the constitution or laws of any state to the contrary notwithstanding.

3. Oaths of Office. The Senators and Representatives before mentioned, and the members of the several state legislatures, and all executive and judicial officers, both of the United States and of the several states, shall be bound by oath or affirmation, to support this Constitution; but no religious test shall ever be required as a qualification to any office or public trust under the United States.

Article 7. Ratification

The ratification of the convention of nine states shall be sufficient for the establishment of the Constitution between the states so ratifying the same.

DONE in Convention by the unanimous consent of the States present the seventeenth day of September in the year of our Lord one thousand seven hundred and eight-seven and of the independence of the United States of America the twelfth. In witness whereof we have hereunto subscribed our names,
G. Washington—President and deputy from Virginia

NEW HAMPSHIRE
John Langdon
Nicholas Gilman

NORTH CAROLINA
William Blount
Richard Dobbs Spaight
Hugh Williamson

MARYLAND
James McHenry
Daniel of St. Thomas Jenifer
Daniel Carroll

PENNSYLVANIA
Benjamin Franklin
Thomas Mifflin
Robert Morris
George Clymer
Thomas FitzSimons
Jared Ingersoll
James Wilson
Gouverneur Morris

NEW YORK
Alexander Hamilton

MASSACHUSETTS
Nathaniel Gorman
Rufus King

SOUTH CAROLINA
John Rutledge
Charles Cotesworth Pinckney
Charles Pinckney
Pierce Butler

VIRGINIA
John Blair
James Madison

DELAWARE
George Read
Gunning Bedford
John Dickinson
Richard Bassett
Jacob Broom

NEW JERSEY
William Livingston
David Brearley
William Paterson
Jonathan Dayton

CONNECTICUT
William Samuel Jackson
Roger Sherman

GEORGIA
William Few
Abraham Baldwin

The first ten amendments constitute the Bill of Rights.
They became an official part of the Constitution in 1791.
They limit the powers of the federal government but not the
powers of the states.

Amendment 1. Freedom of Religion, Speech, Press, Assembly, and Petition (1791)

Congress shall make no law respecting an establishment of religion, or prohibiting the free exercise thereof; or abridging the freedom of speech, or of the press; or the right of the people peaceably to assemble, and to petition the government for a redress of grievances.

Amendment 2. Right to Bear Arms (1791)

A well-regulated militia, being necessary to the security of a free state, the right of the people to keep and bear arms shall not be infringed.

Amendment 3. Housing of Troops (1791)

No soldier shall, in time of peace, be quartered in any house, without the consent of the owner; nor in time of war, but in a manner to be prescribed by law.

Amendment 4. Searches and Seizures (1791)

The right of the people to be secure in their persons, houses, papers, and effects, against unreasonable searches and seizures, shall not be violated; and no warrants shall issue but upon probable cause, supported by oath or affirmation, and particularly describing the place to be searched, and the persons or things to be seized.

Amendment 5. Rights of Accused Persons (1791)

No person shall be held to answer for a capital, or otherwise infamous, crime, unless on a presentment or indictment of a grand jury, except in cases arising in the land or naval forces, or in the militia, when in actual service in time of war or public danger; nor shall any person be subject for the same offense to be twice put in jeopardy of life and limb; nor shall be compelled, in any criminal case, to be a witness against himself; nor be deprived of life, liberty, or property, without due process of law; nor shall private property be taken for public use, without just compensation.

Amendment 6. Right to a Speedy, Fair Trial (1791)

In all criminal prosecutions, the accused shall enjoy the right to a speedy and public trial, by an impartial jury of the state and district wherein the crime shall have been committed, which district shall have been previously ascertained by law, and to be informed of the nature and cause of the accusation; to be confronted with the witnesses against him; to have compulsory process for obtaining witnesses in his favor, and to have the assistance of counsel for his defense.

Amendment 7. Civil Suits (1791)

In suits at common law, where the value in controversy shall exceed $20, the right of trial by jury shall be preserved, and no fact tried by a jury shall be otherwise reexamined in any court of the United States than according to the rules of the common law.

Amendment 8. Bails, Fines, Punishments (1791)

Excessive bail shall not be required, nor excessive fines imposed, nor cruel and unusual punishments inflicted.

Amendment 9. Powers Reserved to the People (1791)

The enumeration in the Constitution, of certain rights, shall not be construed to deny or disparage others retained by the people.

Amendment 10. Powers Reserved to the States (1791)

The powers not delegated to the United States by the Constitution, nor prohibited by it to the states, are reserved to the states respectively, or to the people.

Amendment 11. Suits Against States (1798)

The judicial power of the United States shall not be construed to extend to any suit in law or equity, commenced or prosecuted against one of the United States, by citizens of another state, or by citizens or subjects of any foreign state.

Amendment 12. Electing the President and Vice-President (1804)

The electors shall meet in their respective states, and vote by ballot for President and Vice-President, one of whom, at least, shall not be an inhabitant of the same state with themselves; they shall name in their ballots the person voted for as President, and in distinct ballots the person voted for as Vice-President, and they shall make distinct lists of all persons voted for as President, and of all persons voted for as Vice-President, and of the number of votes for each, which lists they shall sign and certify, and transmit, sealed, to the seat of government of the United States, directed to the President of the Senate; the President of the Senate shall, in the presence of the Senate and House of Representatives, open all the certificates and the votes shall then be counted; the person having the greatest number of votes for President shall be the President, if such number be a majority of the whole number of electors appointed; and if no person have such majority, then from the persons having the highest numbers not exceeding three on the list of those voted for as President, the House of Representatives shall choose immediately, by ballot, the President. But in choosing the President, the votes shall be taken by states, the representation from each state having one vote; a quorum for this purpose shall consist of a member or members from two-thirds of the states, and a majority of all the states shall be necessary to a choice. *And if the House of Representatives shall not choose a President whenever the right of choice shall devolve upon them, before the fourth day of March next following, then the Vice-President shall act as President, as in the case of the death or other constitutional disability of the President.* The person having the greatest number of votes as Vice-President, shall be the Vice-President, if such number be a majority of the whole number of electors appointed, and if no person have a majority, then from the two highest numbers on the list, the Senate shall choose the Vice-President; a quorum for the purpose shall consist of two-thirds of the whole number of Senators, and a majority of the whole number shall be necessary to a choice. But no person constitutionally ineligible to the office of President shall be eligible to that of Vice-President of the United States.

Amendment 13. Abolition of Slavery (1865)

Section 1. Neither slavery nor involuntary servitude, except as a punishment for crime whereof the party shall have been duly convicted, shall exist within the United States, or any place subject to their jurisdiction.

Section 2. Congress shall have power to enforce this article by appropriate legislation.

Amendment 14. Citizenship (1868)

Section 1. Citizenship defined. All persons born or naturalized in the United States and subject to the jurisdiction thereof, are citizens of the United States and of the state wherein they reside. No state shall make or enforce any law which shall abridge the privileges or immunities of citizens of the United States; nor shall any state deprive any person of life, liberty, or property, without due process of law; nor deny to any person within its jurisdiction the equal protection of the laws.

Section 2. Apportionment of Representatives. Representatives shall be apportioned among the several states according to their respective numbers, counting the whole number of persons in each state, *excluding Indians not taxed.* But when the right to vote at any election for the choice of electors for President and Vice-President of the United States, Representatives in Congress, the executive and judicial officers of a state, or the members of the legislature thereof, is denied to any of the male inhabitants of such state, *being twenty-one years of age* and citizens of the United States, or in any way abridged, except for participation in rebellion, or other crime, the basis of representation therein shall be reduced in the proportion which the number of such male citizens shall bear to the whole number of male citizens *twenty-one years of age* in such state.

Section 3. Disability for engaging in insurrection. No person shall be a Senator or Representative in Congress, or elector of President and Vice-President, or hold any office, civil or military, under the United States, or under any state, who, having previously taken an oath, as a member of Congress, or as an officer of the United States, or as a member of any state legislature, or as an executive or judicial officer of any state, to support the Constitution of the United States, shall have engaged in insurrection or rebellion against the same, or given aid or comfort to the enemies thereof. But Congress may, by vote of two-thirds of each house, remove such disability.

Section 4. Public debt. The validity of the public debt of the United States, authorized by law, including debts incurred for payment of pensions and bounties for services in suppressing insurrection or rebellion, shall not be questioned. But neither the United States nor any state shall assume or pay any debt or obligation incurred in aid of insurrection or rebellion against the United States *or any claim for the loss or emancipation of any slave;* but all such debts, obligations, and claims shall be held illegal and void.

Section 5. Enforcement. The Congress shall have power to enforce, by appropriate legislation, the provisions of this article.

Amendment 15. Right to Vote (1870)

Section 1. The right of citizens of the United States to vote shall not be denied or abridged by the United States or any state on account of race, color, or previous condition of servitude.

Section 2. The Congress shall have power to enforce this article by appropriate legislation.

Amendment 16. Income Tax (1913)

The Congress shall have power to lay and collect taxes on incomes, from whatever source derived, without apportionment among the several states, and without regard to any census or enumeration.

Amendment 17. Electing Senators (1913)

Section 1. Method of election. The Senate of the United States shall be composed of two Senators from each state, elected by the people thereof, for six years; and each Senator shall have one vote. The electors in each state shall have the qualifications requisite for electors of the most numerous branch of the state legislatures.

Section 2. Filling vacancies. When vacancies happen in the representation of any state in the Senate, the executive authority of such state shall issue writs of election to fill such vacancies: Provided that the legislature of any state may empower the executive thereof to make temporary appointments until the people fill the vacancies by election as the legislature may direct.

Section 3. Not retroactive. *This amendment shall not be so construed as to affect the election or term of any Senator chosen before it becomes valid as part of the Constitution.*

Amendment 18. Prohibition (1919)

Section 1. *After one year from the ratification of this article the manufacture, sale, or transportation of intoxicating liquors within, the importation thereof into, or the exportation thereof from, the United States and all territory subject to the jurisdiction thereof for beverage purposes is hereby prohibited.*

Section 2. *The Congress and the several states shall have concurrent power to enforce this article by appropriate legislation.*

Section 3. *This article shall be inoperative unless it shall have been ratified as an amendment to the Constitution by the legislatures of the several states, as provided in the Constitution, within seven years from the date of the submission hereof to the states by the Congress.*

Amendment 19. Women's Suffrage (1920)

Section 1. The right of citizens of the United States to vote shall not be denied or abridged by the United States or by any state on account of sex.

Section 2. Congress shall have power to enforce this article by appropriate legislation.

Amendment 20. "Lame Duck" Amendment (1933)

Section 1. Beginning of terms. The terms of the President and Vice-President shall end at noon on the 20th day of January, and the terms of Senators and Representatives at noon on the 3rd day of January, of the years in which such terms would have ended if this article had not been ratified; and the terms of their successors shall then begin.

Section 2. Beginning of Congressional sessions. The Congress shall assemble at least once in every year, and such meeting shall begin at noon on the third day of January, unless they shall by law appoint a different day.

Section 3. Presidential succession. If at the time fixed for the beginning of the term of the President, the President-elect shall have died, the Vice-President-elect shall become President. If a President shall not have been chosen before the time fixed for the beginning of his term, or if the President-elect shall have failed to qualify, then the Vice-President-elect shall act as President until a President shall have qualified; and the Congress may by law provide for the case wherein neither a President-elect nor a Vice-President-elect shall have qualified, declaring who shall then act as President, or the manner in which one who is to act shall be selected, and such person shall act accordingly until a President or Vice-President shall have qualified.

Section 4. Filling Presidential vacancy. The Congress may by law provide for the case of the death of any of the persons from whom the House of Representatives may choose a President whenever the right of choice shall have devolved upon them, and for the case of the death of any of the persons from whom the Senate may choose a Vice-President whenever the right of choice shall have devolved upon them.

Section 5. Effective date. *Sections 1 and 2 shall take effect on the 15th day of October following the ratification of this article.*

Section 6. Time limit for ratification. *This article shall be inoperative unless it shall have been ratified as an amendment to the Constitution by the legislatures of three-fourths of the several states within the seven years from the date of its submission.*

Amendment 21. Repeal of Prohibition (1933)

Section 1. The eighteenth article of amendment to the Constitution of the United States is hereby repealed.

Section 2. The transportation or importation into any state, territory, or possession of the United States for delivery or use therein of intoxicating liquors, in violation of the laws thereof, is hereby prohibited.

Section 3. *This article shall be inoperative unless it shall have been ratified as an amendment to the Constitution by conventions in the several states, as provided in the Constitution, within seven years from the date of the submission hereof to the states by the Congress.*

Amendment 22. Two-Term Limit for Presidents (1951)

Section 1. No person shall be elected to the office of the President more than twice, and no person who has held the office of President, or acted as President, for more than two years of a term to which some other person was elected President shall be elected to the office of the

President more than once. *(But this Article shall not apply to any person holding the office of President when this Article was proposed by the Congress, and shall not prevent any person who may be holding the office of President, or acting as President, during the term within which this Article becomes operative from holding the office of President or acting as President during the remainder of such term.)*

Section 2. *This Article shall be inoperative unless it shall have been ratified as an amendment to the Constitution by the legislatures of three-fourths of the several states within seven years from the date of its submission to the states by the Congress.*

Amendment 23. Presidential Electors for District of Columbia (1961)

Section 1. The District constituting the seat of Government of the United States shall appoint in such manner as the Congress may direct:

A number of electors of President and Vice-President equal to the whole number of Senators and Representatives in Congress to which the District would be entitled if it were a state, but in no event more than the least populous state; they shall be in addition to those appointed by the states, but they shall be considered, for the purposes of the election of President and Vice-President, to be electors appointed by a state; and they shall meet in the District and perform such duties as provided by the twelfth article of amendment.

Section 2. The Congress shall have power to enforce this article by appropriate legislation.

Amendment 24. Poll Taxes (1964)

Section 1. The right of citizens of the United States to vote in any primary or other election for President or Vice-President, for electors for President or Vice-President, or for Senator or Representative in Congress, shall not be denied or abridged by the United States or any state by reason of failure to pay any poll tax or other tax.

Section 2. The Congress shall have the power to enforce this article by appropriate legislation.

Amendment 25. Presidential Disability and Succession (1967)

Section 1. In case of the removal of the President from office or his death or resignation, the Vice-President shall become President.

Section 2. Whenever there is a vacancy in the office of the Vice-President, the President shall nominate a Vice-President who shall take the office upon confirmation by a majority vote of both houses of Congress.

Section 3. Whenever the President transmits to the President pro tempore of the Senate and the Speaker of the House of Representatives his written declaration that he is unable to discharge the powers and duties of his office, and until he transmits to them a written declaration to the contrary, such powers and duties shall be discharged by the Vice President as Acting President.

Section 4. Whenever the Vice-President and a majority of either the principal officers of the executive departments or of such other body as Congress may by law provide, transmit to the President pro tempore of the Senate and the Speaker of the House of Representatives their written declaration that the President is unable to discharge the powers and duties of his office, the Vice-President shall immediately assume the powers and duties of the office as Acting President.

Thereafter, when the President transmits to the President pro tempore of the Senate and the Speaker of the House of Representatives his written declaration that no inability exists, he shall resume the powers and duties of his office unless the Vice-President and a majority of either the principal officers of the executive department or of such other body as Congress may by law provide, transmit within four days to the President pro tempore of the Senate and the Speaker of the House of Representatives their written declaration that the President is unable to discharge the powers and duties of his office. Thereupon Congress shall decide the issue, assembling within 48 hours for that purpose if not in session. If the Congress, within 21 days after receipt of the latter written declaration, or, if Congress is not in session, within 21 days after Congress is required to assemble, determines by two-thirds vote of both houses that the President is unable to discharge the powers and duties of his office, the Vice-President shall continue to discharge the same as Acting President; otherwise, the President shall assume the powers and duties of his office.

Amendment 26. Voting Age Lowered to 18 (1971)

Section 1. The right of citizens of the United States, who are 18 years of age or older, to vote shall not be denied or abridged by the United States or any state on account of age.

Section 2. The Congress shall have the power to enforce this article by appropriate legislation.

Bring your texts up to date!

With up-to-the-minute, innovative, inexpensive, easy-to-use materials from the Close Up Foundation, the leader in citizenship education.

- Student books
- Teacher's guides
- Multimedia curricula materials
- Videotapes
- Posters

Materials available in these areas:

- Current events
- Economics
- International relations
- U.S.-Soviet relations
- The Constitution
- The judicial system
- Congress
- The presidency
- The media
- And more!

No risk guarantee. Discounts available for quantity purchases.

Call toll free today, Monday through Friday, 8:00 a.m. to 5:00 p.m. eastern time (800) 336-5479; (703) 892-5400 in Virginia and Alaska (call collect).

Close Up Foundation
Publications Department, Room HA
1235 Jefferson Davis Highway
Arlington, Virginia 22202